READING WITH OPRAH

READING
WITH
OPRAH

The
Book Club
That
Changed
America

2ND EDITION

BY
KATHLEEN
ROONEY

THE UNIVERSITY OF
ARKANSAS PRESS
· *Fayetteville* ·
2005

Designed by Liz Lester

∞ The paper used in this publication meets the minimum
requirements of the American National Standard for
Permanence of Paper for Printed Library Materials
Z39.48–1984.

The Library of Congress has cataloged the hardcover edition
as follows:

Rooney, Kathleen, 1980–
        Reading with Oprah : the book club that changed America /
    by Kathleen Rooney.
            p.   cm.
        Includes bibliographical references and index.
        ISBN 1-55728-782-1 (hardcover : alk. paper)
        1. Book clubs (Discussion groups)—United States.
    2. Winfrey, Oprah. 3. Books and reading—United States.
    4. Literature and society—United States. I. Title.
    LC6651.R66 2005
    374.22—dc22

                                2004018177

For Martin

CONTENTS

PREFACE TO THE PAPERBACK EDITION

The hardcover edition of this book came out in 2005. Much has happened in the world of Oprah's Book Club since that time.

This updated edition will be published in 2008. More, no doubt, will happen between now and then.

As a scholar who has come to be something of an Oprahologist, this is frustrating, for though I can make myself an authority on the subject, I can never convince myself that I've had the last word on the matter.

Raymond Williams says it is impossible to analyze the artifacts of a culture while it is being lived. In some sense, it is impossible to fully analyze the artifacts of a book club while it is still clubbing. As a writer who is concerned with the vitality of literary culture in America, this inability to come to any final pronouncements on OBC is exciting, for it means that the phenomenon—having already undergone several incarnations—is still growing, changing, and going strong.

So while there is a fair chance that even this new improved edition of *Reading With Oprah* will be at least somewhat out of date already by the time of its release, I consider this a testament to the vital and Protean nature of the book club that changed—and that keeps changing—the way America reads.

In any event, the original text of this book, from the preface up to what is now Chapter 6, remains largely as it first appeared. I have streamlined some of the writing and revised some of the phrasing and language for clarity, but have otherwise left the arguments and evidence unaltered since I still believe them to be sound.

The new material consists of this preface and Chapter 7, which covers the James Frey fiasco and Winfrey's brief turn to (so-called) nonfiction. I have also added an Epilogue, which covers Winfrey's return to fiction with the prize-winning work of Cormac McCarthy and Jeffrey Eugenides, as well as the flowering of literary discussion online, not just in the realm of OBC, but also—for better or for worse—across the literary landscape.

I'd also like to reiterate my gratitude to Larry Malley and Tom Lavoie at University of Arkansas Press for believing in this project.

Kathleen Rooney
Chicago, 2007

PREFACE:
END OF STORY?

It's Thursday, April 4, 2002, at approximately 3:45 p.m. In less than twenty-four hours, virtually everyone in America will have received word of Oprah Winfrey's abrupt decision to cancel her televised book club, but now, as member number two hundred fifty-one in a select studio audience of about three hundred, I find myself privy to this news before it has broken over the general populace.

It is with no small sense of irony that I find myself here at this unforeseeably historic taping. For one thing, I don't even own a TV and have had little direct exposure to *The Oprah Winfrey Show* up until this moment. For another, I'm here not because I'm a fan, but because I'm hurrying to wrap up my research on the impact of Oprah's Book Club on American literary culture. In fact, my very arrival here at Harpo Studios played out something like a game of six degrees of separation, starting last fall when a friend and former Chicagoan mentioned that her mother's cousin's friend knew Oprah's makeup artist, and would I like help getting tickets?

Now—countless e-mails, multiple phone calls, and several months later—I have come to Chicago's West Loop from Washington, D.C., this very morning expecting to receive a typical and formulaic book club segment experience. I plan to take a few notes, write a nice, anecdotal first-person account of the whole thing upon my return home, and be done with it.

Still, along with every other polite, neatly dressed guest present, I gasp with pure, unstaged shock when, immediately after returning from a commercial break, Winfrey stands up and declares "I just want to say that this is the end of the book club as we know it." I sit stunned in my seat listening to the rest of her official statement that will air during her regularly scheduled program on Friday, the statement in which she explains before the cameras that "the truth is, it has just become harder and harder for me to find books on a monthly basis that I am really passionate about."

I hear from Winfrey herself—as will anyone else who watches the show, listens to the sound bites, or reads the papers tomorrow—that "I have to read a lot of books to get to something that I really passionately love, so I don't know when the next book will be. It might be next fall or it could be next year. But I have saved one of the best for last. It's one of my all time favorites and we'll be discussing this selection as usual in about a month. So my final selection is *Sula; Sula* by my favorite author, Toni Morrison."

Unlike most other people who will hear this quote bandied about the press for weeks to come, I happen to be mere yards from Winfrey as she utters it. From my position, dead-center in the third row, I have the advantage of hearing those parts of Winfrey's explanation that will not make the TV edit.

I hear her say during one of the final commercial breaks that six years' worth of book club has been long enough for her, that having to read so many contemporary novels with an eye toward picking one for the show is just too much pressure in conjunction with everything else she has to do, and that she wants to take time now to return to the classics. I hear her say that she spent the previous weekend rereading *The Great Gatsby,* a title to which the audience responds appreciatively with knowing oohs, ahhs, and nods.

Back on the air again at a few minutes before four o'clock, an assortment of staffers pass out copies, both hardcover and paperback, of the final selection. Winfrey reminds all of us in the audience and, of course, everyone watching at home, "After you read it, write me a nice letter. A great Toni Morrison-worthy letter, OK, because in the end she's going to see your letters too," before laughing, thanking us, and plunging into the well-mannered crowd herself to help with the distribution of books. The cameras are rolling as I receive my very own copy of *Sula* straight from Winfrey's hand; I could reach up and touch the sleeve of her fuzzy, pale blue sweater or the crease of her tailored gray trousers were I so inclined.

By slightly after 4 p.m., the show is over. The books have all been handed out, but Winfrey sticks around, as is her wont, to chat with the audience after hours. It is during this unaired window of time that Winfrey's fans have the opportunity to tell their heroine what's on their minds. It is during this time, too, that I witness the saddest part of my in-studio experience, sadder even that Winfrey's initial announcement, sadder because it is heartfelt and wholly unorchestrated.

Rising before posing her question, as we were instructed to do at the beginning of the taping, a well-spoken middle-aged woman in a periwinkle blue shirt addresses Winfrey. I do not catch her name because she is speaking quickly and earnestly, and I couldn't record it anyway because writing materials are not allowed. I do catch that she is a former English teacher, a current mother and homemaker, and a longtime fan of Oprah's Book Club. As such, she thanks Winfrey for having done so much for reading and literature. Then, standing unself-consciously in front of us all, she pleads with Winfrey not to stop now. Recalling Winfrey's rereading of *The Great Gatsby* and her desire to return to the works of dead authors, she wonders if it might be possible to continue to include literature in the show's format by, say, hosting a themed dinner, throwing a Roaring Twenties party, or inviting a Fitzgerald professor to say a few words about the works of F. Scott. There's something strange and desperate and true in her plea, and I want so badly for Winfrey to assent.

Instead, Winfrey explains that she just wants to be a "normal reader" for a while, and that, although she and her staff certainly considered such alternatives, the likelihood that any of them could ever take place is slim. She does not want, she says, laughing, to have to read and select classic novels on the basis of their potential for an accompanying dinner.

By quarter after four, the discussion turns from the announcement entirely. An elderly lady toward the rear of the periwinkle-shirted woman's section stands and asks Winfrey about a particularly attractive pair of snakeskin boots the host wore during an interview a few days earlier. Upon learning both the woman's shoe size and the precise episode during which said boots were worn—originally it is believed to have been a segment featuring Maya Angelou, though it turns out to have been with Michael J. Fox—Winfrey sends a staffer to her dressing room to fetch the footwear.

Shortly after autographing the boots and bestowing them on a beaming Jacquelyn Cosby, Winfrey announces that she must take her leave. She has, she elaborates wearily, some party in New York that she has to fly to by 9 o'clock tonight. It's approximately 4:30 p.m. Without another word about the cancellation of the club, she's gone.

Filing from my section to the studio exit, I can't help considering that this unexpected last chapter in the story of Oprah's Book Club is not dissimilar to the kinds of secrets or surprises divulged in a number of the book club picks. Unlike the best of the Oprah selections, though, this story seems to have a highly unsatisfying conclusion. Winfrey's decision to quit now strikes me as inexplicable, like an author deciding suddenly to stop writing before the narrative is quite done.

Still, it is done—and in the ensuing pages of this book, I'll examine the story of Oprah's Book Club with the care I would devote to the analysis of any complete story.

Over the course of this in-depth meditation on the manifold strengths and small but significant shortcomings of Oprah's Book Club (OBC), I will arrive at a largely positive appraisal of the club as an important and influential cultural institution, one which, via its eclecticism and heterogeneity, has made substantial progress toward effacing and eradicating decrepit, frequently racist and misogynistic cultural hierarchies. I will explore the books themselves, and demonstrate that the majority of OBC texts were of a higher quality than many critics would have us believe. I will investigate how OBC established a set of practical protocols for engaging with literature, which provide a much-needed alternative to those championed by the academy. I will describe how Winfrey established herself as a serious American intellectual who pioneered the use of electronic media, specifically television and the Internet, to take reading—a decidedly nontechnological and highly individual act—and highlight its social elements and uses in such a way as to motivate millions of erstwhile nonreaders to pick up books.

OBC being the sophisticated institution that it is, I will also explore its most prominent weaknesses, specifically how Winfrey's use of television as a means of promoting literacy manages to be simultaneously an enormous asset and a subtle liability, given the way that it flattens complex texts in order to meet the requirements of the televisual format. Relatedly, I will look at the way in which Winfrey's use of television encourages the imposition of competing narratives —specifically the life stories of her audience members and her own mythologized biography—on the narratives of the books themselves, thereby running the risk of applying texts capable of multiple interpretations and uses to a single-minded, socially controlled, and largely therapeutic end. Also, I will explain how Winfrey's unwillingness to discuss explicitly her own position as an intellectual and a monumental arbiter of taste with either her fans or her critics—particularly in the instance of her disinvitation of Jonathan Franzen from *The Oprah Winfrey Show*—has slightly but significantly lessened the hierarchy-leveling impact of her venerable institution.

Finally, I will demonstrate how far Winfrey and Oprah's Book Club have come since 1996, and why OBC in its latest incarnation stands as a testament to the high quality and sheer brilliance of her original endeavor, and how this current version of the club has managed to refine itself while still maintaining the distinctive non-hierarchical character that makes it such a valuable cultural institution. The act of reading has long been venerated—and rightly so—as an autonomous exercise of freedom, imagination, enlightenment, and creativity, one that cultivates benefits not only for the atomized individual but also for society as a whole. In an era in which so many find themselves lamenting the decline of popular engagement with literature and literacy in favor of electronic media and other sources of distraction and satisfaction, Winfrey has proven through her admirably democratizing book club that there are in fact large and largely untapped portions of the population who are willing and eager to interact with literary texts, and through them, with each other. As a culture, we want and need to engage with literature in order to learn, as well as to entertain and enrich ourselves—to discover our humanity and that of others without feeling insulted or put off by hierarchical distinctions telling us what we can or cannot, should or should not read. Since 1996, via OBC—with all its interconnected strengths and weaknesses—Winfrey has helped us do just that.

At the time of Winfrey's April 2002 announcement, of course, I had no way of knowing that within little more than a year, OBC would be back on the air, under the same name, but in a significantly altered form. Now that the original incarnation of the club has ended and the new version has taken its place, I can effectively show how OBC Part I originated, how it evolved, what it meant while it lasted, and why it had to end this way, as well as how OBC Part II emerged in its aftermath, largely immune to the criticisms leveled against its predecessor. In doing so, I expect to prove that, like any good novel, this story—the story of Oprah's Book Club—is full of complexity, conflict, nuance, and aspects about which to feel ambivalence.

CHAPTER ONE

The Stories of Oprah: Oprah's Book Club and American Literary Culture

Over the course of the past few years, whenever I've found myself home in the Chicago area, I've worked as a sales associate at Anderson's Bookshop in Naperville, Illinois, a shop with the proud history of being one of the region's oldest independent booksellers, a shop whose paychecks are still personally signed by Mr. Tres Anderson. The bookshop's employee restroom is covered in those free publicity posters sent out by publishers to advertise books. One of the posters is for *The Birth of a Whale,* another is for *Let's Count the Raindrops,* another is for *River Horse: Across America by Boat,* and still another is for *Willow Bark and Rose Hips: An Introduction to Edible and Useful Wild Plants of North America.* My favorite, though,—which is to say the one with which I had the most sympathy, at least until relatively recently—is a poster put out by McGill University Press, a glossy spread of such esoteric titles as *The Theology of the Oral Torah, Deformed Discourse, Mad Cows and Mother's Milk: The Perils of Poor Risk Communications,* and *Colonial Empires and Armies 1815–1960,* emblazoned with the slogan "Books You Won't See on *Oprah.*"

Initially, my own sentiments were similar to those implied by this slogan: that books which garner the approbation of the academic and cultural elite tend to be worlds apart from those hawked by certain TV talk show hosts, and that, somehow, the former are superior because of this distinction. Lately, though, I've come to view this poster as an illustration of the continuous discrepancy between what goes on at the front of the store—that is, blockbuster sales of the fifty-four books that have been awarded the approval of Oprah's Book Club—and the attitudes expressed at the back. Generally speaking, the majority of literature customers choose to praise and purchase reflects values that are a far cry from the ones held by those more ostensibly in the know.

In any case, my purpose in exploring the ramifications of OBC on American literary culture is very different now than when I began this project. At first, I—like many others who consider themselves to possess intellectual, and therefore privileged, tastes—was antagonistic and dismissive toward, even scornful of, the way in which Oprah Winfrey, the queen of daytime TV, had managed to position herself as one of the nation's most influential arbiters of literary taste. Who did she think she was, anyway? What right did she have to tell people what they should read? And why were all the books she picked so depressing? I was inclined to agree with those critics—Tom Shone of the *New York Times Book Review* and *Talk* magazine, Richard Roeper of the *Chicago Sun-Times,* and Bill Ott of *American Libraries* magazine, for instance—who suggested that OBC represented a debasement of the state of American literature, or a subversion of so-called good literary taste.

Now, with a book-length manuscript, a good-sized bibliography, and the majority of the Oprah novels behind me, I feel prepared, even eager, to argue that OBC, at least in its first incarnation, was in fact a crucible for the heated clash between high and low literary taste. By studying it as such, we stand to discover substantial evidence that such arbitrary and binaristic classifications as high and low may actually have the same limits, boundaries, and scope. In other words, we stand to learn something akin to what David Foster Wallace cites Mexican poet and essayist Octavio Paz as attempting to reveal with a concept he calls meta-irony: "that categories we divide into superior/arty and inferior/vulgar are in fact so interdependent as to be coextensive" (Wallace 42).

That said, I discovered over the course of my research that there were, in fact, valid complaints to be made against OBC, they just weren't the ones people seemed to be making. The assertion that the problem with OBC had to do with the books it typically selected—that, for instance, as Susan Wise Bauer suggests, OBC's misery-laden selections were "ultimately dishonest, offering false consolation that can only lead to deeper despair" (74)—was invalid, as was the assertion that the problem with OBC had to do with the celebritization of its selected authors. The assertion that the problem with OBC had to do with the fact that one person, particularly an entertainer, should not wield so much power in the literary world was invalid. The assertion that the problem with OBC had to do with the commercialization of literature—"many publishing industry executives say the TV show magnate and one of *Forbes* magazine's 400 richest Americans has single-handedly taken fiction to new commercial heights" (Fitzgerald 24)—was invalid, and so was the assertion that the problem with OBC was its use of TV as a vehicle for literature.

Likewise, I found that the praise of OBC was not always adequate in addressing the actual features of the club, even when it came directly from OBC-selected authors themselves, many of whom were kind enough to speak with and/or write to me regarding the matter. Fittingly, in fact, I conducted my first such interview with the club's inaugural author, Jacquelyn Mitchard, whose first novel, *The Deep End of the Ocean,* became the first selection of OBC in September 1996. Sitting in the cramped and cluttered back office of Anderson's before a signing for her novel *A Theory of Relativity* one evening in late June 2001, Mitchard gamely answered the series of questions I had prepared for the occasion. Enunciating clearly for the benefit of my handheld tape recorder, Mitchard pointed out that "people say there's a stereotypical Oprah book in the sense that it's often about a woman who, through her own wits and grit, pulls herself out of difficult circumstances. And some critics have said, 'Lighten up already,' and, you know, do a good mystery or whatever. But that is her particular mission, and, though some of the selections would not have been my cup of tea, some of the selections have been absolutely marvelous. I don't think anyone was ever harmed by reading any of them" (interview with the author). Transcribing the interview a few days later, this nobody's been hurt yet business struck me as an insufficient analysis of the specific ways OBC proved itself advantageous to contemporary literature.

In his own e-mail reply to my questions regarding his *Oprah* experience, Robert Morgan—whose novel *Gap Creek* became an OBC selection in January 2000—pointed out, "I have heard it said that one person shouldn't have so much power in the publishing world, but it's hard to think of anyone who has been hurt by the Oprah Book Club" (e-mail to the author). Again, simply stating—albeit correctly—that OBC hasn't actually damaged any individual readers doesn't quite hit upon the beneficial cultural significance of the club.

Also in response to one of several questions I posed via e-mail, Pearl Cleage—whose novel *What Looks Like Crazy on an Ordinary Day* became an OBC selection in September 1998—pointed out, "I don't think being chosen by the Oprah Book Club makes celebrities out of authors. I'm not a celebrity. I'm a working writer, living in the same house, shopping at the same grocery store, standing in line at the post office, sitting on the front porch talking to my neighbors, just like always. Being picked doesn't change who you are. It changes how many books you're likely to sell" (e-mail to the author). I appreciated her response and found this heartening to hear. Still, I felt as though some critics' apparent discomfort with OBC's tendency to foreground the relationship of authors' real lives and personalities to their fictional novels remained unaddressed. All in all, while not essentially incorrect, such apologies for OBC understated the complexity of the way the club actually functioned.

In short, I learned quickly over the course of my study that OBC was an institution about which virtually everyone felt compelled to have an opinion, but about which most people didn't actually know very much. From its inception in September 1996, OBC was commandeered as a rallying point around which both cultural commentators and common people positioned themselves in perpetuation of America's ongoing struggle of highbrow versus lowbrow. Both sides made reductive use of the club to galvanize themselves either as populist champions of literature for the masses or as intellectual defenders of literature from the hands of the incompetent. Both sides lobbed cheaply persuasive anecdotes to support their respective stands.

Members of the pro-OBC camp, for instance, heralded triumphant testimonials of the club's power to compel participants—many of whom had not read a book since they were forced to in high school—to return to active literacy, though they seldom paused to consider how exactly the club instructed these participants in their new pursuit. In turn, members of the anti-Oprah corps criticized and decried OBC selections without having read a representative sample of them.

Through it all, little analytical or empirical evidence regarding the true nature of the club itself and its impact on the culture in which it was situated was offered; this, then, is precisely what I want to get at in my study. I want to explore and expose the actual character and merit of OBC in such a way as to reveal to both sides, and everyone in between, what the club is and what it isn't, what it means and what it doesn't. If I wanted to put the matter crudely, I might suggest that OBC features enough of a combination of stereotypically highbrow and lowbrow components as to render it fairly middlebrow. But I don't intend to put it crudely. Instead, I intend to prove that OBC is a vastly more complex and even consequential phenomenon than either its supporters or its detractors may realize. In doing so, I hope to make the case that the vertical hierarchy by which we so frequently rush to classify the literary arts in particular and culture as a whole is unnecessarily, anachronistically rigid. If we are willing to let it, OBC—with its sometimes surprising heterogeneity and eclecticism—stands to prove that there exists a far greater fluidity among the traditional categories of artistic classification than may initially meet the eye; that we needn't shove every text we encounter into a prefabricated box labeled "high," "low," or "middle."

In order to apprehend OBC's capacity to reveal how essentially silly and antiquated traditional classifications of artistic taste actually are—as well as to better understand Winfrey's attitudes and our own toward the cultural work she has undertaken—we must turn first to the origins of those classifications. In his groundbreaking work on the subject—entitled, fittingly, *Highbrow/Lowbrow: The Emergence of Cultural Hierarchy in America*—cultural historian Lawrence Levine explains the ignominious genesis of these "adjectival categories created in the late nineteenth century" as follows:

> "Highbrow," first used in the 1880s to describe intellectual or aesthetic superiority, and "lowbrow," first used shortly after 1900 to mean someone or something neither "highly intellectual" nor "intellectually refined," were derived from the phrenological terms "highbrowed" and "lowbrowed," which were prominently featured in the nineteenth-century practice of determining racial types and intelligence by measuring cranial shapes and capacities. A familiar illustration of the period depicted the distinctions between the lowbrowed ape and the increasingly higher brows of the "Human Idiot," the "Bushman," the "Uncultivated," the "Improved," the "Civilized," the "Enlightened," and, finally, the "Caucasian," with the highest brow of them all. (221–22)

Admittedly, the majority of people probably aren't even aware of the frankly embarrassing baggage attendant upon the adjectives they toss around so lightly. Still, bearing this etymology in mind, it seems somewhat preposterous that such initially racist, imperialist, conservative, and generally terrible terms should still carry so much weight today. For although the meanings of these descriptors have been refined over the ensuing years, they retain a kind of mindless bluntness that continues to inform conversations about culture to this day.

Indeed, literary taste is typically judged as good, bad, or somewhere in between based on factors of perceived cultural and/or economic legitimacy. These factors traditionally tend to be at odds with, or even mutually exclusive of, each other. Describing this phenomenon in his seminal essay "The Field of Cultural Production: The Economic World Reversed" the late French sociologist Pierre Bourdieu asserts that there exist three basic competing principles of artistic legitimacy. First, he says, there's what he calls the specific principle of legitimacy, which is to say "the recognition granted by the set of producers who produce for other producers . . . i.e. by the . . . world of 'art for art's sake,' meaning art for artists" (Bourdieu 51). Next, he continues, there's the principle of legitimacy corresponding to "bourgeois" taste. By this he means the recognition "bestowed by the dominant factions of the dominant class and by the private tribunals," as well as public and state-guaranteed ones, including schools and universities "which sanction the inseparably ethical and aesthetic (and therefore political) taste of the dominant" (Bourdieu 51). Thirdly, he concludes, there's the principle of legitimacy commonly known as "popular," by which he means the preferences of average consumers, known collectively as the mass audience.

Obviously, there exists some overlap between the first and second of these categories. So-called serious writers, for instance, may champion the aesthetic value and attendant superiority of, say, *Finnegans Wake* and similar works, but so too may such novels be taught in such bourgeois strongholds as upper-level literature classes at major universities. Conversely, there exists less overlap among the former two categories and the latter, more popular one. Huge swaths of the population may love reading the latest John Grisham on the train or at the beach, for example, but it remains unlikely that you'll find such novels being taught—widely, anyway—at the college level, or see them appearing on the short-lists of preeminent annual literary prizes. In any case, whether or not you agree with Bourdieu's specific delineation of these categories, the important thing here is to note that, when it comes to artistic and literary taste, some kinds of legitimacy are more legitimate than others.

The literary field is a site of continuous struggle between what Bourdieu defines as the two principles of hierarchization, the first of which consists of those "bourgeois" and "popular" artists who dominate the field economically and politically. The autonomous, or "high" art for art's sake artists typically in possession of the least economic and political capital comprise the second. The members of this second category, says Bourdieu, "tend to identify with [a] degree of independence from the economy, seeing temporal failure as a sign of election and success as a sign of compromise" (40). In short, the smaller the audience, sales, and public recognition with which a particular work meets, the more secure its status as so-called high art; the lower a work's economic capital, the higher its cultural capital. Conversely, works that attain for themselves a wide popular readership, and thus large sales figures, frequently find themselves in possession of vast quantities of economic capital while at the same time becoming impoverished in terms of perceived cultural validity. To put it simply, traditionally serious art cannot simultaneously be salable art. In keeping with this trend, then, autonomous producers tend to set themselves deliberately apart from "bourgeois" and especially "popular" writers and artists whom they frequently view as inferiors or even enemies.

Bearing this in mind, it comes as no surprise that Winfrey—known in some circles as the "Midas of the Midlist" for her ability to turn modestly successful yet critically overlooked novels into overnight bestsellers—met with so much overt hostility from the American literary intelligentsia. For whenever a new literary force makes its presence felt in the field of literary production—as OBC has certainly done—the result is a change in the power relations and positions within that field. "The whole problem," says Bourdieu, "is transformed since its coming into being, i.e. into difference modifies and displaces the universe of possible options; the previously dominant productions may, for example, be pushed into the status either of outmoded [*declassé*] or of classic works" (32). Winfrey, with her creation of what amounted to the world's largest, most potentially inclusive book club, certainly transformed and rearranged the literary universe.

For regardless of how the gatekeepers of tradition, the canon, and high culture may have felt about it, the original incarnation of OBC had an indisputably significant impact upon the nation's culture and economy. With over thirteen million regular viewers per book segment, and even more readers (Max 6), the televised club exercised a measurably high influence over the reading public, over authors, and over the publishing industry itself. Moreover, the club provided an opportunity to examine how the televisual can be used to promote the literary, how various types of media inform each other, and how socio-cultural attitudes—particularly, in this case, attitudes regarding race, women, class, family, God, organized religion, and, of course, Winfrey herself—both produce and are produced by literature.

Indeed, supporters of OBC would say that the club actually created literary taste, as well as demonstrated the impulse of

Americans to intellectual satisfaction and self-improvement. And, for the most part, they'd be right. On the surface, anyway, it's difficult to argue that OBC was anything other than a qualifiedly "good thing" for contemporary literature and its readers. Essentially, thanks to her book club, Winfrey managed to do a lot for the previously underrepresented masses, at least those masses comprised chiefly of American women, who, incidentally, are responsible for approximately 70 percent (McCormick 38) of all purchases of literary fiction. As Anna Quindlen—who saw her novel *Black and Blue* become an OBC selection in April 1998 and who was good enough to respond at length to each of the questions I posed to her regarding that experience—observes, "I'm particularly disdainful of the critics who complain that the selections focus on 'women's issues' or 'women's books,' and wonder where they were over the years when virtually the entire canon focused on 'men's books.'" (e-mail to the author) There are also, she continues, "a number of surveys showing that women buy far more books, take more out of the library, and read more than their male counterparts, so to the extent that Oprah focuses on women she is also focusing on likely readers. This seems to me an affirmative good, for her and her books" (e-mail to the author). Not only did Winfrey give these women already engaged in active readership a potential forum from which to take reading suggestions and in which to discuss them, she also made it her mission to tap into the potential readership of those members of her audience who had not yet, for whatever reasons, discovered the pleasures of active readership on their own. OBC novelist Robert Morgan goes so far as to suggest that "the greatest value of the Oprah Book Club is that it has millions of people reading who might not otherwise, or reading better books than romances or thrillers. That seems a good thing to me" (e-mail to the author).

Fittingly, Winfrey managed to accomplish this encouragement of literary taste through a means all her own, using her unique position as an influential television personality to press her viewership to engage in readership as well. One of the chief ways in which she did so was by acknowledging the fact that women—the gender of which her audience is predominantly comprised—frequently find themselves on the receiving end of gender-based prejudice, discrimination, harassment, violence and hardship. Thus, the books she selected for her club resonated with, reflected, and represented the frequently burdensome reality of contemporary women's lives. In Jane Hamilton's *The Book of Ruth*, for instance, the mentally retarded yet mostly good-hearted Ruth must overcome the emotional abuse of her hateful mother and the physical abuse of her piggish husband. In Janet Fitch's *White Oleander*, Astrid must face not only maternal neglect, but also the mind-bogglingly miserable conditions of California's foster-care system. In Sheri Reynolds's *The Rapture of Canaan*, Ninah must survive an unwanted pregnancy and the subsequent wrath of the cultish Church of Fire and Brimstone into which she has been born. The list goes on and on, addressing time and again the miseries inflicted on women at the hands of hands of history, poverty, disability, their husbands, their families, and their governments.

I would like to note at this point that *all* taste is dictated, if not by recognized cultural authorities at the so-called top, then from somewhere. All reviewing of or advocacy for a particular book— whether it appears on the book's jacket, in the *New York Times Book Review*, or elsewhere—may be construed as suggestion or even gentle coercion from those in positions of cultural power to those at lower levels. Worthy of note, too, is the fact that most people seem fairly comfortable with this long-established tradition by which we, the public, are told how and what to read by various powers that be, many of whom are members of some kind of specialized literary class. Worthy of asking, then, is why widespread signs of discomfort seemed to surface only when said power manifested itself in the form of a middle-aged black woman, and, more precisely, a middle-aged black woman with lots and lots—her net worth in September 2003 was estimated at $1.1 billion ("*Forbes* 400")—of money.

"Money," wrote Virginia Woolf, "dignifies what is frivolous unpaid for" (Woolf 108). And while her observation was accurate in terms of the attempts of female authors to gain legitimacy through sales at the time of her composition of "A Room of One's Own," money's role in the contemporary hierarchy of legitimacy of taste seems somewhat more complex. As editor Cathy Davidson observes in *Reading in*

America: Literature and Social History, "questions of literacy are always charged and political" (12). Moreover, "literacy is never simply a rate that can be quantitatively measured, but is an exceptionally complicated social process as well as the embodiment of significant social ideals" (Davidson 12). Indeed, Winfrey's unprecedented ability to turn each and every book she touched into an O-stickered bestseller seemed to be one of the chief sources of detractors' disgust with the club. "Winfrey is the Midas of the Midlist," explains Susan Fleming-Holland, a publicist for Simon and Schuster. "Once the announcement is made, it's like a tidal wave. All we can do is get out of the way" (qtd. in Bayles 3). Unbeknownst to her, Fleming-Holland also seems to be explaining how, even though Winfrey picked a multitude of critically acclaimed books (including Nobel Prize winner Toni Morrison's *Song of Solomon* and Jane Hamilton's PEN/Faulkner winning *The Book of Ruth*) her picks still managed to be subject to critical scorn once they received her approbation. In short, OBC books tended to exhibit an inversely proportional relationship between their cultural capital—low—and their economic capital—high. I feel this says much about how complex and often counterintuitive the interconnectivity among money, art, race and gender really is.

Generally speaking, white male artists are best-equipped—that is, financially and socially secure enough—to adopt a cultural pose that implies they'd rather not have an audience at all than have one comprised of your run-of-the-mill, mainstream, bestseller-reading, pop-music-listening bourgeois masses. Women and people of color still need, on the other hand, to earn a kind of monetary keep to prove their value. The critical backlash against the selections of OBC serves as a textbook case of a warped hierarchy of legitimacy, but American culture abounds with additional examples of similarly skewed value attachments. For instance, American hip-hop and rhythm and blues artists often tend to represent themselves as being strongly materialistic, for example, by taking vocal pride in their earned financial successes and by the avid and conspicuous consumption of luxury goods; for the predominantly black artists who make this music, such material things signify legitmation via the marketplace, and, therefore, success. By contrast, American indie rock and emo artists seem to disdain such popular legitimation: they seek to maintain an exclusive, "underground" listenership, they dress in thrift shop chic, and they affect disinterest regarding audience size and financial gain. In other words, only those in positions of power can afford to be dismissive of such basic economic concerns because their position is secure and in need of little to no legitimation.

The trick of producing and disseminating a list of favorite novels based on fairly arbitrary criteria is in fact one of the oldest in the taste-arbitrating book. Even Winfrey's method of book selection—she is, by all accounts including her own, simply a voracious reader who recommends novels from which she herself derives the most enjoyment—had numerous and prominent antecedents. John Carey's recently published *Pure Pleasure: A Guide to the 20th Century's Most Enjoyable Books* is one of the more honest among them. "Admittedly, there are book snobs, and they do a lot of damage," explains Carey in his introduction to the collection. "They link reading in the public mind with swank and false refinement. That goes, too, for the lists of 'great books' concocted by panels of experts and published from time to time in the literary press. Who are these daunting league-tables meant for? Not, surely, other human beings. They seem more like end-of-term reports, dispatched to the Almighty, to show Him how well His earthly creatures are doing on the cultural side" (Carey, *Pure Pleasure* xii). This is precisely the manner of book snobbery in which detractors of OBC engaged as they decried Winfrey's selections and her authors, dismissing and ahistoricizing them in order to defend an established literary hierarchy.

Carey intends his own list, he continues, to be an antidote to all this highbrow posturing. For its contents are "not chosen on grounds of 'literary greatness,' the testimony they bear to the human spirit, or anything of that kind, though no doubt some would notch up reasonable scores even by those standards. Instead, I took pure reading pleasure as my criterion—the pleasure the books have given to me, and the pleasure I hope others will get from being reminded of them" (Carey, *Pure Pleasure* xiii). Correspondingly, virtually all of Winfrey's selections seemed chosen with a view toward readability and enjoyment, managing too, more often than not, to be both entertaining and edifying along the way. The chief difference between Carey and Winfrey remains, of course, that Carey—a recently retired fellow of Oxford University, frequent contributor to *The London Times,* and author of multiple academic volumes—is universally perceived as a member of the public intellectual sphere, whereas Winfrey—the most successful daytime talk show host in the history of the format, publishing magnate, and head of her own production company—unfortunately is not. (Actually, in response to my e-mail request for his perceptions of Winfrey and her club, Carey replied, much to my chagrin, "Alas, I know nothing about the OWBC, so my opinions are not worth having.")

I want to assert now that Oprah Winfrey is, in fact, an intellectual force. Although the televisual means by which she has secured her status are unconventional, her identity as such is very much in step with the traditional sense of the word. Like any good intellectual, Winfrey is a demonstrably intelligent, erudite, and well-spoken person. Additionally, she teaches—both informally on her daily talk show and formally at Northwestern University—and has produced a substantial body of influential work in the form of her show, her magazine, and the very life she has led. Winfrey even articulates what amounts to a coherent ideology: "The message has always been the same: that you are responsible for your life. Now we've evolved into talking about how to live your best life. That's the theme of my magazine. That's also the theme of my talk show—to get people to take charge. To get people to realize that things are not just happening to them willy-nilly" (qtd. in Clemetson 44). If intellectuals generate new ideas that are initially somewhat at odds with a culture's conventional wisdom through means that may be considered subversive, then Winfrey certainly qualifies as one, to the extent that her program is vastly different from typical talk show fare. In the mission statement for her show, for instance, she declares her intention "to use television to transform people's lives, to make viewers see themselves differently and to bring happiness and a sense of fulfillment into every home" (*Oprah Winfrey Show* fact sheet). Moreover, her use of television to conduct a widely inclusive discussion of books was not merely unprecedented, it was also revolutionary.

here was nothing intrinsically new, scary, or alienating about
the Winfrey assumed in literary culture, nor about the intel-
position she adopted. If anything, OBC had its antecedents
in what Levine describes as "a rich shared public culture that once
characterized the United States," a culture "less hierarchically organized, less fragmented" (9), and generally more democratic, in which
members of every class enjoyed such entertainments as opera,
Shakespeare, symphonic music and museums that we would today
term "highbrow." Rather, the revolutionary element of her program
had to do with who she is, how she actually accomplished her literary goal, and the scale on which she met that goal. More than any
other cultural authority, Winfrey promoted the bridging of the high-
low chasm that cleaves the American literary landscape. As Jacquelyn
Mitchard explained during our interview at Anderson's:

> There are lots of people who say they would never want their
> book to be Oprahfied, because they would never want the false
> blip and the sort of commercialization of their fiction . . . which
> they consider "serious." But I also think that's silly because, as
> Joni Mitchell said, "Art isn't art if only 16 [sic] people know
> about it." You know, you don't write for yourself. It's a perfor-
> mance, so why not have as many people see it as possible? . . .
> Nureyev and Fonteyn didn't say, "Only really smart people can
> come to the ballet." (Interview with the author)

Analogously, Oprah invited everyone to the ballet. Impressively,
many of those invited actually showed up. Oprah managed with
grace and ease to succeed in creating new readers where the book
industry had failed. Producer Alice McGee claimed to receive "five
letters a day from people saying that they hadn't read a book in 20
years until Winfrey made them pick one up," while "Barnes & Noble
reports that 75 percent of people who came in for a Winfrey book
bought another title as well" (qtd. in Max 8). Moreover, according to
Rachel Jacobsohn, who runs a national information exchange service for book club members, "there are around 500,000 bookclubs in
America today, twice as many as in 1994. They have between five
million and 10 million members. She attributes the growth to

Winfrey" (Max 8). Clearly, Winfrey was fighting the good fight for the creation of a new American readership—racking up her victories no doubt thanks to her televisual weapon of choice. For the use of TV as a deliberate means to such a flourishing literary end was unheard-of before Winfrey took the field. Indeed, Mitchard told me, some of the people who read *The Deep End of the Ocean* "hadn't read a book since high school, and because Oprah Winfrey was so powerful and so respected by them, they took her word for it, they read it, and they were blown away by the idea that a so-called serious book could be as much fun to read as a mystery or a romance" (interview with the author).

The testimonials of those who, by their own admission, hadn't read for years until Winfrey told them to were powerful, and went far to make the case for the unquestionable "goodness" of OBC; however, they also contributed to the idea that OBC was somehow an exclusively low phenomenon, beneficial only to the relatively uneducated, to the previously mindless watchers of TV. This was hardly the case. Mitchard puts it best when she recounts, "One time, a writer said to me, would I rather have the approbation of my peers or of a bunch of suburban housewives? And I said suburban housewives, hands down. I believe that mid-list readers are very intelligent people, and they live in the real world. And I write the books that I want to read. So I'm certainly not writing for critics or academics—not that I disdain them. I just am not. I'm writing for readers, ordinary readers." So, the categories of ordinary readers and smart readers are not mutually exclusive.

On this point, Cathy Davidson observes, "the whole matter of who should learn what has (in America as elsewhere) a long and troubled history. The Company of the Massachusetts Bay established guidelines for the education of its young (specifically its young men) even before leaving England" (9). She goes on to discuss Allan Bloom's *The Closing of the American Mind: How Higher Education Has Failed Democracy and Impoverished the Souls of Today's Students* and E. D. Hirsch Jr.'s *Cultural Literacy: What Every American Needs to Know,* two major works of critical nonfiction that were on the bestseller lists at the time of her 1987 writing. These two pedagogical—and in Bloom's case vitriolic—volumes "aptly illustrate some of the most persistent contradictions in American theories of education and literacy. In a democracy, should one evaluate the success of the educational system by how well how many can read? Or should the nation particularly concern itself with providing an excellent education for a ruling elite— the best for the brightest? And are these different agendas really mutually exclusive?" (Davidson 9–10). As evidenced by some circles' scornful reactions to Winfrey's goal of expanding active literacy well beyond the classroom, it remains clear more than twenty years later that we are still quite far from a national consensus on the matter.

These questions of who should be reading what—as well as what value should then be placed on the readers and their chosen reading material—are tricky. Try to be too specific or prescriptive about it, and you come across as a big, fat, culturally conservative, hegemony-enforcing jerk. Indeed, Davidson points out that Bloom suggests that "Only Great Books (defined largely as works of classical philosophy and European high culture) can ostensibly open American minds (defined—and this is a subtext running throughout Bloom's book—as the minds of, essentially, white men, as if no other minds could either warrant or repay the effort to educate them into an awareness of their own proclaimed primary place in the culture)" (10). Winfrey, to her credit, never troubled over which minds were worth opening. Rather, through her promotion of literature that more often than not combined pleasurable readability with thought-provoking content, she welcomed them all.

While I'm at it, I'd like to add that readable literature is not by definition unworthy of critical respect. In the first place, the books Winfrey picked for the club frequently combined accessibility with substantial artistic merit. Also, "Winfrey didn't invent the kind of fiction she promotes, a genre Marty Asher, the editor in chief of Vintage Books, calls 'accessible literary fiction.' Publishers have been selling it for 15 years with some success, especially since the breakthrough of *The Color Purple*. But the scale of Winfrey's ability to reach readers is unprecedented" (Max 7). Furthermore, much of the literary fiction Winfrey selected was often significantly more enjoyable than so-called challenging contemporary literature. Actually, for what it's worth, many of the novels Winfrey selected were every bit as *challenging* as so-called challenging contemporary novels. Barbara Kingsolver's *The Poisonwood Bible* is just as sophisticated— with regard to its structure, plot, characterization, and even thematic appeals to outlying socio-political concerns—as Jonathan Franzen's *The Corrections.*

Since no discussion of accessible literary fiction in America can be complete without citing the work of Janice Radway, I'd like to quote now from her essay "The Book-of-the-Month Club and the General Reader," wherein she observes of the BOMC:

> In spite of the esteem it now enjoys within the publishing world, the club's reputation in what might be called the literary world remains that of the quintessentially "middlebrow" forum. . . . The Book-of-the-Month Club offers, in such a view, neither the best works of contemporary literature, nor the worst examples of mindless trash. Its books, rather, fall into that large, amorphous middle ground of the unremarkable but respectable. It is worth keeping in mind, however, that . . . midrange books are seen by such commentators not simply as different from those occupying higher positions but as failed attempts to approximate the achievement of the best books." (Radway 260)

Even though Radway is clearly referring to the BOMC, her characterization could pertain almost equally well to OBC, which should in no way be filed mistakenly under the dismissive category of middlebrow. For "to label the club middlebrow . . . is to damn it with faint praise and to legitimate the social role of the intellectual who has not only the ability but the authority to make such distinctions and to dictate them to others" (Radway 260). Far from presenting works that were all of a middling piece, OBC recommended books that were readable and enjoyable, yes, but that were also well-written and arguably good if not great.

I feel the need to pause here and clarify that I firmly believe that literary taste—which is to say the personal faculty of discerning what is aesthetically appropriate and valuable—is a necessary and practical capacity for an individual to possess, so long as it is constructed as thoughtfully and autonomously as possible. In this sense, then, certain informal hierarchies and categorizations of artistic value prove useful for the purposes of discussion, organization, and the task of deciding what—out of millions of available options—to read. I want to clarify, too, what I was getting at with my earlier assertion of the inherent interdependence and coextensiveness of levels within various literary hierarchies, and to discuss how exactly these hierarchies function. In short, I want to show you that these systems of literary classification must be understood as fluid rather than rigid. Interestingly enough, the best way to do this seems to be by setting up a kind of sample hierarchy of my own.

Thus, I give to you now an offhand, but hopefully illuminating, five-level system of contemporary fiction classification, on the first and lowest level of which we can include comic books and pornography. Moving on, we can place such genre fiction as mysteries, thrillers, sci-fi / fantasies and romances on the second and slightly higher level. At level three, we can locate the various sentimental and formulaic novels one typically finds shelved in the mass-market paperback sections of bookstores. These are the novels whose authors clearly seek to write more than mere genre pieces, but whose books simply tend, for various reasons, toward the mediocre. At level four we can situate the earnest, sincere, good but not great novels one finds shelved nearby in the more literary contemporary trade paperback section. Here we have novels that tend to feel more weighty and to be more intellectually and artistically ambitious than the ones in the previous level, but that are prevented from joining the ranks of level five by such flaws as less skillful writing, less complicated ideas, and / or less sophisticated voices.

Finally, at the fifth and topmost level, we can place both successful and failed serious literary novels, which is to say books that are either arguably great or at least approaching greatness. Among the former, we can include Virginia Woolf's *Mrs. Dalloway,* Vladimir Nabokov's *Lolita,* Thomas Pynchon's *The Crying of Lot 49,* Paula Fox's *Desperate Characters,* Don DeLillo's *White Noise,* Haruki Murakami's *The Wind-Up Bird Chronicle,* Daniel Handler's *The Basic Eight,* and most of the work of Toni Morrison. Among those who aim high but fall slightly short, we can list numerous works by gifted writers whose books possess undeniable cultural enterprise, but that miss attaining the kind of prophetic voice exhibited by the truly great.

Clearly, this hastily thrown up hierarchy proceeds from those hackish, genre-type works that characteristically exhibit little to no ambition beyond one to entertain, up through those more stylishly written works of a large and contemplative scope with a great deal of moral, cultural, and intellectual ambition. Still, to assume that because this is the trend in the hierarchy certain categories may be disregarded or presumed worthless—or automatically worth less than others—is to miss out on the usefulness of cultivating discriminating taste in the first place, as well as to miss out on a lot of good literature. For within each of these categories there exist works that break this trend, or which, put another way, transcend their genre.

To summarily reject the comic books contained in the first level, for instance, would be to cast off the sophisticated graphic novels of Daniel Clowes, Art Spiegelman, Chris Ware, and Lynda Barry, just as to summarily reject the porn of level one would be to dismiss the highly literary *The Story of O* by Pauline Réage, *Story of the Eye* by Georges Bataille, and *Delta of Venus* by Anaïs Nin. Similarly, one would be hard-pressed to deny the superior attributes of such works as Umberto Eco's *The Name of the Rose* or those of the novels of Raymond Chandler, Dashiel Hammett, James M. Cain, Dennis Lehane, Orson Scott Card, Ursula LeGuin, and Diana Gabaldon, when evaluating this hierarchy's second level. As for the novels in the third and fourth tiers, many are published with more than one cover and targeted toward more than one type of reader. Indeed, the very fact that these books tend to be shelved in more than one place in bookstores—usually among both mass market and trade paperbacks—suggests that they may have more than one place in this particular hierarchy. Similarly, the status of the great and the slightly sub-great novels outlined in the fifth and final tier are hardly immune to contention.

Now that I've finished briefly setting forth this hierarchy, I want to issue a disclaimer, that being: these kinds of taste issues are intricate and difficult to articulate, save by example, which is what I'm really getting at. I do not intend the itemized portions of this list to be taken terribly seriously, or to be treated as if I have attempted to set them in stone. I have delineated these categories chiefly to make the point that such categories are extremely complicated to delineate; I have taken this time to create a superficially predictable hierarchy to prove that the works such hierarchies seek to contain are frequently unpredictable.

All in all, I'm sure that a good number of you disagree, maybe even passionately, with my classifications. If that's the case, then good job. You understand that such hierarchies, as helpful as they may sometimes be, must not be trusted blindly or adhered to mindlessly, and that's the mark of a discriminating, which is to say thoughtful, consumer of literary fiction. So too is it the mark of Oprah Winfrey, who chose her initial book club selections from all over what might be considered the rather arbitrary hierarchy of contemporary fiction. In fact, I'd argue that one of the best attributes of the first OBC was its ability to surprise, in the sense that it could feature, for instance, Anita Shreve's absurd *The Pilot's Wife* back-to-back with Bernard Schlink's *The Reader*. For whatever you can say about the consistency—or lack thereof—of Winfrey's literary taste, you have to admit that it is, by all appearances, fairly autonomous: she does her best to be a thoughtful, discriminating, and independent selector of literature.

Nonetheless, the detractors of the first club persisted. But who were these people, anyway? At least some of them, Mitchard suggested when I asked her:

> are literary purists who believe that anything that is read by more than a few people who breathe extremely rare air must be mediocre. Like the *New York Times* critic . . . Michiko Kakutani, who would believe that anything that could attract a popular audience—and is, the word that is often used is "accessible"—therefore must be mediocre. And to that I would say Mark Twain is accessible, and so is Charles Dickens, and, you know, so is Leo Tolstoy—my mom used to say, *"There's a book that takes the fun out of adultery,"* about *Anna Karenina*.

So that is a hollow criticism. And then there's another group of people whose books are not in danger of being chosen for that singular pleasure who are just sour grapey about it. (interview with the author)

Still, the fact that such widespread criticism of, or at least subtle discomfort with, OBC existed indicated to me that Winfrey's project was not without room for improvement.

In fairness, no one—not even Oprah Winfrey herself—can please everyone all the time, nor should one expect to. Still, there were identifiable reasons why so many people remained displeased with her project, even if those reasons may not have been the ones that initially suggested themselves. Literary critic Gayatri Chakravorty Spivak once observed in an interview that "there is an impulse among literary critics and other kinds of intellectuals to save the masses, speak for the masses, describe the masses. On the other hand, how about attempting to learn to speak in such a way that the masses will not regard as bullshit . . . ?" (56). Via her self-proclaimed mission to get the country reading again, Winfrey acted on her impulse as a powerful and influential intellectual force to describe, speak for, and ultimately save the masses. Nonetheless, it is highly unlikely that Spivak would be entirely comfortable with Winfrey's approach to literature for a popular audience.

In the same interview, Spivak continues, "What can the intellectual do towards the texts of the oppressed? Represent them and analyze them, disclosing one's own positionality for other communities in power" (56). While Winfrey undoubtedly was able to use OBC to provide herself a language in which to analyze books and address her audience without compelling them to rise as a unit and change the channel, this language was by no means free of condescension, hypocrisy, or any other manifestation of the all-too-familiar bullshit to which Spivak refers. Moreover, by failing to explain freely and explicitly to the public—her admirers and her detractors alike— where exactly she was coming from, and what exactly she was trying to do, Winfrey in effect allowed OBC to be an alienating phenomenon rather than a genuinely empowering one.

OBC was a "good thing" that stood to become much better, but could have done so only if Winfrey had undertaken to admit and acknowledge that what she did, though not political, was political in its ramifications. In addition to being implicitly feminist—in seeking to better the cultural situation of female readers—OBC also seemed to be promoting the cultural viability of underclass readers and readers of color. Simply put, Winfrey neither succeeded in fully addressing the needs of the reading masses, nor did she discuss her own indisputable position of privilege over those masses or disclose her own goals, aims, and assumptions to others in similar situations of influence and authority.

The fallout of this failure may be somewhat crudely classified as twofold. First, in terms of her highbrow detractors—the ones who suggested, erroneously, that among other things, she pandered to a kind of television-swilling lowest common denominator via sentimental novels that peddled the crippling notion of self-pity and preached the smug doctrine of self-help—she did herself and her club an immense disservice by failing to reply overtly and intelligently to the aspersions they cast. Secondly, in terms of her readers themselves, Winfrey sadly underestimated her audience's ability and willingness to comprehend and to discuss the significance of their participation in such a revolutionary club, resorting more often than not to what amounted to little more than *Reading is Fundamental— and Fun!*–style sloganeering. This in turn was tied to Winfrey's tendency to underestimate her audience's ability to appreciate intelligent discussion of OBC-selected books themselves, and to resort instead to the imposition of various extraneous competing narratives—including those of her show, herself, and her readers— upon the novels.

Returning now to the first bit of Spivak's assertion, even a casual assessment of Oprah Winfrey's cultural position confirms that she is an intellectual, although to venture more deeply into the first fold of her failure is to discover that she's simply not perceived as one. To put an even finer point on it, other intellectuals refuse to identify Winfrey as one of their own largely because she refuses to disclose her own identity in relation to theirs. In the interest of further clarifying what

I intend by my application of the appellation "intellectual" here, I turn to the illustrative example of the early nineteenth-century writer, critic, and self-appointed arbiter of mass taste Arnold Bennett. In an endeavor not dissimilar to the one to which Winfrey has committed herself, Bennett, in his book *Fame and Fortune,* analyzed a number of contemporary bestsellers, "to show that their popularity rests on genuine qualities which demand respect, and which only those besotted with the 'dandyism of technique' could ignore" (Carey, *Intellectuals and the Masses* 154–55). Intrinsic to Bennett's intellectual project was the notion that there exists, between the popular and the highbrow reader, no essential difference, or as he would have it, "not only is art a factor in life; it is a factor in all lives. The division of the world into two classes, one of which has a monopoly of what is called 'artistic feeling,' is arbitrary and false" (Carey, *Intellectuals and the Masses* 155). As I would have it, the notion that this division is arbitrary and false is one that Winfrey seemed, based upon her selections for the club, to share; however, the still-extant antagonism between the two types of "brows," as it were, could have been far more effectively eradicated had Winfrey spoken more directly to this end. Turning once more to Bennett, then, we see that:

> In politics, he displayed a matching optimism: the spread of education will heal the rift in English culture. "The abyss between the mentality of the true leaders and the mentality of the people narrows and must narrow every year." His own contribution to narrowing the abyss was book reviewing, which educated the taste of the English public. Without being either patronizing or elitist, he introduced his readers to what he believed was truly valuable in modern literature. Writing for the *New Age,* he addressed a cross-section of the public that included "board-school teachers, shop assistants, servants, artisans, and members of the poor generally." (Carey, *Intellectuals and the Masses* 156)

Here, in the twenty-first-century United States, Winfrey had within her reach the ability to narrow the rift in American literary culture. Her book club could have performed a great feat in the filling of the abyss between the so-called lowbrow and highbrow mentalities of American literary consumers. Here, unfortunately, I must insist upon the inclusion of the word "could," since in spite of all she did to encourage, promote, and legitimize mid-level American taste, her stance persisted in setting her loyal middlebrowers apart from genuinely challenging literary discussion.

For while her club provided a strong start toward building a tradition of low- to middle-class, predominantly female readers, Winfrey was not entirely like Bennett in that she essentially failed in the creation of a true middle-ground site for the discussion of all kinds of literature by all kinds of people, one that avoided at all costs the hollow, archaic, and detrimental divisions of high versus low taste. Winfrey's book club was far too reliant upon an overly simplistic "if we can't be in your club then we'll just have our own" reaction to the so-called literary establishment. Admittedly, this attitude was not entirely unsuccessful. Her fan base was stunningly devoted, as evidenced by the fact that the show received as many as ten thousand letters each month from people eager to participate in on-air discussion, as well as the fact that by the time each book club segment was televised, five hundred thousand viewers had read at least part of the novel, and almost as many bought the book in ensuing weeks (Max 36). Nonetheless, this very same attitude fostered and perpetuated a forum for discussing literature that was less integrated, more exclusionary, and ultimately less effective than it could have been at creating a genuinely open space of literary discussion in America. For while Winfrey resembled Bennett in that she offered the public complex and compelling reading material, she remained woefully dissimilar to her predecessor in that she refused to allow her readers to discuss that material in any but the most superficial fashion—at least when it came time for the taping of an actual OBC segment.

In episode after episode, Winfrey instructed her audience to experience the books in terms of how they personally related to the main characters, focusing less on the novels themselves and more on how their own life stories could be understood and improved in the process. Now I'm not suggesting here that Winfrey and her readers should have modeled their approach to literature after that of the academy, in the sense that "a select body of required texts would be elucidated by a trained scholar (the professor as hierophant expounding on mysteries hidden to the uninitiated)" (Davidson 2). Nor am I suggesting that they should have espoused any kind of dogmatic academic protocol—like, say, New Criticism—to interpret texts, for such schools of analysis are invariably reductive and flattening in their own right. In fact, the club—both Winfrey and its members at large—did produce its own sophisticated set of protocols for choosing, reading, and engaging with popular literature. The problem was that said protocols became virtually undetectable on OBC segments themselves, getting lost in the translation from real life to the small screen. Once the tape started rolling, neither Winfrey nor her readers seemed permitted to remark critically on the selections, or to advance beyond any but the most immature, advertisement-like, unconditionally loving responses to every single novel they encountered. Thus, unlike Bennett, Winfrey may have subtly perpetuated the very rift she sought to heal by giving the appearance of encouraging her audience to misread, or at least to under-read, the books she selected.

This is not to suggest that Winfrey's goal of championing authentically challenging literary discussion would have been an easy one, even if she had been able to improve her handling of reader response. To the contrary, she should have been able to expect the very authors she fed to turn promptly around and bite her hand. Once again, an examination of the Bennett prototype reveals that a less-than-grateful reaction on the part of the so-called challenging authors whose works such arbiters of taste seek to disperse is only to be expected. For even as he "admired, supported, and defended T. S. Eliot, Proust, James Joyce, E. M. Forster and Aldous Huxley, and boosted the unknown William Faulkner" (Carey, *Intellectuals and the Masses* 156), a number of these self-consciously intellectual intellectuals reacted by denigrating him at every available opportunity as a man entirely subject to the whims of the masses, as one embarking on a power trip with his own glorified tastes in tow, or as one so weakminded as to be obsessed with human interest and self-betterment. In short, these intellectuals in turn turned on him, a circumstance not unheard-of today.

Selected author Jonathan Franzen's remarks disparaging the club—and Winfrey's reaction to those remarks—provided a case in point. "I feel like I'm solidly in the high-art literary tradition," Franzen said in just one of a series of statements wherein he expressed doubt regarding the legitimacy of the Winfrey phenomenon, "but I like to read entertaining books and this maybe helps bridge that gap, but it also heightens these feelings of being misunderstood" (qtd. in Kirkpatrick, "Winfrey Rescinds," screen 1). Understandably—although not, perhaps, most wisely—Winfrey replied with a cool yet polite dis-invitation. "Jonathan Franzen," she explained in an official statement, "will not be on the *Oprah Winfrey Show* because he is seemingly uncomfortable and conflicted about being chosen as a book club selec-tion" ("Winfrey Cancels"). Her graciously backhanded response seemed too dismissive and non-confrontational considering the size of the matter that had been broached. For her failure to disclose, at long last, her own position in order to confront an issue—where does Oprah's Book Club fit in the hierarchy of American literary culture?—which had been practically begging for debate since the club's 1996 inception, can only be described as irresponsible, shortsighted and, I'm sorry to say, boring. This could have been some really riveting TV, to say nothing of its impact on the advancement of a truly inclusive approach to literature. Although I will address the entire fiasco in much more depth in the following chapter, I want to stress now that Winfrey could and should have acquitted herself even more gracefully by remaining steadfast in her resolve to have Franzen do the club seg-ment, thereby finally taking the opportunity to address some of the antipathy of which she had been the target for so long.

Not only did Winfrey fail to disclose her positionality at the helm of a significant literary movement to others in similar positions of power, but she also failed to do so before the eyes of her own audi-ence. While I commend Winfrey for her efforts to provide some kind of nonhierarchical, non-taste-codified space for her readers, I abhor that she attempted to do so in what amounts to a rather dumbed-down vacuum. The project in which Winfrey engaged herself was without a doubt an intellectually ambitious one, at least in light of the way she attempted to span the age-old intellectuals versus the masses, high versus low culture divide. Her refusal to more openly acknowl-edge this aspect of her project, however, seemed to encourage these archaic divisions rather than to efface them. For Winfrey rarely discussed with her book club participants some of the frequently voiced criticisms of the club, especially those rooted in the insupportable presumptions regarding the institution made by those outside it. Such presumptions—assertions that the club's selections were too depressing, too woman-oriented, too bourgeois, too middlebrow, too selfhelpy, too whatever—could all have been dispelled had Winfrey only acknowledged and responded to them, say, on the show. Yet hardly a word in defense of the club was spoken by anyone officially affiliated with it, and absolutely no words pertaining to taste or how it is created and regulated were ever uttered on the show. This, in turn, seemed to reflect certain presumptions on the part of Winfrey herself—specifically that, first and foremost, her club needed no defense, and secondly that her audience wouldn't be capable of understanding such concerns.

Admittedly, there is the distinct possibility that Winfrey's club didn't need a defense, at least inasmuch as it could not be characterized as anything but a smashing success in terms of the show's viewership and sales of the selections. It is the second presumption, though—the one that Winfrey appeared to make about her own audience—that concerns me more. For while it was none too surprising that Winfrey never discussed issues of literary taste with her audience, the sad corollary was that she never discussed issues of genuinely sophisticated approaches to reading with them. To make use of Spivak's term just once more, Winfrey seemed determined to present texts via methods that involved a fair amount of bullshit, which is essentially what I meant earlier by my mention of the imposition of extraneous competing narratives on the novels.

Carey has written that "the imaginative power reading uniquely demands is clearly linked, psychologically, with a capacity for individual judgement and with the ability to empathize with other people. Without reading, these faculties may atrophy" (Carey, *Pure Pleasure* xi). In this light, it seems at first glance fair enough that Winfrey should have opted to use human interest and empathy as the lenses through which she taught her audience to perceive literature. Upon closer examination, though, it becomes apparent that the problem with this technique was its failure to direct her audience to look beyond what these rather rudimentary methods can reveal. By encouraging her readers to sympathetically impose their own life stories over the ones they encountered in books, Winfrey caused OBC to have less to do with the books and more to do with the self-help narrative of her show itself. Indeed, according to *The Boston Globe* of May 29, 1997, whatever else it may have been, OBC was certainly part of Winfrey's larger mission to transform the character of the show, for "In less than three years, Winfrey succeeded in changing the meaning of her career. Where once 'Oprah' connoted the spilling of toxic revelations about corrupt relationships, now her first name—as noun, verb or adjective—might stand for self-improvement" (Canellos 1). Moreover, Winfrey:

> as much as anyone, convinced America that "dysfunction" described the national condition. Then, having diagnosed breakdowns in families, relationships and self-esteem, Winfrey aimed for cures. Affirmation replaced dysfunction, and to the surprise of many, millions of Americans began toning their lives to her new themes: Responsibility, gratitude, and respect. (Canellos 1)

Winfrey, then, via her simplistic, "how did this book make you feel?" approach, habitually represented genuinely good novels as little more than self-help texts to be consulted in her ongoing treatment of all that ails America.

The personal narratives of her readers and the self-help narratives of *The Oprah Winfrey Show* itself were not the only ones Winfrey imposed upon her selections, nor—though they were substantial— were they the largest ones. Winfrey related her own biographical narrative to the books as well. Everyone with a passing awareness of OBC knows that Winfrey has always loved books, and that—to hear her tell it—novels were essentially her only friends growing up. Everyone knows this because Winfrey's affinity for novels received as much publicity as the novels themselves did. Whenever the topic of OBC arose in an interview, Winfrey had an anecdote about reading's profound and poignant effect on her troubled formative years at the ready, such as, for instance, how she was delighted to find in Maya Angelou's *I Know Why the Caged Bird Sings* a book that reflected her own experiences. Leading by example, Winfrey urged her audience to view fiction not as an opportunity to engage intimately with a strange and complex other-consciousness, but rather to perceive it as being merely about the reader.

Another aspect of her own project that Winfrey could have discussed with her audience—as well as her fellow-occupiers of power—was the fact that her power is decidedly televisual. According to John Carey in his book, *The Intellectuals and the Masses:*

> Among European intellectuals hostility to newspapers was widespread. . . . The mass media aroused "the cheapest emotional responses," [T. S. Eliot] warned; "Films, newspapers, publicity in all forms, commercially-catered fiction—all offer satisfaction at the lowest level." . . . For some male intellectuals, a regrettable aspect of popular newspapers was that they encouraged women. In the Nietszchean tradition the emancipation and education of women were signs of modern shallowness. (7–8)

Similarly, owing to her revolutionary use of television as a format through which literature may reach a mass audience—revolutionary because TV has allowed her to assume a cultural role that would have been unreachable by traditional channels—Winfrey vexed those who resented the fact that much of the mass she reached consisted of middle-aged women home to watch her program. Just as the newspaper was scorned as an inferior medium of the masses at the turn of the twentieth century, television is perceived as a less privileged medium than print today. Even though television possesses as much power to extend the opportunity for knowledge to vast segments of the population as newsprint, traditional print sources of literary review are still considered, by many, to be superior to Winfrey's televisual mode of presentation simply because they are older.

Just because this rationale for disliking Winfrey's medium of choice was misguided doesn't mean that there weren't other, perfectly valid reasons to find it suspect. For more than virtually any other aspect of OBC, the fact that the club was a televisual institution stood as a simultaneous source of incredible power and a site of almost insurmountable weakness. The shortcomings that resulted from OBC's status as a TV segment stemmed not only from the nature of the medium itself, but also from the simplifying way in which Winfrey chose to apply it. In fact, as Winfrey herself will tell you, she has been aware from an early age of TV's unfortunate tendency to conflict with literature. According to a *Newsweek* special issue profiling the "Newsmakers of 1996," "the stepmother who raised Winfrey to be the compulsive reader she is—young Oprah had to write book reports for her—clearly saw TV as the enemy of literature. 'I was only allowed to watch for an hour . . . "Beaver" and "Andy Griffith." The rest was reading'" (Gates 77). Moreover, according to a *Mirabella* article included with the press kit sent to me by *Oprah Winfrey Show* senior publicist Audrey Pass, Winfrey freely acknowledges that her secret to finding the time to be so thoroughly successful and well-read is that "I don't watch TV, ever" (qtd. in Streitfield 50).

As I've mentioned above, Winfrey treated fictional, novelistic events primarily as things that happen to real people, doing so in large part because this approach to literature plays well on-screen. In fairness, the roots of elite resentment of such flagrant appeals to human interest are deep ones. According to Carey, such disgust descends almost directly from attitudes initially expressed in such early twentieth-century treatises as Clive Bell's *Art* and Ortega y Gasset's *The Dehumanization of Art.* Such works taught that "only people incapable of aesthetic emotion look for human interest and other such 'sentimental irrelevancies' in artistic works," as well as that "'the passion and pain of the man behind the poet' is the province of the degenerate masses, not the specially gifted minority" (Carey, *Intellectuals and the Masses* 215). Theory, he continues, declares literature and art to be "self-referential" and "self-reflexive," and in so doing perpetuates the notion that they have little connection to the lives of ordinary people.

Winfrey's effort to connect literature to the lives of her readers, then, can be seen as an attempt to roll back what Levine has termed "the sacralization of culture" in which "audiences were to approach the masters and their works with proper respect and proper seriousness, for aesthetic and spiritual elevation rather than mere entertainment was the goal" (146). She actively opposed the idea that literature as a "high art" was something to be tiptoed around, bowed down to and feared, or worse yet, simply ignored as something better left to trained professionals.

So the case can be made that her use of television was a necessary evil, in the sense that it inspired people to see the relevance of literature to their own lives and caused them to take an interest and participate in the club. Bearing this in mind, though, one must not lose sight of the fact that the way in which Winfrey used TV to present literature was most definitely an evil, the very one by which she entangled so many competing narratives in her presentation of the books. Television served as the means by which Winfrey managed to turn book discussions into little more than book advertisements, and to turn solid literary fiction into so much theatrically sympathetic autobiography and self-help. Even beyond that, the human interest presented by TV is disturbingly un-human, to the extent that it is wholly unlike that of books, which are rich, private, and full of imagination. Television does not appeal to the individual imagination; it is unavoidably glib and superficial in a way that the best books are not.

Thus while Oprah Winfrey went to great lengths to promote American literacy in general, and to foster a strong female readership in particular, she failed, in terms of disclosure of her own position as a powerful intellectual force and cultural authority, to go even further to address the issues of agency and taste that were raised by OBC. Still, her implicit assertions that literature should not be left completely in the hands of university specialists—and by extension that there is more than one right way to interact with a text—stand to go a long way toward the promotion of greater fluidity among traditional hierarchical artistic categories. For that reason, I intend to spend the rest of this book analyzing the club itself, the contemporary texts it presented from 1996 to 2002, and its turn to "great books" in its latest incarnation in such a way as to clarify perceptions about the entire institution, as well as its impact on American literary culture.

CHAPTER TWO

Jonathan Franzen Versus Oprah Winfrey: Disses, Disinvitations, and Disingenuousness

"Jonathan Franzen will not be on the *Oprah Winfrey Show* because he is seemingly uncomfortable and conflicted about being chosen as a book club selection. It is never my intention to make anyone feel uncomfortable or cause anyone conflict. We have decided to skip the dinner and we're moving on to the next book."

> —*Oprah Winfrey, the New York Times, October 23, 2001*

"I was delighted that Oprah Winfrey picked *The Corrections* for her Book Club. I'm glad many of her viewers are reading and enjoying it, and I'm sorry to learn that there won't be a dinner for this particular selection. I was never conflicted by any of this, although the printed logo on the dust jacket did make me uncomfortable. I'm a writer, not a spokesperson. . . . I'm sorry if, because of my inexperience, I expressed myself poorly or unwisely."

> —*Jonathan Franzen, the New York Times, October 23, 2001*

Since I began work in earnest on this book in December 2000, I've become keenly aware that it's just not hip to be comfortable with Oprah's Book Club. At Oxford, where I began reading each and every Oprah selection, my tutors and classmates encouraged me to take this project as an opportunity to deliver a scathing critique of OBC, essentially, to go in for the cultural kill. An exhaustive study of OBC was worth pursuing, they told me, so long as I used it as a chance to expose the club for the cheesy, sentimental, middlebrow institution they perceived it to be. Back in Illinois, on returning from the United Kingdom and mentioning the undertaking to old friends, I lost track of the number of times I was asked if I was joking. To dignify the club via scholarly research was, they insinuated, amusing. And going for dessert at Kramerbooks and Afterwords Café one night in Washington, D.C., I found the host and several of the wait-staff sporting navy blue T-shirts silkscreened with enormous O's and the words "NOT AN OPRAH BOOK" in hot pink letters. "You know how people say that Oprah's Book Club is very boring and monotonous?" explained the host when I asked him about the meaning of the slogan. "Well, we're saying that we have more—that we're more diverse than that." And, even though my first inclination was to disagree with him, the thing was, I *did* know how people said that.

In fact, such sensibilities were one of the areas I was attempting to address in my project, but anti-OBC snobbery—prevalent as I knew it to be—was difficult to point out or pin down in much more than an anecdotal fashion, let alone to analyze effectively. Anti-Oprah grousing—a bookstore customer's dismissal here, a slam in a literary supplement there—had proven itself to be by nature so diffuse and so difficult to measure discretely that I began to worry. My book—which had rapidly grown into a more sympathetic, even borderline defensive, view of OBC than I had anticipated—might come across as paranoid. In short, cultural cynicism regarding OBC was not such a concrete thing as I would have liked.

Or at least it wasn't until October 22, 2001, when an insulted Oprah Winfrey officially disinvited an outspoken Jonathan Franzen from the dinner segment of her book club. This was an unprecedented move in the history of OBC. Few things could have elated me more, given its applicability to my project, yet I was appalled by its implications for American literary culture at large. I had longed for concrete proof of just how galvanized the pro- and anti-OBC camps really were, and now it lay before me; to that extent, I was delighted. Yet the dispute sounded to me like the first shots in what I knew would be another inconclusive battle in America's ongoing cultural war, one more unproductive eruption of crossfire in the country's messily intertwined high culture versus low culture, television versus literature, men versus women conflicts. Sadly, for the most part, this is exactly how it has turned out. For this booklovers' spat did not, observes Salon.com's Laura Miller, occur in a vacuum:

> America's book culture too often seems composed of two resentful camps, hunkered down in their foxholes, lobbing the occasional grenade at each other and nursing their grievances. One side sees itself as scorned by a snooty self-styled elite and the other sees itself as keepers of the literary flame, neglected by a vulgarian mainstream that would rather wallow in mediocrity and dreck. Each side remains exquisitely sensitive to perceived rejection from the other, and the fact that one is often characterized as female and the other as male resonates with the edgy relations between the sexes of late. (Miller, "Book Lovers' Quarrel, screen 2)

And even though Franzen himself repeatedly expressed regret at appearing to draw a distinction between high and low literary culture —"Mistake, mistake, mistake to use the word 'high,'" he admitted in an October 26, 2001, telephone interview with the *New York Times*— the cultural damage had once again been done. "Both Oprah and I want the same thing and believe the same thing, that the distinction between high and low is meaningless,'" he continued. (Kirkpatrick, "'Oprah' Gaffe" screen 3) It's pretty to think that this is the case, and that ultimately, all the disses and the ensuing disinvitation turned out to be an opportunity for American readers to explore their obvious ambivalence about taste distinctions in general. But as the aftermath of the situation has shown, regardless of how he and Winfrey may feel, plenty of readers remain content to embrace reductive binary oppositions when choosing how they'll be entertained and what it means when they make these choices. Nonetheless, it remains worthwhile to take a blow-by-blow look at what exactly happened to create such a high-profile falling out in the fall of 2001, to understand the incident for what it really was, and to see what it still has the power to show.

In his now-notorious essay, "Perchance to Dream: In the Age of Images, a Reason to Write Novels," Jonathan Franzen wrote: "Exactly how much less novels now matter to the American mainstream than they did when *Catch-22* was published is anybody's guess. Certainly, there are very few American milieus today in which having read the latest work of Joyce Carol Oates or Richard Ford is more valuable, as social currency, than having caught the latest John Travolta movie or knowing how to navigate the web" (38). This essay appeared in *Harper's* magazine in April 1996. Oprah Winfrey launched her televised book club in September of the same year. In doing so, she made clear just how much the novel could be *made* to matter to the American mainstream. Winfrey eventually went so far as to expose the work of the aforementioned Oates to quite a large milieu when she selected *We Were the Mulvaneys* as the OBC pick for January 2001. That being the case, one might logically surmise that the man who'd written those sentences would be thrilled, or at least reservedly appreciative, when Winfrey selected his critically lauded third novel, *The Corrections*, for the club, and thus for a similar increase in its value as social currency. And he was. At first.

Franzen told *People* magazine that on the afternoon of August 31, 2001, when Winfrey dialed him up in his Manhattan apartment to let him know that his book had been chosen, "she introduced herself and said that she really, really loved the book and that the characters stayed with her for months afterwards. The conversation lasted no more than two minutes. I called my girlfriend in California and it was like, 'Oh my god'" (Schindehette 83). This reaction, almost adolescent in its giddiness, seemed to make perfect sense, coming as it did from a writer whose two prior novels, 1988's *The Twenty-Seventh City* and 1992's *Strong Motion*, sold roughly fifty thousand copies combined (Schindehette 84), and who once lamented—bitterly and in print—over the pain of "receiving sixty reviews in a vacuum," the "consolation for no longer mattering to the culture," and the failure of his culturally engaged novels "to engage with the culture I'd intended to provoke" (Franzen, "Perchance to Dream" 38). Even before Winfrey publicly announced her pick, *The Corrections* had attained bestseller status, with over three hundred thousand copies in print (Keller, "Author's Rejection" 20). After she made her announcement at the end of the September 24 edition of her show—which had profiled previous OBC pick *Cane River* and its author Lalita Tademy—the in-print total rose to eight hundred thousand copies, with that latest half-million books bearing the OBC logo (Keller, "Author's Rejection" 20). Thus did Franzen find himself receiving praise from the mainstream to match his longstanding critical approbation, not to mention selling even more of what was already a successful book. Both of these achievements seemed to be ones Franzen had long sought to consider his own.

In 1996, Franzen wrote that the only mainstream American household he knew well was the one in which he grew up, and that:

> I can report that my father, who was not a reader, nevertheless had some acquaintance with James Baldwin and John Cheever, because *Time* magazine put them on its cover, and *Time*, for my father, was the ultimate cultural authority. In the last decade the magazine whose red border twice enclosed the face of James Joyce has devoted covers to Scott Turow and Stephen King. These are honorable writers, but no one doubts it was the size of their contracts that won them covers. The dollar is now the yardstick of cultural authority, and an organ like *Time*, which not long ago aspired to shape the national taste, now serves mainly to reflect it. ("Perchance to Dream" 38-39)

This said, one would think that Franzen would have felt gratified by Winfrey's aspirations to fill the cultural void he believes to have been left by *Time*'s transition from arbiter to reflector of taste. For Winfrey sought to shape the taste of her audience, rather than merely to mirror it, as the very selection of such novels as Franzen's own indicates. Moreover, given her predilection to pick midlist and even obscure books by little-known authors, there can be no doubt that contract size had nothing to do with her decision-making process. In effect, Winfrey took the initiative to serve for millions of contemporary readers as precisely the kind of cultural authority that *Time* was for his father. While the dollar is and very likely always will be a yard-stick of a *certain kind* of cultural authority, it is similarly fair to acknowledge that, as far as the call for other kinds of cultural authorities is concerned, OBC certainly did its part to answer. All in all, then, for a writer who'd complained of his history of report cards of "A's and B's from the reviewers who had replaced the teachers whose approval, when I was younger, I had both craved and taken no satisfaction from; decent sales; and the deafening silence of irrelevance'" (Franzen, "Perchance to Dream" 41), as well as copped to having once begun an essay entitled "My Obsolescence" ("Perchance to Dream" 40), OBC should have seemed a chance at a kind of sudden, school-yard popularity for a kid who had previously been a self-acknowledged teacher's pet.

Certainly, after Franzen's many declarations of how badly he yearned to engage with the culture, his decision to then turn around and punch that culture in the face when it wanted, finally, to hang out could be regarded as counterintuitive at best. Nevertheless, this is exactly what he appeared to do. Only weeks after agreeing to appear on the show some time in the weeks following Winfrey's September 24 announcement, Franzen, in the middle of a sixteen-city book tour, began to make dubious remarks pertaining to his OBC status. In a letter to me dated December 6, 2001, Franzen wrote with respect to these remarks that he "wanted to make sure that you've found your way to the few halfway sensible discussions of it amid all the paddling and mischaracterizing and selective quotation" (letter to the author). Clearly I noticed during the flurry of heated coverage, that the media served the fiasco with relish and that the American public ate it up with a spoon, but I noticed, too, that even in complete context, full quotation, and charitable interpretation, it is absolutely impossible to conclude that Franzen, in the days leading up to his disinvitation, was inoffensive. The extensive trail of doubting comments he left in his wake during his publicity blitz was certainly enough to make anyone aware that he had come, for whatever reasons, to the conclusion that his Oprah selection was at least as much of a stigma as it was a distinction.

Much of the foundation for the fiasco was laid during an

October 4, 2001, book tour stop at Powell's, an independent book superstore in Portland, Oregon. During a now-infamous and oft-quoted interview that ran on the powells.com Web site, interviewer David Weich told Franzen, "I had recommended *The Corrections* to a friend. A few days later, Oprah announced that it would be her new book club pick. My friend emailed me to ask if I really thought he should read it" to which Franzen replied, simply, "Now I've signed a big label deal and I'm playing stadiums how good can I be?" (Weich, screen 6). "Exactly," continued Weich:

> But this is someone I very much respect, and I don't think his asking that question can be considered at all unusual. I'm sure that thousands of people won't read this book for no other reason than the fact that Oprah recommended it. If you're that popular, the thinking goes, if you speak to the masses, you can't possibly be saying anything too intelligent. Whereas from where I sit the authors that matter are the ones that can say something intelligent and thought provoking that a reasonably smart person can digest and enjoy. If you need a scholarly background to decode it, it might be great art, but to what end? You might as well be writing in Latin. (Weich, screen 6)

Interestingly enough, Franzen seemed at first to handle this line of questioning with grace and finesse. "That's one of the perverse, not to say fetishistic responses to the obliteratively ubiquitous presence of buying stuff in our lives," he replied, "to say 'I don't buy the popular stuff, I buy the small label stuff,' as if that makes you a any less of a consumer. But I'm somewhat guilty of it myself, and it follows a pattern. Certainly in music, suddenly the band you like because it was *not* produced goes to a major label and becomes heavily produced. It's hard to think of a major label Mekons recording, for example. It's impossible because they would never do it" (Weich, screen 6-7). Thus, Franzen, to his credit, appeared to be taking the discussion in the direction of a not especially original, yet still pertinent, and above all non-Oprah-specific exploration of American consumerism and taste in general.

Then, in the middle of this perfectly serviceable answer, he agrees:

> But I'm with you, I don't think the same applies to fiction. The problem in this case is some of Oprah's picks. She's picked some good books, but she's picked enough schmaltzy, one-dimensional ones that *I* cringe, myself, even though I think she's really smart and she's really fighting the good fight. And she's an easy target. But as far as being popular, yeah, I think Dave Barry is really funny. And *[The] Silence of the Lambs* is a really smart book. But of course everybody who's sold out and been co-opted, as I obviously have, says the same thing, and it makes for a pathetic spectacle. (qtd. in Weich, screen 7)

For Franzen to have referred to certain of Winfrey's selections "schmaltzy" and "one-dimensional" and to have called Winfrey herself "an easy target" could be construed as unkind, and even unwise, but his candor in this incident alone could hardly be considered damning. Immediately following this response, Weich steered the interview in a totally different direction, mentioning, "I noticed one of my favorite authors in your Acknowledgements, Donald Antrim," precipitating a lively discussion of the two men's reading habits. The interview ends shortly thereafter, with Franzen having said nothing further regarding the book club, and certainly nothing at all worth being demonized or disinvited over. Indeed, it's not unreasonable to believe that had Franzen simply left his OBC skepticism at that, Winfrey would never have been so insulted, the show would've have gone on, and my study would've been substantially less satisfying.

But he didn't leave it at that. His interviewers kept asking him leading questions, to be sure, but Franzen took it upon himself to follow said leads again and again. In his notorious October 12, 2001, interview with Jeff Baker in the *Portland Oregonian*, he curiously suggested that not only was he uncomfortable with his OBC designation, but also that said designation wouldn't prove to be worth all that much anyway since "we feel it does as much for her as it does for us" (Baker). When pressed to elaborate on what he meant by this statement, he continued, "well, it was already on the best-seller list

print a
w/ wv emblems⇒

and the reviews were pretty much all in. What this means for us is that she's bumped the sales up to another level and gotten the book into Wal-Mart and Costco and places like that. It means a lot more money for me and my publisher" (qtd. in Baker). His dismissiveness on this point appears more transparently silly when one considers just how *much* more money Winfrey's commendation meant for him and his publisher. According to the *New York Times*, Winfrey's selection helped prompt Franzen's publisher Farrar, Straus and Giroux, to print "an additional 500,000 copies. Authors typically earn more than $3 a copy toward their advance and royalties, so Ms. Winfrey's selection may have been worth more than $1.5 million to Mr. Franzen" (Kirkpatrick, screen 3). That hardly seems a negligible sum, yet when prompted to explain what his selection means, in turn, for Winfrey, he replied only that, "it gets that book and that kind of book into the hands of people who might like it" (qtd. in Baker). While the aforementioned comments alone would have taken a massive effort to explain away, Franzen's arguably most regrettable statement of all came when he attempted to explain to Baker what exactly he meant by "that kind of book." In doing so, Franzen stated that his selection for OBC, "heightens this sense of split I feel. I feel like I'm solidly in the high-art literary tradition, but I like to read entertaining books and this maybe helps bridge that gap, but it also heightens these feelings of being misunderstood" (Baker). One could wonder at this point why his publisher, having gone to so much trouble to give him such a carefully crafted publicity campaign—in effect, to make him so highly visible to audiences of *all* kinds—did not also make clear to Franzen the responsibilities attendant upon accepting the Oprah designation, or at least suggest that he might conduct himself more thoughtfully. Still, no one intervened, and Franzen kept talking.

On October 15, 2001, this time during an appearance on NPR's *Fresh Air*, Franzen persisted in giving his ambivalence a bit too much rope, and ended up hanging himself yet again—and, yet again, it seemed a terrible and unnecessary shame that he did so. For, even as he allowed himself to slip into the rather suspect practices of literary posturing and the implicit privileging of one audience over another, he made several shrewd observations about gender and the consumption of fiction, among them that:

> It has been a source of pain that there are interesting male novelists out there—and I'll just leave myself out of the statement for the moment—who don't find an audience because they don't find a female audience because it is—I mean, so much of reading is sustained in this country, I think, by the fact that women read, while men are off golfing or watching football on TV or, you know, playing with their flight simulator or whatever. (Gross 2)

Nonetheless, any potentially enlightening discussion of gender's role in the readership of novels seemed doomed to get lost in the inevitably ensuing flap over his perceived snottiness elsewhere in the interview.

In response to Terry Gross's question, "Were you surprised when Oprah chose your new novel . . .?"—which she framed with reference to his seminal 1996 *Harper's* essay, observing, "you wrote that most fiction readers are women. You said writers like Jane Smiley and Amy Tan are confident of an attentive audience, whereas all the male novelists that you know of, including yourself, are clueless as to who could possibly be buying your books"—Franzen said:

> It went beyond—yeah, I guess surprise is a word. I was so—it was so unexpected, that I was almost not surprised. It was like, "Oh, hey, Oprah, thank you for calling. Yeah? Oh, that's nice." And then I put down the phone because it literally never once crossed my mind that this might be an Oprah pick, partly because she seldom chooses hard covers, partly because she does choose a lot of female authors and partly because, as, you know, the reviewer in *The New York Times* said, you know, this is—"This feels too edgy to ever be an Oprah pick." And so it had never occurred to me. (2)

Frivolous, self-flattering preoccupations with such fatuous abstractions as "edginess" aside, some of the fears Franzen voiced about the consequences of his OBC selection seemed, in fairness, somewhat legitimate. For instance, "now I'm actually at the point with this book where I worry—I'm sorry that it's—I had some hope of actually reaching a male audience," he continued, "and I've heard more than one reader in signing lines now in bookstores say, 'You know if I hadn't heard you, I would've been put off by the fact that it is an Oprah pick. I figure those books are for women, and I never touch it.' Those are male readers speaking. So I'm a little confused by the whole thing right now" (2). Still—overwhelming and unsettling as it must have been for Franzen to have found his own name added to Winfrey's relatively short list of male authors—it's difficult to hear such statements without thinking he would have been well-advised to have kept at least some of that confusion to himself, or at least not to have been so eager to voice it in such half-baked and embittered terms.

While explicating his opinions on the wide and disparate audience for his novel, Franzen crassly expressed the belief that some readers are simply superior to others. In fact, when asked by Gross, "I wonder if you've been—if you feel like you've reached a lot of readers that ordinarily wouldn't have found your book and if, in doing so, you've gotten interpretations of your book that are surprising?" he replied:

> First and foremost, it's a literary book. And I think it's an accessible literary book. It's an open question how big the audience is to which it will be accessible, and I think beyond the limits of that audience, there's going to be a lot of, "What was Oprah thinking?" kind of responses. They, themselves, over there at "The Oprah Show," they have no idea how they're going to arrange the show because they've never done a book like this, and they're waiting to hear from their readers. (2)

Whether or not the producers of *Oprah* were having to think really hard about the format of their segment on *The Corrections* is neither here nor there; however, the resounding answer to any "what was Oprah thinking?"–style questions seemed to be that her thinking was right on target, that she'd picked a book that was both excellent in its own right as well as for the purposes of her club, and that in doing so she'd helped Franzen's novel earn such high praise as that found in Gross's own introduction wherein she described it as "one of those rare books which is both a literary and a popular success" (1).

Still, the worst of this interview was yet to come, and come it did in the form of Franzen's reply to Gross's final Winfrey inquiry, wherein he said of his experiences with the production of the show that, "I've done the sort of bogus thing where they follow you around with a camera and you try to look natural. And I've done a two-hour interview, which will be boiled down to three minutes or so. But, no, the show with—which I've never seen until they sent me a tape—the little coffee klatch and then the full audience stuff, that has not happened. Won't happen till November" (3). Television is, by nature, a reductive medium—by now, everyone and their mother knows that. So, while, it was fine—if a bit needless and uninspired—for Franzen to call attention to that reductiveness, it was wholly uncalled-for for him to be so belittling and dismissive of his audience. Moreover, this comment, taken in conjunction with others he made elsewhere—when he said in the *Philadelphia Inquirer*, for instance, that *The Corrections* is "a hard book for that audience," (qtd. in Schindehette 84), and thus that the kind of female readers drawn by the show were unintelligent, and therefore undesirable—make the position Franzen appeared to be taking virtually indefensible. In short, no matter how much Franzen may have intended his comments merely to discuss gender and fiction in America, or how many apologies he issued later, it remains difficult to see how his remarks could have been taken as being anything but insulting.

All in all, Franzen's vocal ambivalence prompted those following the situation to wonder why in the world he had accepted the OBC seal of approval in the first place. In fact, he stated in the October 12, 2001, edition of the *Portland Oregonian* that, "the weekend after I heard I considered turning it down," (Baker). Also in the *Oregonian*, he expressed what turned out to be highly controversial reservations about allowing the OBC logo to appear on the dustjacket of the book:

> I see this as my book, my creation, and I didn't want that logo of corporate ownership on it. It's not a sticker, it's part of the cover. They redo the whole cover. You can't take it off. I know it says Oprah's Book Club but it's an implied endorsement, both for me and for her. The reason I got into this business is

because I'm an independent writer, and I didn't want a corporate logo on my book. (Baker)

Ultimately, to assuage this concern, Franzen's publisher, Farrar Straus and Giroux, agreed to release some copies of the book with the Oprah label and some without it. And even though Jonathan Galassi, Franzen's editor at FSG, remarked that "the logo never bothered me, but it is not my book. The jacket itself is advertising" (qtd. in Kirkpatrick, "'Oprah' Gaffe," screen 4), Franzen apparently was not the only one upset by the OBC seal. According to Steven Zeitchik in a *Publishers Weekly* online newsletter dated October 28, 2001, Book Soup manager Denise Bonis told the *New York Times* that she had had to special-order non-Oprah editions for particularly sensitive customers, prompting Zeitchik to observe that while "there's always been an issue among design purists over incorporating the Oprah logo into jacket art . . . one really has to wonder who these readers are inviting to their houses that this would be an issue" (Zeitchik, e-mail newsletter).

In all seriousness, though, also at issue was whether or not OBC required the placement of the logo on selected books. According to the *Chicago Tribune*, an assistant to Winfrey said the TV show host did not require the logo, whereas Jeff Seroy, vice president and publicity editor of FSG, said, "Our understanding was always that the logo was not optional. If it is, that was not apparent" (qtd. in Keller, "Author's Rejection" 20). Assistant director of publicity for Warner Books, Tina Andreadis—who worked with Winfrey's staff when Lalita Tademy's *Cane River* was selected for OBC on June 20, 2001,—said the logo placement on the cover is "a given. And you want it. Honestly, this whole Jonathan Franzen thing is the first time I've heard of anyone not wanting the logo" (qtd. in Keller, "Author's Rejection" 20). While it may very well be the first time Andreadis or anyone else has heard an author express such logo-based apprehensions, it is most definitely not the first time an author has felt them. Lake Bluff, Illinois-based author Tawni O'Dell, whose novel *Back Roads* was the OBC pick for March 2000, said of her own reservations that:

I didn't know what to think. The image I had was that Oprah books were fluffy. After it happened, most people said, "This is great, this is wonderful." But some people did say, "Your book was a serious book. This will alienate male readers." And they were concerned that critics would write me off with, "Oh, it's an Oprah pick." (qtd. in Keller, "Author's Rejection" 20)

Nonetheless, O'Dell continued, "Still, I can't imagine saying no. Anybody who does what she does to get people to read is wonderful" (qtd. in Keller, "Author's Rejection" 20). Franzen, on the other hand *did*—obviously and vocally—imagine saying no.

It was only a matter of time then before Winfrey herself, in turn, imagined saying—and then did say—no to Franzen. Just weeks after hailing the novel publicly as "a work of art and sheer genius" (qtd. in Schindehette 84), and remarking that Franzen seemed to have poured so much into the novel that "he must not have a thought left in his head" (qtd. in Franzen, "Meet Me in St. Louis" 74), Winfrey disinvited the author from her show. A spokeswoman said Winfrey was aware of the comments that Franzen had made in a variety of interviews ("Winfrey Cancels"), and the *New York Times* reported that Winfrey's decision stemmed from "occasional public comments by Mr. Franzen that she felt disparaged her literary selections as middlebrow or unsophisticated." (Kirkpatrick, "Winfrey Rescinds," screen 1). Thus, in a statement in *Publishers Weekly* that appeared in an e-mail newsletter the night of Monday, October 22, Winfrey cancelled Franzen's scheduled appearance on the talk show (Kirkpatrick, "Winfrey Cancels," screen 2). Somewhat pointedly, she did not revoke her selection of the book itself, however; *The Corrections* remains in the Oprah canon, if you will, and can still be found among the complete list of OBC picks on her Web site, www.oprah.com.

FSG and Franzen himself apparently were somewhat blindsided by Winfrey's decision not to air the dinner segment, which seems understandable, inasmuch as up to that point, neither Winfrey nor any member of her staff had commented upon Franzen's remarks. Surprise aside, though, Franzen released a prompt and cordial statement of his own through FSG on Tuesday, October 23, 2001. In this statement—this apology, really—Franzen explained, among other things, that:

> I try to explore complicated emotions and circumstances as honestly and fully as I can. This approach can be productive on the page, but clearly hasn't been helpful in talking to the media, many members of which used the occasion of my book tour to raise questions about Oprah's Book Club and the supposed divisions among American readers. The conflict is preexisting in the culture, and it landed in my lap because of my good fortune. . . . I continue to be grateful to Oprah for her love of *The Corrections*. (qtd. in Zeitchik e-mail newsletter)

In just about everything he says here and elsewhere in the statement, he's right. The high versus low cultural conflict underscored by the dinner-cancellation debacle *was* preexisting in the culture, and neither he nor Winfrey can honestly be blamed for bringing the divide to light. Moreover, Franzen was right when, in an October 23, 2001, telephone interview with the *New York Times*, he said, "Oprah Winfrey is bent on demonstrating that estimates of the size of the audience for good books is too small, and that is why it is so unfortunate that this is being cast as arrogant Franzen and popular Winfrey—I like her for liking my book" (Kirkpatrick, "Winfrey Rescinds," screen 2). It really *was* unfortunate that the situation had been so consistently cast that way—although perhaps not for exactly all of the reasons that he thought it was.

Certainly it was upsetting to see cultural commentator after cultural commentator handle this controversy not as an opportunity to substantively discuss America's alleged cultural divisions, nor to expose said divisions' possible innate fallacies, nor to take this incident as anything more than an opportunity to revel in op-ed-page pandering and petty name-calling. I feel no compulsion to engage in any of that, but I do feel compelled to point out, before going any further, how disingenuous both Franzen and Winfrey were in their own respective handlings of this unfortunate impasse. The very format of Winfrey's show, for instance, pivots around making people uncomfortable, to the point of on-air tears and hugs. Or, as Chris Lehmann, editor of the *Washington Post's* "Book World" would have it, "This, mind you, is a woman who, in the course of her day job . . . routinely prompts suffering guests to weep before a mass audience and then places them into the creepy public solicitude of her therapeutic aide-de-campe, 'Dr. Phil' McGraw, a man all too easy to imagine presiding over a show trial" (Lehmann, "The Oprah Wars" 40). Thus, it was disingenuous of her to offer little by way of explanation for her cancellation other than that "it is never her intention to make anyone uncomfortable."

Similarly, it was disingenuous for Franzen—the author of three novels, a frequent contributor to the *New Yorker* and *Harper's,* and someone who wrote of his realization that "the money, the hype, the limo ride to a *Vogue* shoot weren't simply fringe benefits" to a novelist such as himself (Franzen, "Perchance to Dream" 38)—to attribute much of his own behavior in this situation to his unfamiliarity in dealing with the media, or to pose, in effect, as some kind of cultural naïf. In resorting to such irresponsible and phony behavior, both Winfrey and Franzen merely helped the very media they'd been criticizing as more than a little unfair in their fixation on high versus low cultural binarisms to continue in that way. What could have been an opportunity for a candid discussion of the status of America's literary culture was reduced to just another occasion for casting aspersions and an even deeper digging into the trenches of cultural warfare.

Certainly, neither Winfrey's nor Franzen's position in this situation was entirely unassailable; however, Franzen remained the one most compelled, for obvious reasons, to apologize; and apologize he did, quite profusely. Following the disinvitation in late October 2001, Franzen wrote an actual letter of apology to Winfrey herself, of which he said to *People* magazine "I can only presume it was hurtful for her to read that I was anything but purely grateful. . . . I should have expressed myself simply and graciously. I messed up" (Schindehette 84). Still, while Franzen sensibly presumed that his candor must have been hurtful to Winfrey, in the days immediately following the October 22, 2001, announcement many of his observations—"You can't talk to reporters you don't know the same way you talk to family and friends—you really only learn by burning your hand on the stove" in a phone interview with the *New York Times* (Kirkpatrick, "'Oprah' Gaffe," screen 2), for instance—sounded surprising, if not insincere. Indeed, the most baffling aspect of Franzen's apologies and remarks since the falling out was his own apparent bafflement at the way public opinion—popularly, in the media, and even among his fellow people of letters—swayed so soundly against him. Given that, in the days leading up to the disinvitation, Franzen left a trail of anti-Oprah comments like a swimmer bleeding carelessly in the ocean, it can be little wonder that the media sharks began to circle, then feast. Thus, I find it extremely difficult to swallow Franzen's assertions that, among other things: "I kind of lived in this bubble from which I wrote the book, then I stepped out into the world. . . . Suddenly, you find yourself in the middle of discussions that have been going on for years" (qtd. in Keller, "Franzen vs. the Oprah Factor" 3), and that "I said things that ended up hurting Oprah Winfrey's feelings and far too late it was pointed out to me that this was happening" (qtd. in Kirkpatrick, "Winfrey Rescinds," screen 2). To his credit, Franzen wrapped this last statement up by saying, "I feel bad for a number of reasons because I really don't like to hurt people, and I feel bad because the person being hurt is actually a really good person for American reading and writing" (qtd. in Kirkpatrick, "Winfrey Rescinds," screen 2). Essentially, it's easy to believe that Franzen is truly sorry for what he did, but practically impossible to believe that he was totally unaware he was doing it.

Fortunately, by November 2001, Franzen's expressions of regret regarding the disinvitation had grown both more self-aware and more culturally-aware. On Sunday, November 12, 2001, while he was in the city for an event sponsored by the Chicago Humanities Festival, he explained in an interview with *Chicago Tribune* cultural critic Julia Keller that:

> A few expressions of discomfort on my part are now being read as my scathing criticism of the book club. But I don't think Oprah Winfrey and I disagree. There is no opposition here, because there is truly no category of person in the world to whom I'm more naturally sympathetic and more grateful to as

a writer than readers. I've looked into the question of who reads literary novels in America. I know the distinction between high audiences and low audiences is false. I'm not trying to cast myself as a victim. I have no one but myself to blame. ("Franzen Vs. the Oprah Factor," 3)

Furthermore, in an interview with Jeff Giles of *Newsweek,* which ran in the November 5, 2001, issue of the magazine, Franzen stated: "I don't have any preconceptions about what kind of reader makes a good reader for my work. Anybody who enjoys the book is a friend of mine, and that specifically includes Oprah Winfrey" (69). Upon adding that "the last thing the literary community in America needs is some divisive little battle about this" and having it pointed out to him that, whether consciously or not, he had fired the first shot himself, he answered, "It's a disaster and I can't tell you how bad I feel about it" (69). I feel it should be noted here that while Franzen may in fact have fired the so-called first shot, so too did he assume the largest peacekeeping role in the ensuing melee.

Following the disinvitation, Franzen began defending Oprah's contributions to the American literary community in much the same repeated, rapid-fire fashion he had previously employed against OBC. Nary an interview or a public appearance could go by without his mentioning in some way how incredibly and genuinely sorry he was to have in any way maligned Winfrey or her club, or to have appeared to take a position indicative of a belief in cultural hierarchy. In perhaps his greatest gesture toward healing the cultural rift he himself helped to expose and exacerbate, Franzen said, upon winning the National Book Award (in the company of Andrew Solomon for his *The Noon-Day Demon: An Atlas of Depression* for nonfiction, Alan Dugan for his *Poems Seven: New and Complete Poetry,* and Virginia Euwer Wolff's *True Believer* for young people's literature) "I'd like to thank Oprah Winfrey for her enthusiasm and advocacy" (qtd. in Weeks, C1). When asked shortly thereafter whether or not he would allow his publisher to slap a shiny gold NBA Winner sticker on the cover of *The Corrections,* Franzen replied that he didn't think it would be productive for him to get into sticker discussions, indicating perhaps he'd learned at long last that sometimes the best answer to a leading question is no answer at all.

It can be argued, then, that knowing when to keep one's big mouth shut is central to the discussion of this situation. For if Franzen threw fuel on this particular fire by saying entirely too much, Winfrey in turn contributed paradoxically to the conflagration by saying virtually nothing at all. Even as the nation's opinion columns and letters to the editor pages brimmed over with populist, pro-Oprah rhetoric as embodied by such statements as "Poor Oprah. Only Gutenberg has done more to put good fiction in the hands of ordinary people, but Oprah and her books—some of them really good, none of them truly awful—are still disdained by many vigilantes of high culture" (Schimch 1), Oprah herself remained pointedly still. And although Franzen's copious apologies leading up to, and at, the National Book Awards—where, incidentally, just two years earlier Winfrey was honored for her contribution to reading and literature—provided Winfrey with multiple opportunities to weigh in on the subject, little more came from the OBC camp than the original disinvitation and a curt mention from a rep in *People* magazine that "she's moving on" (Schindehette 84). Well and good as it is to want to leave an unpleasant situation behind, even Winfrey's own Dr. Phil might suggest that it's none too healthy to do so without addressing the problem itself first.

In any case, Winfrey's silence on the matter proved scarily, imperiously, and inscrutably deafening. True, this silence could be interpreted as dignity, decisiveness, or even courage, but so too could it be attributed to fear, laziness, or the outright inability to think of anything to say. For even though "most authors are careful not to offend Ms. Winfrey" since her book club "sends legions of her viewers into bookstores," "she has often made best-sellers of previously low-selling, but critically acclaimed authors," and "her selections have included highly regarded writers like Toni Morrison, Wally Lamb and Isabel Allende" (Kirkpatrick, "Winfrey Rescinds," screen 1), she came across as arrogant and ignorant herself when she appeared to expect foot-kissing gratitude as the only possible emotional response her notice might evoke in an author. To this end,

Franzen said, "I feel as if I'm not the first writer to have experienced some minor discomfort over the selection. I'm just the first one who was unwise and insensitive enough to mention some of that discomfort in public" (Giles 68). And while "unwise" and "insensitive" were certainly apt descriptors of Franzen's behavior in this situation, so too could Winfrey's own conduct be called insensitive. For here at last she found herself facing an opportunity to address many of the complaints frequently raised against her approach to literature, her treatment of authors as celebrities, and even the very existence of her club in the first place, among other things. Instead, she treated this potentially critical juncture with an uncharacteristically icy reserve and a failure to disclose her own positionality within any kind of cultural hierarchy.

In fairness, given the two alternatives of near constant speech or almost absolute silence over the affair, Oprah probably made the wisest choice, or at least the one that best allowed her own interests to emerge unscathed. For when all this began, she was arguably in the right, having made, in *The Corrections*, "a bold and generous choice for a book that is also bold and generous. If the author has on this occasion lacked the nerve and imagination of his creation, well, writers are human beings, too, and sometimes they screw up" (Miller, "Book Lovers' Quarrel" screen 3). In a sense, though, Oprah too lacked nerve and imagination; in a way, she screwed up as well. Had she either allowed Franzen to appear on the show after all, or at least allowed herself to comment more publicly on the situation as it unfolded, she could have moved OBC beyond its binary, either you love it or you love to hate it status quo. Beyond that, it would have made for some truly fascinating television. Nonetheless, Oprah made it more than clear that she would not be willing to discuss the matter any time soon, and her decision has held.

Cultural commentators on the other hand proved themselves every bit as determined to talk about the collapse as Winfrey was not to. Sadly, their approach to it typically involved little more than reveling in superficial, ad hominem attacks against Franzen, as *Chicago Tribune* columnist Mary Schmich does when she writes: "Maybe you've even run across Franzen's official photo during his burst of fame. He's a handsome guy. He looks as if he might show up in one of those high-art fashion ads that wants you to believe that the brooding, cleft-chinned model is a Harvard grad student because who else would wear such earnest glasses and not have time to shave?" (Schmich 1). Others cited out of context the most offensive quotes uttered by Franzen over a period of weeks and took him easily to task for them, as did one literary agent in *Newsweek*, quoted as saying, "most of the people I hear talking about all this now refer to Franzen along the lines of 'that pompous prick'" (Giles 68). Still others pulled the occasional holier-than-thou, populist pose in defense of Winfrey and her perceived readership, as did Jonathan Yardley, when he wrote in his *Washington Post* opinion column of his disgust with writers who "are troubled over guilt by association with what they regard as inferior work" and who "feel that their books are being read by the wrong people, i.e. housewives from Oklahoma who don't know SoHo from TriBeCa and, worse, don't *care*" (Yardley, "The Story of O, Cont'd" 21). In doing so, they managed to avoid any substantial analysis of what was really at issue—specifically, what if any kind of artistic cultural hierarchy exists in America, why it exists, and what it signifies for our society—almost entirely.

In fact, a great deal of this glib, misleading criticism served as often as not to further entrench rather than call into question the notion of high versus low cultural contentiousness in America. Weighing in on Franzen's response to his novel's selection as an OBC pick, for instance, the flak.com Web site posted an editorial stating that:

> Such a reaction should come as no surprise coming from a guy who hangs out with David Foster Wallace and Donald Antrim and lists Don DeLillo and Thomas Pynchon as his major influences. Such a close identification with grad-school darlings immediately locates Franzen clearly on one side of America's long-entrenched literary divide—the literati versus the hoi-polloi, sophistication versus mass consumption. Right down to his wardrobe—thick-rimmed geek glasses and tweed jackets abound—Franzen really wants to be one of these guys, among them, someday read by bluestockings and Ph.D. candidates. And he seems, like DeLillo and Pynchon, to want to comment on

society, to try and capture its ethos in print, but otherwise keep his hands clean of popular culture. ("Franzen's Dilemma")

Cheap and shortsighted as this editorial is, it's far from the only piece of commentary about the debacle that, instead of helping dispense with the notion of high and low as being unfailingly clear cut and constantly clashing, actually fostered precisely such vapid distinctions. Taking his own tasteless stab at the subject, *Amistad* novelist David Pesci wrote: "If Jonathan Franzen was a 3-year-old this would be a moment for an extended timeout where he would be told to contemplate such things as manners, gratitude and his truly staggering intellectual narcissism. Of course, Franzen is an adult, at least biologically. But the analogy works since he's acting like a spoiled whiny little brat with a full diaper" (Pesci 21). While I'm hesitant to agree that Pesci's analogy is good for anything—it hardly casts new light on the issue of taste distinctions in America—it certainly served to cast hurtful aspersions against a man who, when all is done and spoken, probably didn't deserve them. Similarly, turning once more to Schmich's column on the issue, we hear her ask about Franzen with rhetorical glee, "Sounds like a brat who accepts an invitation for a free cruise then whines that some of the guests are beneath his social class, doesn't he?" (1).

Opinion writers were hardly the only ones who seemed to glory in such relatively depthless coverage. Writing of critic Harold Bloom's remark that he would be "'honored' to be invited on Winfrey's show and that "it does seem a little invidious of him to want to have it both ways, to want the benefits of it and not jeopardize his high aesthetic standing," David Kirkpatrick of the *New York Times* referred to Bloom as a "defender of that high-art literary tradition," thereby effectively validating the existence of the very institution Franzen had been so derided for once mentioning in affiliation with his own work (Kirkpatrick, "'Oprah' Gaffe," screen 2). Similarly, a number of Franzen's fellow OBC-selected authors were eager to toss in their two cents worth on the subject, resorting to disappointing if not entirely surprising masses versus the elite divisions to do so. "I was angry on behalf of the club. And I was appalled as a reader who appreciates the incredible amount that Oprah Winfrey has done for books," proclaimed Chris Bohjalian (qtd. in Schindehette 84), whose anger, while certainly a valid response to Franzen's clumsily committed slight of OBC, should not have been his only one, inasmuch as it was irrational, unanalytical, and therefore unsuited to an issue as complicated as the one at hand. Moreover, genuine as his sympathetic anger may be, Bohjalian—who saw sales of his 1997 *Midwives* jump from 100,000 to 1.6 million copies after it became an Oprah pick (Schindehette 84)— had less impetus to express ambivalence of the sort voiced by Franzen, who had already hit the bestseller list pre-Oprah.

Andre Dubus III expressed his reaction to the falling out in terms of a precast high-low power structure, declaring: "It is so elitist it offends me deeply. The assumption that high art is not for the masses, that they won't understand it and they don't deserve it—I find that reprehensible. Is that a judgement on the audience? Or on the books in whose company his would be?" (qtd. in Kirkpatrick, "'Oprah' Gaffe," screen 3). Reprehensible as any such elitist assumption—which I don't think was necessarily being made by Franzen in this case—definitely would be, reprehensible too was the way in which virtually everyone who commented upon the situation felt compelled to scramble as far as possible to either one side or the other of the high-low spectrum, thereby perpetuating the very institution they claimed to hate.

Clearly, it's big fun for columnists and critics to seize events such as this one as opportunities to whip out their poison pens and write witty, acerbic little indictments of elitism, because nobody likes an elitist. But that's just the thing—*nobody* likes an elitist. As Lehmann noted in his own rare, right-minded editorial:

> One is, in American Kulturkampfs, either with "the people" or their "elitist" enemy (even though in the actual American social order, one is about as likely to encounter a genuine self-professed "elitist" as, say, a practicing Owenite). This is the plodding script by which all manner of controversies over public taste and aesthetic standards have played out for decades—from the near-identical [Robert] Mapplethorpe, Andres Serrano, and Brooklyn Art Museum dustups to clashes over "political correctness" in

the American university. In all such set-pieces, the right claims
heroically to defend—even as the left in populist ardor, claims to
"subvert" or "appropriate"—the products of mass culture from
the precious disdain of the shifty elitists lording over their nasty
taste hierarchies. (Lehmann, "The Oprah Wars" 40)

Thus, regrettably, most of the ink spilled over this cultural disaster
proved futile, with the ones doing most of the spilling merely revisit-
ing rote arguments while allowing the real issue to go unbroached.
Flak.com wrote that Franzen was "unprepared for the full impact of
what being a social novelist entailed. He wrote a novel that commented on the state of contemporary society, and yet he didn't fore-
see how contemporary society would comment on the book." In
fairness, he can't be expected to have foreseen how society would
comment on his book, but one can imagine he might've hoped it
would do so in a more evenhanded, less knee-jerk manner.

Indeed, one of the only commentators who got even remotely
close to the crux of the matter—that high and low cultural distinctions are an increasingly archaic and impotent vestige of a hierarchical past—was *Harper's* magazine editor Lewis Lapham, and even he
seemed to do so almost tangentially or inadvertently. After describing
Franzen as "a guy from the country who shows up at court wearing
the wrong shoes," Lapham added that "it was part of the avant-garde
literary tradition that came out of the '20s—that the writer was this
genius in whose presence one behaved oneself, that a hush fell over
the room. It still had some force through the 1960s, but now the gar-
ret is a thing of the past. A good writer is a rich writer and a rich
writer is a good writer" (qtd. in Kirkpatrick, "'Oprah' Gaffe," screen
2). Similarly, author Rick Moody—who has never been an OBC pick,
but who has written *The Ice Storm*, *Purple America*, and *Demonlology*—
asserted that contemporary literary success depends less upon intan-
gible, abstract distinctions of highbrow versus mass acclaim, and
more on the measurable, concrete distinction of financial gain.
Asked whether or not he would appear on Winfrey's show Moody
answered unconditionally in the affirmative: "If you want to sell
700,000 copies, then you have to play ball with the 700,000-copy

vehicles, and then you are in Oprah-land" (Kirkpatrick, "'Oprah' Gaffe," screen 3). Furthermore, he continued, "I am published by the AOL-Time Warner empire. If you are being published by one of the big houses, you can't object that you are not commercial in some way: what book doesn't have the publisher's logo on the spine?'" (qtd. in Kirkpatrick, "'Oprah' Gaffe," screen 3). In other words—even though numerous artists, commentators and the so-called general public seem reluctant to admit it—cultural capital and economic capital are increasingly becoming one and the same.

America is a rich country with an extremely high literacy rate. Attitudes held with regard to this literacy, then, are an indispensable way of describing and understanding American culture and values. Franzen's own rather awkward and embarrassing attempt to articulate his ambivalence about OBC was precisely the sort of self-questioning behavior that befits a culture that is itself so transparently ambivalent about its own tastes. Frequently arbitrary taste distinctions such as high and low certainly do exist and simply cannot be expected to disappear, that much is true. Yet also true is the fact that these distinctions as they are typically drawn are far too stark and reductive. Bearing that in mind, then, if there's anything that the Franzen fiasco should have taught us, it's that taste-based ambivalence in America bears discussion, and that running around making self-congratulatory proclamations along the lines of either "I hate the Oprah Book Club—I'm with the high artists!" or "I love the Oprah Book Club—I'm with the masses!" doesn't cut it. It is possible, for instance, to voice objections to OBC—to appreciate how she encouraged so many people to read, while also calling into question how she approached literature itself, say—and not to be simultaneously a snob. So too is it possible to be a diehard OBC devotee—to admit to having read and enjoyed all of her picks—and not be simultaneously ignorant or unappreciative of the work of such decidedly non-Oprah authors as Don DeLillo or David Foster Wallace.

At a certain point in her column on the incident, Mary Schmich began to make a bit more sense. She observed that, "Ordinarily, disputes involving serious authors are of interest primarily to those of the high-art literary tradition. This one's making the news partly because Oprah is Oprah but also because it stirs up mud in the American cultural divide" (Schmich 1). At last, someone—besides the practically self-flagellatingly apologetic Franzen himself—gratifyingly conceded that the nation's so-called cultural divide is in fact muddy. For whatever else the disinvitation might be worth, the incident *should* have been taken as a rich and rare opportunity to study this muddiness in order to attain an understanding of why we, as Americans, feel so compelled to cling to cultural divides in the first place.

Assuredly, the Winfrey-Franzen affair has much to teach us about the extent to which taste—literary and otherwise—along with attendant attitudes regarding such factors as commercialism and hipness, has to do with self-perception, identity formation, and socialization. People speak frequently about issues of taste—the books they read, the music they listen to, the movies they've seen, the programs they watch—both with people they've just met and people they've known for a great while, with the latter category often tending to be comprised of individuals whose tastes mirror their own. As long ago as 1757, philosopher David Hume argued in his classic essay, "Of the Standard of Taste," that people with the best taste frequently have the best—and the most—friends, because, "a very delicate palate, on many occasions, may be a great inconvenience both to a man himself and to his friends: But a delicate taste of wit or beauty must always be a desirable quality; because it is the source of all the finest and most innocent enjoyments, of which human nature is susceptible. . . . Wherever you can ascertain a delicacy of taste, it is sure to meet with approbation" (236–37). In short, we like to take recommendations on how to entertain, instruct, and improve ourselves from people we love and/or whose opinions we respect, since the things being recommended affect, whether directly or indirectly, how we judge ourselves and others. As Bourdieu correctly observes, in his landmark work *Distinction: A Social Critique of the Judgement of Taste*, "taste classifies, and it classifies the classifier" (6). Laura Miller of salon.com notes the effect these tendencies can sometimes have on literature:

> The sad and petty truth is that far too many book lovers don't

really want a good book to reach a large audience because that would tarnish the aura of specialness they enjoy as connoisseurs of literary merit. I'm not just talking about egghead critics here, since there are just as many people who stand ready to condemn "hip and trendy" or "too clever" books they've never taken the trouble to read. ("Book Lovers' Quarrel" screen 2)

Thus, when examined more carefully, the disinvitation reveals that Winfrey and Franzen were not the only ones acting arrogantly; so too was anyone who used the incident to stake his or her claim entirely on either side of the cultural divide.

To read at all in a culture so dominated by visual media is, in a sense, to wear a badge of special distinction, which is part of the reason it's so upsetting that America's literate subculture possesses such a tendency to conduct itself in a detrimental, divisive, and cliqueish fashion. Indeed, as Miller rightly observes:

What makes Franzen's gaffe so unfortunate is that *The Corrections* is the kind of book that bridges the gap between high- and middlebrow readers, between people who like brainiac puzzle novels and those who want stories of family and emotional life. Enid Lambert, the mother character in the novel, is the book's great achievement of a sentimental Middle American woman that's smart and unflinching but ultimately sympathetic. Oprah trusted that the readers she sent to *The Corrections* would connect with that sympathy and at the same time be able to handle Franzen's savage take on contemporary life. ("Book Lovers' Quarrel," screen 3)

As evidenced by sales figures for *The Corrections* and enthusiastic feedback on the oprah.com Web site, many OBC readers rose to the occasion. Sadly, given Winfrey's abrupt cancellation of the author dinner and studio audience participation segments, these readers never had a fair chance to see the book discussed, at least not officially.

The Corrections is a truly thought-provoking novel, which makes the cancellation of its discussion—and thus of any insight such discussion would have yielded on the book in its own brilliant right— sad in and of itself. Add to that the fact that matchless opportunities to discuss a host of other pertinent issues were also squandered, and the cancellation becomes even sadder. Observing that the disinvitation spoiled a chance to flesh out attitudes regarding gender and the consumption of fiction, Janice Radway, professor of literature at Duke University and author of *A Feeling for Books: The Book-of-the-Month Club, Literary Taste, and Middle Class Desire,* said:

> Oprah is obviously a serious reader with particular goals and interests in mind. She's criticized by high-art critics or even cultural-studies scholars, because they say when she picks a book like *Beloved,* she's not looking at its aesthetic complexity—she's making it sentimental, confessional. That seems like a pointless criticism to me. When you write a book and put it out, that book can be read in many ways by many different people. People are always thumbing their noses at women's reading. It's a dismissal of women's engagement with literature, rather than recognizing that it's a particular and very vital way of making literature a part of daily life. ("Deconstruct This" B4)

Analogously, regarding the missed forum to discuss how OBC actually presented literary fiction—possibly even with a more diverse audience than usually watches the show—Jerry S. Herron, director of the American studies program at Wayne State University, wrote:

> Instead of getting mad at Franzen, Oprah should have said, Come on the show. . . . There are other writers who would conceivably have a stake in exactly this conversation about high art and entertainment. This is really a debate about the role that literature plays in our society and who has the right to adjudicate the quality of literature and to promote literature. That's a tailormade question that would invite writers and college literature professors to have conversations about just those matters. And they're nowhere. ("Deconstruct This" B4)

The cancellation also destroyed an opportunity to discuss the impact of OBC in the celebritization of authors. Some novelists—including DeLillo, one of the writers Franzen himself most admires—categorically refuse to appear on television, while others—including Franzen's friend David Foster Wallace, who once insisted that Franzen be at his side during a segment with television host Charlie Rose—agree to appear only reluctantly. Many writers are ambivalent about television, for as Moody explains, "literature wants want television has. But if you could say what you needed to say in that medium, you wouldn't need to write a book" (qtd. in Kirkpatrick, "'Oprah' Gaffe," screen 3). It would have been fascinating to hear more about why exactly these contradictory pulls between televised celebrity and literary reclusivity exist.

Finally, to have actually allowed *The Corrections* show to go on could have shed some much-needed light on what on earth went so, so wrong between Franzen and Winfrey. For as Schmich observed, there was more going on than may initially have met the eye:

> Among certain residents of the cultural ozone, it's considered better to have your book applauded by 12 English professors than to have it read by a few million ordinary American women. If all those Oprah-watching women like it, it can't be all that good, can it? Franzen's remarks smelled of that kind of snobbery until I read them in context. Then I understood that his mistake was not so much snobbery as indiscretion. (1)

As it stands, the show never did and never will go on, and as a result, the entire situation lacks to this day the kind of context it so desperately deserves. To this end, Lehmann notes:

> One of the more painful ironies here is that the ambivalence Franzen voiced over the book club actually meshed quite clearly with the subject of *The Corrections* itself. . . . Why then should it be so unthinkable to bring up the book club itself—surely the most powerful market force in American publishing—for the same kind of discussion? Why not have Franzen appear on the show and air his views about the book club with its members? Why not, in other words, use this as a near-unprecedented opportunity to give a mass public a direct stake in a literary dispute? ("The Oprah Wars" 40)

Why not, indeed? Why not take this unequalled chance to explore and perhaps even explode extant notions of elitism and aesthetic hierarchy in American literary culture? Because ultimately—as far as I or anyone else can tell—Oprah Winfrey said no.

I have to add, though, that as much as the decision of whether or not to have Franzen on the show was in Winfrey's hands, I can't hold her totally to blame. Even before she began her official book club, Winfrey was quoted as saying how in awe she is of authors and their creations, that "writers are in a class by themselves. I have the ultimate respect for them" (Johnson 6). As romantic as such declarations occasionally struck me, I'd be lying if I said I didn't understand how she felt. In fact, when I found out that Franzen was doing a signing at Politics and Prose in Washington, D.C., on October 11, 2001, I set out for the event, a contingent of staffers from the college literary magazine I edited in tow, giddy with the kind of enthusiasm most typically exhibited by groups of people on their way to a rock show. We arrived well before he was supposed to begin, took our places among the already standing-room-only crowd, and waited, speculating and disagreeing excitedly about what passage he'd choose to read, what his voice would sound like, what he'd be wearing, and how tall he'd be. Yet we all agreed that no matter how anything else turned out: he would be funny; he would be cool. And, as we listened to him read about Gary Lambert, amateur kitchen video-surveillance, mixed grill, and ANHEDONIA, we knew that we had been right.

After the brief question-and-answer portion, we waited toward the end of the lengthy and serpentine signing line—my companions to get their books autographed; me both to get my book signed and to hand him the eleven-question survey I'd been distributing to each and every Oprah author since I began this project. When it was my turn, with my left hand I gave him—carefully, so he wouldn't see the pencil-scrawled notes of sentences and page numbers I'd made all over the front flyleaf—my book to sign, which he did: "To Kathy 10.11.01, Jonathan Franzen." With my right hand, I gave him the questionnaire and explained in what I hoped was a concise and illuminating fashion why I was giving it to him, what I hoped to learn by doing so, and that I'd be very grateful if he could fill it out and send it back to me whenever he got the chance. "That sounds fascinating," he said upon graciously hearing me out and slipping the survey into his briefcase, at which point I was confident—even though he was in the middle of a sixteen-city book tour, and even though he certainly had other things to write than answers to my somewhat generalized questions—that I would hear back from him.

I left the signing elated—I recall jumping self-indulgently up and down outside the store at the prospect of receiving another author reply—and went with my friends for dinner at a Chinese place down Connecticut Avenue from Politics and Prose, where we stayed very late, eating and talking. I was supposed to take my GRE the following morning and then drive several hundred miles to Ithaca, New York, the following afternoon, but I didn't care; I didn't care because I. Had met. Jonathan Franzen. Our conversation kept turning and returning inevitably to the reading: how excellent it was, how cool Franzen seemed, how convinced we were that he'd respond to my questions.

Thus, I was more than a little inclined to cry say it ain't so when I learned slightly less than two weeks later that, as a result of his having publicly disrespected OBC all over the country—in the notorious *Oregonian* interview, for instance, no more than a day after we'd gone to see him—he'd been unceremoniously disinvited from the *Oprah Winfrey Show*. I couldn't believe that an author who had seemed so articulate and thoughtful could be so careless and contemptuous. Even worse, I was sure that, given the fact that he had managed to embroil himself in something of a nationwide cultural war, he'd never reply to my survey. I went back and re-read my questions (among them: "What do you make of detractors—those people who criticize the selections, etc.—of the Oprah Book Club? As in who do you think—critics? Other authors? Readers in general?—make complaints against the club, and do you believe that any of these objections are valid ones?"). I concluded that it was no wonder he didn't want to answer.

But then he did. In a letter dated December 6, 2001,—which my little sister called and read to me over the phone from our parents' house in Illinois, where I'd been asking authors to send their replies — he wrote:

> A belated response to your hand-delivered letter and question-
> naire. You'll probably understand why I'd just as soon not fill the
> latter out, but I'm wondering how this fall's fiasco has affected

your project, and I want to make sure that you've found your way to the few halfway sensible discussions of it amid all the paddling and mischaracterizing and selective quotation . . . and the attendant self-righteous populist posturings. (Franzen, letter to the author)

He helpfully went on to suggest that I check out, among other things, a column on the subject in the online *American Prospect* as well as "an essay of mine, kind of halfway on the subject" (Franzen, letter to the author) in the December 24 and 31 issue of the *New Yorker*.

In the essay, entitled, "Meet Me in St. Louis: An Author's Televised Homecoming," Franzen does paint a rather convincing portrait of the pain, both physical—"now, on Monday morning, as I stand in the shadow of an Arch that means nothing to me, the rash has coalesced into a flaming, shingles-like band of pain and itching around the lower right side of my torso"—and psychological—"I could see the back of my old house. . . . I couldn't stand to look for more than a second"— of being coerced to go home again for the benefit of the *Oprah Winfrey Show* cameras (71-72). Here and throughout the essay—his medium of choice—he seems to address some of the points he may have been trying to make in his earlier, more controversial comments. Television, he suggests—and rightly so—is frequently sappy, sentimental and emotionally false. Nonetheless, he still seems willing to disclose a lot more, specifically a lot more emotionally intimate information and almost human interesty detail to the audience of the *New Yorker* than he was to that of the *Oprah Winfrey Show*.

As I read the essay—which I suggest anyone with any interest in the topic take a look at in its entirety—I couldn't help but think that over the course of his encounters with the Winfrey production team, Franzen seemed to behave almost like one of his own characters. At the essay's opening, he describes "my third book, *The Corrections*" as "a family novel about three East Coast urban sophisticates who alternately long for and reject the heartland suburbs where their aged parents live" (Franzen 71). He goes on to recount how, during his dealings with "one of Winfrey's producers, a straight-shooter named Alice" he has it explained to him that in order "to produce a short visual biography of me and an impressionistic summary of *The Corrections* the producers would need 'B-roll' footage to intercut with 'A-roll' footage of me speaking" and that they would like to shoot some of said B-roll in his former St. Louis neighborhood (Franzen 71). What, he asks, about "filming me here in New York?" (71), going so far as to suggest to Alice that, "between my apartment and my studio, in Harlem, which I share with a sculptor friend of mine, there was quite a lot of visual interest in New York!" especially since—even though he has written two novels about the place—"St. Louis doesn't really have anything to do with my life now" (71). In short, here and throughout the rest of the essay, Franzen comes across as mildly obsessed with conveying the image of his *own* East Coast sophisticate lifestyle.

Still, it seems as silly and unimaginative to obsess about and identify oneself with reductive coastal versus center distinctions as it does to do so with similarly reductive high versus low cultural ones. But more than that, it seems in this case almost to imitate the *Oprah Winfrey Show's* approach to fiction—which is to say, to fixate on the author's personal tie to the subject of a novel, to act as if fictional scenarios are events that really happen, and to behave as if the author has at least some small thing in common with one or more of his or her characters.

Toward the end of the essay Franzen explains both his ambivalence regarding the OBC designation and the ambivalence apparently inherent in his typical mode of conduct, writing:

> Beginning the next night in Chicago, I'll encounter two kinds of readers in signing lines and in interviews. One kind will say to me, essentially, "I like your book and I think it's wonderful that Oprah picked it," the other kind will say, "I like your book and I'm so sorry that Oprah picked it." And, because I'm a person who instantly acquires a Texas accent in Texas, I'll respond in kind to each kind of reader. When I talk to admirers of Winfrey, I'll experience a glow of gratitude and good will and agree that it's wonderful to see television expanding the audience for books. When I talk to detractors of Winfrey, I'll experience bodily the discomfort I felt when we were turning my father's

oak tree into schmaltz, and I'll complain about the Book Club
logo. ("Meet Me in St. Louis" 75)

Here, as at so many other points during the unfolding of the epic
Winfrey-Franzen affair, attention is called to the issue of why people
express taste and how they choose to do so. For not only is expressing taste a passing of judgement on a cultural artifact or institution,
it is also the subjection of oneself to judgement. Franzen in this
instance, evidently out of fear of being misjudged himself, seemed
to misjudge Winfrey and her club. Winfrey in turn seemed to misjudge what an excellent opportunity this misunderstanding might
have provided to discuss why people feel the way they do about OBC
in particular and about literature at large.

CHAPTER THREE

Raise Your Hand if You Haven't Done All the Reading: The Novels of OBC

"For the pocketful of small change it's worth, I don't much care for most of the books she anoints. As anyone who has seen her show is surely well-aware—I watched it once and nearly gagged on all the treacle and psychobabble— she has a powerful taste for earnest high-mindedness and is drawn to books of that ilk. . . . But she doesn't pick genuinely bad books. If I were forced to choose—perish the thought—between reading a year's worth of Oprah selections or the top dozen books on the fiction bestseller list, I'd make a beeline for Oprah. The literary taste of the American mass market is execrable. Oprah Winfrey is doing her part to elevate that."

—Jonathan Yardley, the Washington
Post, November 5, 2001

"They all seem to me to be very solid, honorable books, with feeling and some kind of substance."

—Robert Gottlieb, former editor of Knopf
and the New Yorker regarding the
selections of OBC, the New York
Times, October 29, 2001

Whether they choose to be stridently snotty and uninformed about it like Jonathan Yardley, or quietly sensible and discerning like Robert Gottlieb, it seems that just about everyone feels compelled to weigh in with an opinion about the merits, or lack thereof, of the selections of Oprah's Book Club. The most vocal commentators tend to be the ones who criticize the picks out of hand, as Yardley does, without ever having read a substantial number of them, thereby making the careless mistake of conflating the content and quality of the show on which the novels are presented with the content and quality of the works themselves.

Others, in their haste to push all of the widely diverse selections into a single, easy-to-label category seem either unable to accept or eager to deny the eclecticism and heterogeneity of the books of OBC. These critics would rather dismiss them out of hand as sentimental and middlebrow for mere ease of classification, rather than taking the time to ponder, as Ted Striphas puts it, "how a stark, ambiguous German novel like Bernhard Schlink's *The Reader* (1997) could sit side-by-side . . . with Breena Clarke's *River Cross My Heart* (1999), which one journalist dismissed as 'a poorly written, sentimental novel from a diversity bureaucrat at Time, Inc.,' let alone four selections by Nobel Prize winning author Toni Morrison" (296). In their evidently willful failure to fully consider the logic behind Winfrey's eclectic selections, these critics overlook the ingenious way in which the club worked independently of traditional highbrow versus lowbrow literary hierarchies. In doing so, they miss an invaluable opportunity to gain insight into "how high art so easily could comingle with mass culture, let alone how millions of *Oprah* viewers were so unfazed by this seeming contradiction" (Striphas 297).

Still others narrowly criticize the picks by reading just a few of them with an eye toward interpreting them through an extremely limited and dismissive lens, as do the "whiners" described in an article in *Book* magazine who complain "about the selections, which are considered a little heavy in the trauma and misery department—'penny dreadfuls for the Therapy Age,' as one critic recently called them" (Abramson 41). As it turns out, the aforementioned critic is none other than Tom Shone who, in a piece thinly disguised as a *New York Times* review of Anita Shreve's novel *The Last Time They Met*, delivers a scathing attack on the books of OBC, writing, "One hesitates to ask what Oprah will make of the new book, which feels fractious and fraught with questions of literary status, as if Shreve were anxious to elevate herself above all the healing-and-redemption packages that Winfrey selects" (Shone 34). Next, apparently because one cheap shot isn't enough, he quotes Shreve as having written, "She admired a negligee and remembered nights with other negligees, and still the sadness, that cloud, was not swept away" (qtd. in Shone 34). He then adds, "if you had to guess that Shreve was an Oprah-anointed author from one sentence, it would be that one I think: the brief glance at the pleasures afforded by this world, the delicate hint of more spiritual matters, the glum refusal to have anything resembling fun. There is nothing new in this, of course; looked at one way, Oprah's Book Club offers us a return to High Victorianism—they are penny dreadfuls for the Therapy Age" (Shone 34).

As Shone himself says, though, this is only true if the picks of the OBC are looked at *one way*, which, in addition to being a reductivist approach to literature, is certainly the wrong way to approach the wide range of complex novels selected by Winfrey since 1996. Moreover, this OBC-assassination-attempt posing as book review was published on April 22, 2001, by which time the club had "anointed" 17 more authors after Shreve. Among them were Robert Morgan, Sue Miller, Barbara Kingsolver, Andre Dubus III, and Joyce Carol Oates, all of whom are skilled and respectable literary writers, none of whom place any kind of cartoonish over-emphasis on healing and redemption. Additionally, Shone never makes specific mention of any other OBC picks, nor does he take steps to substantiate his preposterous claim that "the Oprah list offers us that rather ominous thing: not a world without pity, but a world composed of nothing but" (Shone 34). In fairness, the show itself might be guilty of perpetrating the crime of excess pity, but by and large the books on the list are not. Thus, Shone's allegations reveal far less about the true nature of the picks of OBC than they do about his own underinformed bias against them.

Unapprised as he is, Shone is hardly alone in his baseless complaints against, and distorted representations of, Winfrey's selections. In an article in the April 2001 issue of *American Libraries* magazine, Bill Ott even goes so far as to propose what he jokingly refers to as "Oprah Cure: Bill's Book Club," writing, "You're a devoted member of Oprah's Book Club, but lately you've been feeling off your feed. You just can't bear another inspiring yet oh-so-depressing tale of a single mother whose daughter is kidnapped or worse, but who works through her pain and finds strength in the midst of tragedy" (Ott 102). Here, I have to interrupt Ott to point out that not only is he inaccurate in his categorization of OBC picks as simple tales of struggle then triumph over adversity, but also in his characterization of the club itself as a tell-tale symptom of an ailing culture, as some kind of taste disease for which such auto-appointed authorities as himself must condescendingly propose treatment. Yet propose he does, continuing: "You will never be asked to read a novel that could be described by the word poignant. Our books are irreverent not inspirational, ironic not idealistic, sensual not spiritual, uproarious not uplifting. We can't guarantee you won't find meaning in these books, but if you do, it will sneak up gradually, not slap you upside the head" (Ott 102). Such smug criticism amounts to little more than a misdiagnosis of the selections in question, for virtually none of the books of OBC may be stripped down to functioning on a merely inspirational level.

Moreover, Ott's critique exhibits a woefully poor grasp not only of the substance of the club itself, but also of literary fiction in general, for there are libraries-full of solidly good and truly great literature—the works of Hardy, the Brontës, and even F. Scott Fitzgerald, for instance—which is hardly irreverent, but rather achingly sad and, I daresay, poignant. As E. M. Forster writes in his seminal classic *Aspects of the Novel*—based on a series of superb lectures on the art form delivered under the auspices of Trinity College, Cambridge in 1927—"The intensely, stifling human quality of the novel is not to be avoided; the novel is sogged with humanity; there is no escaping the uplift or the downpour, nor can they be kept out of criticism. We may hate humanity, but if it is exorcised or even purified the novel wilts; little is left but a bunch of words" (24).

Speaking less to the art of the novel in general, and more specifically to the case in question, German author Bernhard Schlink—whose extremely human novel *The Reader* was selected for the club in February 1999—wrote to me that "The Oprah Book Club makes people read and that, I think, is a great thing. It is so great that I don't care too much about the criticism that I sometimes hear smart people raise in a smart way. I don't expect someone in Oprah's position to always pick great books. But as little as I can follow her selections, many of her books are really worthwhile and they are also books that make you want to read more" (letter to the author).

Although these smart people who raise their complaints in a smart way may not be worth caring about too much, they are not the only ones committing highly selective readings of the books of OBC. Other misguided complainers include smart people who raise their objections in a premature and incomplete way, such as Gavin McNett of Salon.com, who wrote in 1999 that most of the OBC picks "play on base sentiment" and only help readers "learn what they already know" (qtd. in Chin 112). I'll address these assessments in extensive detail later in this chapter, when I examine several of the novels themselves, but for now, I have to say that neither of them is wholly, or even mostly, correct. Yet such evaluations represent precisely the kind of hastily registered critical opinion that encourages people who may have little to no firsthand knowledge of the club to dismiss OBC as consisting entirely of books that are just too simple or too sad to read.

Even as the original incarnation of OBC drew to a close, having exhibited along the way a great deal of growth and variety in its selections, critics who drew negative conclusions about the picks early on have rarely bothered to revise their initial evaluations. Among these critics is novelist Susan Wise Bauer, who in December of 1998 wrote an article entitled "Oprah's Misery Index," wherein she observed that Winfrey's picks tend toward overt sentimentality to the extent that they "intend to connect the reader to the story by appealing to shared emotional experiences" (Bauer 71). And although she was evenhanded enough to add that "to characterize the Oprah novels as 'sentimental' ought not to denigrate either their power or their importance," as well as that, since the novels are directed toward a primarily female audience, it can be no wonder that they preoccupy themselves "with dead and missing children, and the continual exploration of difficult family ties (as opposed to job problems, say, or the frustration of ambition)" (Bauer 71), she nevertheless contributes to the misconception that misery, sentiment, and nebulous "women's issues" are *all* these novels have to offer.

Such commentary as Bauer's contributes to the perception of the club's expansive list of novels as being little more than sentimental, sensitive, smarmy, schmaltzy and just about any other similarly derogatory s-adjectives you can think of. By pigeonholing the works as just for women, she attendantly classifies them as being second-rate, and certainly not serious. Although she makes no mention of the books' merits in terms of language, style, or structure, Bauer adds that "an evocative picture of emotion is as powerful as a well-reasoned argument," and that "the Oprah novels are more than simple exercises in empathy. They too have a cause: to find meaning in suffering" (72). Charitable as she's obviously attempting to be here, these statements imply that OBC picks in particular and so-called "women's lit" in general tend to function without logic or reason, hearkening back to disquietingly archaic notions of women as emotional creatures upon whom appeals to ideas are lost.

Dozens of new books have been selected since Bauer wrote her article. Yet recent reviews indicate that the problem with criticism regarding OBC picks is not only that people registered their complaints too early and with too much finality, but also that even contemporary critics can't get past the idea that Winfrey's selections are somehow too depressing to be good. Approaching the picks from just such a limited angle in a July 13, 2001, *Wall Street Journal* article entitled "Read Them and Weep—Misery, Pain, Catastrophe, Despair . . . and That's Just the First Chapter," Cynthia Crossen dismisses OBC protagonists as little more than "the sum of their problems" and claims that, as a body of literature, Winfrey's selections:

> are predictable and parochial. She knows what her audience wants—tragedy and redemption—and that's what she serves. Does she know for a fact that members of her flock wouldn't occasionally want to read about success, fulfillment or happiness, or can't grapple with the vast gray area between black and white that they wouldn't be tempted by fiction that incorporates careers, politics, world affairs, higher education, sports, business or the environment? (Crossen W15)

Here, and elsewhere throughout the article, Crossen comes across as hypocritical at worst, poorly read at best. For one thing, Winfrey's audience wants more than mere tragedy and redemption—which is hardly the lowest common denominator of literature anyway.

Rather, OBC devotees seemed to want richly drawn, fully realized characters, moving purposefully and plot-fully through sophisticatedly rendered and vividly described worlds. Moreover, Crossen seems unaware that successful, fulfilled, happy and above all unconflicted people don't exactly make for the most interesting protagonists, or the most riveting novels. J. D. Salinger's Holden Caufield, for instance, is a deeply messed-up—albeit winsome, funny and vulnerable—young man; Paula Fox's titular *Desperate Characters,* Sophie and Otto Bentwood, provide no working model of a healthy marriage; Richard Yates's *Revolutionary Road* could never be read as a map to the American Dream; Dostoevsky's Raskolnikov is far from a paragon of personal satisfaction, and, for that matter, *Crime and Punishment* is a veritable poster-book for tragedy and redemption if ever there was one. In short, many if not most canonically good novels are about people who are, for lack of a better word, depressed, and/or who must choose either to struggle or not to struggle with various problems and issues. Thus, anyone slamming the picks of OBC for depicting too much misery comes across as ignorant, sanctimonious, or both. As for careers, politics, world affairs, higher education, and all the rest, perhaps if Crossen had bothered to read a substantial number of the selections, she'd know that the majority of them do in fact address these subjects, frequently at the same time, while also creating the kind of moral gray area for which she professes to long.

What's more, Crossen fairly pulls the rug out from under her own argument by conceding that, "there's nothing wrong with creating fictional works of misery—Charles Dickens, John Steinbeck and Theodore Dreiser turned wasted lives into enduring literature. But a steady diet of melodrama and tragedy only reinforces some peoples' feeling that life doesn't offer much in the way of compensation for its miseries," ending the article by saying, "surely a book club that influences the reading habits of millions of Americans could open its gates to a wider world, where men aren't always the enemy, women aren't punching bags and children laugh giddily as they sled down a snowy hill" (Crossen W15). All in all, Crossen and virtually every other critic who has condemned the picks of OBC for wallowing excessively in pity and misery sound more guilty of craving a sentimental, Hallmarky world than Winfrey herself ever has. Beyond that, though, they are engaging in a damaging and dishonest project, as bad as any other school of criticism, which seeks to impose itself upon texts rather than bothering to interpret what the texts actually *say*.

Half the time, too, it seems that, like slackers in a high school English class, these critics are scrambling to write a paper without actually having done the reading. If they had kept up with the assignments of OBC, they might realize—as does Sue Miller, whose altogether good novel *While I Was Gone* was the OBC selection for May 2000—that while, "there is a typical Oprah book . . . she offers a number of surprises too. I think the books she chooses are for the most part mainstream and pretty accessible" (letter to the author). In a letter in which she delivers itemized answers to each of my eleven questions regarding her OBC experience, Miller wrote of the club's selections, "The language is clear and conventional. The themes are centered primarily in women's lives. Again, I think she knows her audience. I think a few books have been pretty weak, some very good, some middling, a few extraordinary. But for the most part, they are serious books which have elsewhere gotten quite respectable reviews."

Indeed, OBC picks are typically written by women, and tend to feature strong female protagonists—often experiencing comings-of-age, or enduring hardships and emotional challenges that compel them to plumb the depths of their identities as individuals—but this in and of itself is hardly anything for which the club should apologize. As Daisy Maryles, executive editor of *Publishers Weekly*, observes, "She tends to choose books with major subjects, tough themes, dealing with personal issues—these are not light stories" (qtd. in Fitzgerald 27). For what it's worth, neither the female nor the male authors of OBC always write from the point of view of their own gender. Several of the novels by females feature male protagonists, as in Morrison's

Song of Solomon and Tawni O'Dell's *Back Roads.* On the other hand, many of the male authors choose to employ female points of view, as does Wally Lamb in *She's Come Undone,* Bret Lott in *Jewel,* and Robert Morgan in *Gap Creek.* In total, out of the forty-three works of contemporary adult fiction selected by OBC as it existed from 1996–2002, just ten were written by men while thirty-three were by women.

Bearing this in mind, I'd like to cite Jonathan Franzen citing the work of Shirley Brice Heath, which he does in his 1996 *Harper's* magazine essay, "Perchance to Dream: In the Age of Images, a Reason to Write Novels." Heath—a former MacArthur Fellow, a linguistic anthropologist, and a professor of English and linguistics at Stanford University—performed an in-depth sociological study of the audience for fiction in America. After finding that the majority of the "serious" readers she interviewed had had to deal in some way with unpredictability in their personal lives, she determined unpredictability to be a defining feature of substantive works of fiction. She discovered in this study that "therapists and ministers who counsel troubled people tend to read the hard stuff. So do people whose lives have not followed the course they were expected to: merchant caste Koreans who don't become merchants, ghetto kids who go to college, men from conservative families who lead openly gay lives, and women whose lives have turned out to be radically different from their mothers'" (Franzen 15). This last category, notes Franzen, is especially large, for "there are, today, millions of American women whose lives do not resemble the lives they might have projected from their mothers,' and all of them, in Heath's model, are potentially susceptible to substantive fiction" (15). Winfrey's own life—her tumultuous rise from poverty and obscurity in segregated Mississippi to her current station as one of the wealthiest, most influential people on the planet—has followed a decidedly unpredictable course. On what generally must be a smaller scale, so too have the lives of her mostly female audience.

This audience, then, is encouraged to read in the way that the May 1998 author selected for OBC, Edwidge Danticat, does: "There are a lot of us who feel some part of us, an important part, was salvaged by reading. Oprah says that when she reads about people who are going through similar experiences to her own, she feels less alone. A lot of us share that feeling" (qtd. in Farley 82). Given what Heath discovered in her research on serious fiction readers, it is difficult to see why certain critics decry Winfrey's selection of novels that—via their depictions of the lives of characters who may be very circumstantially similar to ourselves, or who may be similar only in that they too struggle with problems—are designed to strike a very human chord within their audience. As Forster observes, "Since the novelist is himself a human being, there is an affinity between him and his subject-matter which is absent in many other forms of art" (44). Moreover, "in daily life, we never understand each other. . . . But people in a novel can be understood completely by the reader, if the novelist wishes. . . . And this is why they often seem more definite than characters in history, or even our own friends" (Forster 47). A novelist's very human affinity for his characters is passed on, not surprisingly, to the novel's readers. It is imperative to note, too, that in her interviews:

> Heath uncovered a "wide unanimity" among serious readers that literature "makes me a better person." She hastened to assure me that, rather than straightening them out in a self-help way, "reading serious literature impinges on the embedded circumstances in people's lives in such a way that they have to deal with them, and in so dealing, they come to see themselves as deeper and more capable of handling their inability to have a totally predictable life." (Franzen 15)

Thus, since in many cases the very impulse to read may very well be delineated in terms of this type of self-improvement, it seems untenable to censure Winfrey for selecting books with this type of betterment for her audience in mind.

One of the things—but certainly not the only thing—genuinely good books can do for us as readers is inspire us to higher levels of morality, in the sense that they put us through the paces of moral awareness, affiliation, and disaffiliation; this is what good OBC picks do, too. Good books don't present us with flat characters enacting formulaic plots; rather, they encourage us, often via round characters vastly dissimilar to ourselves, to grapple with ideas and situa-

tions different from our own. Winfrey gravitates tow
on highly plausible or factual events written by a
extensive real-life research to develop their plots, sett
acters. And while not all realistic fiction is good fiction
mimetic work chosen for OBC is.

With regard to the selection process itself, sometimes
will suggest a book, but for the most part the pick ends
book Winfrey—a lifelong reader, an insatiable bookstore cr ...ser, and
an avid peruser of reviews—has discovered herself. Toni Morrison,
who has visited Oprah at her Indiana farm, reports: "Except for other
writers,' I have very seldom seen a home with so many books—all
kinds of books, handled and read books. She's a genuine reader, not
a decorative one. She's a carnivorous reader" (qtd. in Johnson 6). At
the height of the club's popularity, Harpo, Winfrey's Chicago-based
production company, received hundreds of novels monthly from
publishers and authors craving exposure on the show. Some books
have been chosen concurrently with their initial publication, as was
the case with *The Corrections,* whereas others, such as Morrison's
Song of Solomon, were already several years old at the time of their
selection. According to a spokeswoman for Oprah, "the only real criteria we have is that the author has to be alive, so that he or she can
appear on the TV program" (qtd. in Fitzgerald 27). This criterion is,
so to speak, a whole other can of worms, one which I intend to open
in the following chapter on Winfrey's use of television as a forum
for literary fiction. At present, though, it is critical to concentrate on
the books themselves. As Jerry S. Herron, director of American studies at Wayne State University says, "Everything on Oprah is not the
kind of pop schmaltz that she often gets characterized as producing" ("Deconstruct This" B4).

For the record, I am only analyzing fiction, and therefore will be
leaving the club's two autobiographical works—Maya Angelou's *The
Heart of a Woman* and Malika Oufkir's *Stolen Lives*—out of all further
discussion. Bill Cosby's children's books will also be left out of the
analysis, even though I read and enjoyed them, because my focus is
adult literary fiction. All of the aforementioned books, though, testify
to the beneficially heterogeneous nature of Winfrey's selections. Of

forty-three works of contemporary fiction selected by the original incarnation of OBC, thirty-one were reviewed in the *New York Times Book Review*, a critical publication I've chosen to incorporate into my analysis because of its status as a widely read and respected arbiter and indicator of literary taste, a status that makes it both a natural complement and foil to OBC. All of these reviews—with the exception of the ones for *Where the Heart Is* by Billie Letts, *The Pilot's Wife* by Anita Shreve, and *Here on Earth* by Alice Hoffman, which were negative, and Jane Hamilton's *A Map of the World*, Mary McGarry Morris's *Songs in Ordinary Time*, and Anna Quindlen's *Black and Blue*, which were mixed—were decidedly, even glowingly, favorable. So it seems that in many cases, it is only after the books receive the designation of OBC and are considered within that particular cultural context that they undergo a critical reevaluation and a fall from certain favor.

Now, since I didn't go to the trouble of spending over a year reading all those Oprah novels just to tell you what the *Times* has to say about them—and since you may not have read all that many Oprah books yourself, even though you may be quick to voice an opinion about their quality—I'm going to tell you what I personally thought of the selections. And while I'm certainly not going to try to persuade you that each and every one of them was brilliant—because, frankly, they weren't—I *am* going to try to convince you that for the most part, they weren't remotely as terrible as so many people seem bound and determined to believe; many of them, in fact, were excellent.

Lest I should seem a hypocrite for urging Winfrey to do something I myself refuse to do, I have to pause here to disclose where I'm coming from—to be completely honest about the frame of reference in which I am encountering OBC. I hope this disclosure will serve as an antidote to those critics who would summarily dismiss the club without any indication whatsoever that they have made an earnest attempt to study or comprehend it.

In the original draft of this chapter, I announced with great fanfare that I was "qualified" to distinguish good literature from bad, owing to my extensive literary education, including my undergraduate degree in English and creative writing and my soon-to-be completed MFA in writing, literature, and publishing. After giving the matter further thought, though, I realized that trying to "prove" my "superior" ability to engage with texts was a decidedly old-fashioned gesture. For in doing so, I was tacitly buying into the reactionary belief that only a minority of trained professionals can interact critically with texts, and that, by extension, such texts are in some way imperiled by the attentions of the marginal, the inexperienced, or the unscholarly. In other words, I had to ask myself: does the mere fact that a member of Oprah's Book Club may deal with fiction in a *different* way than a member of the academy negate the value of her experience of literature, or degrade her enjoyment and interpretation thereof? And I had to answer myself: probably not. In fact, it would be short-sighted of me to treat this group of millions of enthusiastic, intelligent readers as irrelevant or inferior simply because of their presumably non-specialist status.

If anything, perhaps my list of alleged credentials is itself a handicap of sorts, an obstacle preventing me from experiencing literature in any way other than the one in which the academy has instructed me. Maybe a traditional insistence upon a borderline New Critical approach to texts doesn't make one superior; perhaps it just makes one overly narrow in one's focus. For some people can't or—gasp!— don't want to study literature in a university setting, and these are the people for whom Winfrey's approach to fiction might be highly beneficial. Indeed, Lawrence Levine points out that as early as the mid-1800s, "Walt Whitman consistently fought this . . . cultural hierarchy. He insisted that culture should not be 'restricted by conditions ineligible to the masses,' should not be created 'for a single class alone, or for the parlors or lecture-rooms,' and placed his hopes for the creation of a classless, democratic culture in the leadership of the new 'middling' groups—'men and women with occupations, well-off owners of houses and acres, and with cash in the bank'" (Levine 225). Winfrey deserves to be commended, then, for reaching out to precisely such groups as these, and for treating literature not as private property to be surrounded with barbed wire and defended by an elite fighting force of trained academics, but rather as public space, open to us all.

In any case, consider yourself warned that the rundown of

books that follows is only one woman's opinion. Still, I believe that it is an important opinion to give in order to provide the reader with a better overview of the books themselves, as well as a better sense of where I'm coming from, and why I agree with Levine that:

> My own interest is not in attacking the notion of cultural hierarchy per se. Obviously we need to make distinctions within culture as within every other realm of human endeavor, although I do spend a fair amount of time wondering if by making those distinctions as rigidly as we tend to, we are not limiting the dimensions of our understanding of culture, which could be furthered by having a more open and fluid set of divisions more conducive to facilitating truly complex comparisons we presently lack. Our comparative understanding might be furthered as well by adding to the almost exclusively aesthetic criteria of the present hierarchy, thematic criteria (the message of various forms of expressive culture), functional criteria (how various forms of expressive culture work), and quantitative criteria (to what extent various forms of expressive culture are diffused through the society). (7–8)

That said, I have to start by telling you that even though I set about this project intending to read all OBC-selected fiction, I haven't actually done it, and I'm probably not going to. To be honest, I found some of the books—five of them—to be not exactly awful but just unreadable. For the record, there were five just plain awful ones, too, but I managed to finish them anyway, and will therefore deal with them later. For now, though, I have to say that I simply could not get all the way through *Stones from the River* by Ursula Hegi, *Paradise* by Toni Morrison, *I Know This Much is True* by Wally Lamb, *River Cross My Heart* by Breena Clarke, and *Cane River* by Lalita Tademy. Rarely do I leave a book unfinished, for no matter how bad a novel may be, and no matter if it's for a project or my own entertainment, I generally find myself compelled to finish it. In fact, OBC selections aside, I can count the books I've started but haven't finished on one hand. They are as follows: Joseph Heller's *Catch-22* (I know, I know; I'm sorry, but I got to the Major Major Major Major part, and couldn't take it—*it* being the ballsy manliness, the absolutely embarrassing depiction of women, and so forth—anymore), Toni Morrison's *Beloved* (again, I apologize, but I've honestly started it on five separate occasions now and have never been able to get past Chapter Two), and Sir Walter Scott's *Waverley* (which I was supposed to read recently as part of a Nineteenth Century Novel course; upon reaching page forty-nine I decided that I just didn't have time in the middle of writing this book to get tremendously worked up over Flora and Fergus MacIvor, Rose and Bailie Macwheeble, or any of the rest).

In any case, it's only fair to explain what exactly made these five OBC picks so unreadable. Proceeding, then, in chronological order of their selection, I'll start with Ursula Hegi's *Stones from the River*, chosen in February 1997. Hegi's novel centers on the travails of Trudi Montag, a dwarf from the war-torn German town of Burgdorf, who is the protagonist of a story that the *New York Times* enjoyed for its portrayal of a woman who is "above all, a human being who longs for friendship and love," and who, "rejected and brutalized," manages to "resist the temptation to luxuriate in hatred, as her Nazi neighbors do" (Ruta 2). Personally, I found all this a bit much to heap on one character, and couldn't help thinking how derivative the dwarf-story was of Günter Grass's classic *The Tin Drum*. Thus, I didn't get much beyond the second and third sentences wherein Trudi speaks of her life "before she understood the power of being different. The agony of being different" (Hegi 9), before I realized I probably wasn't going to finish the whole thing. I happened to be in Germany when I began reading the novel, and this helped me press forward a few pages more, but by the time I got to her rather stereotypically unhinged mother and passively neglectful father, I knew I couldn't keep slogging through so much stock dysfunctionality no matter how much well-researched, minutely rendered local history the next 525 pages might contain.

As for *Paradise*—Toni Morrison's novel about an imaginary utopia in the form of the all-black town of Ruby, Oklahoma, population 360—I feel compelled to state that even though I include it in my list of OBC unreadables, the *Times* described the novel, Morrison's first since she received the Nobel Prize for Literature in 1993, as "possibly her best work of fiction to date" (Allen 6). Even though I enjoyed *Song of Solomon,* an OBC pick in October 1996, and even though I list April 2000 pick *The Bluest Eye* in my top ten Oprah favorites, I found *Paradise* unnecessarily cryptic and impenetrable in its style and composition.

In fact, upon *Paradise's* selection in January 1998, so many readers wrote in to say that they didn't understand the novel that Winfrey arranged to have Morrison, a professor at Princeton, host an on-the-air master class attended by Winfrey, her best friend Gayle King, and twenty audience members who sat on the floor and couch while Morrison lead the discussion. "Are we supposed to get this on the first read?" King demanded at one point, and Winfrey jokingly raised another woman's hand to signal "over our heads," at another (Max 5). The necessity of rereading, the unreliability of the novel's various narrators, the significance of the fragment of Gnostic text that serves as the book's epigraph and other assorted questions were bandied about as Morrison refused to explicate her intent beyond saying, "If it's worth writing, it's worth going back to" (Max 5). And while, with some books—James Joyce's *Ulysses,* for instance, or even *The Sound and the Fury* by Morrison antecedent William Faulkner—this may be the case, with others it is less the sign of challenging reading than it is the sign of maddeningly obscure and needlessly muddled writing. I'm not suggesting the audience comprising OBC isn't up for a challenge, but rather that they probably don't want to put up with deliberately and unnecessarily obfuscating texts. And even though Winfrey herself relished this particular segment declaring, "I loved the *Paradise* gathering. I just thought it was really interesting television in terms of being with a lot of other people who were stimulating, really good thinkers" (Max 6), it ranks as one of the lowest-rated book club shows to date. Still, Winfrey's handling of the *Paradise* discussion illustrates the unique eclecticism of her selection process, as well as her attunement to the needs of her audience. Her candid admission of the difficulty of the book and her permitting readers more time to engage with the text than with other selections seems to suggest that "beyond merely acknowledging and making allowances for the fact that certain titles might prove more challenging for readers than others, the choice of books often was influenced directly by the relative difficulty of the preceding one" (Striphas 303).

Unreadability reared its ugly head twice in 1998, the second time taking the form of *I Know This Much is True,* Wally Lamb's June-selected tale of the recently wifeless, childless, and soon-to-be mother-less Dominick Birdseye and his schizophrenic twin, Thomas. At 902 pages in paperback—including "A List of Sources Consulted" (Lamb 899) as well as information for "readers wishing to learn more about or to assist people with schizophrenia and other serious mental ill-nesses" (902)—this self-consciously topical misery-fest appeared at first glance to be lacking many of the qualities of a quintessentially good novel, a judicious editor being first among them. Nevertheless, I approached the book with the intention of giving each and every one of the plentiful pages the attention it deserved, which I proceeded to do. Until I reached page five, that is, at which point:

> With his left hand, Thomas enacted each of the steps he'd rehearsed in his mind. Slicing at the point of his right wrist, he crunched through the bone, amputating his hand cleanly with the sharp knife. With a loud grunt, he flung the severed hand halfway across the library floor. Then he reached into his wound and yanked the spurting ulna and radial, pinching and twisting it closed as best he could. He raised his arm in the air to slow the bleeding. When the other people in the library realized—or thought they realized—what had just happened, there was chaos. (Lamb 5)

Even if I didn't harbor an almost pathological fear of blood and, by extension, injuries which result in spurting a lot of it, I'm confident that I would still find this episode not merely gratuitously shocking and grotesque, but also cheap, off-putting, and above all sensational in a way that truly good literature simply isn't. In short, I found this passage supremely manipulative; I felt jerked around by an author who never gave me a chance to achieve an understanding of or sym-pathy for the protagonist in any kind of subtler, more skillful way. Thus, reopening the book that I had disgustedly flipped shut and skimming through the remaining 898 ramblingly gloomy, poorly edited pages about said protagonist's pathetic life, I concluded—even though Lamb's previous pick, *She's Come Undone,* earned a place in my OBC top ten—I'd already had more than enough to do with *I Know This Much Is True.*

Unreadability didn't strike again until sixteen months and ten novels later in October 1999, when Breena Clarke's *River Cross My Heart*—a well-researched, heartfelt novel of African American life in Washington, D.C.'s Georgetown neighborhood in the 1920s—entered the OBC canon. Clarke's novel starts slowly and proceeds to suffer steadily from the lack of an engaging, or even authoritative, narrative voice, as well as the fact that it's laden with such flat, poorly paced, repetitive sentences as "The girls were not supposed to go in the river. Parents regularly warned their children not to swim there. Alice and Willie Bynum, knowing Johnnie Mae's fondness for swimming, had warned her off the banks of the Potomac" (Clarke 6). If for no other reason than it's set near where I was living at the time, I really wanted to like, or at least finish, the novel. Sadly, Clarke wrote the book so stiltedly and in such an awkwardly childlike voice that I just couldn't do it.

Coincidentally, Lalita Tademy's *Cane River*—the third and most recent book containing reference to this particular geographic feature—rounds out the list of OBC unreadables, earning its spot for many of the same reasons as the previous river novel. Despite the sound ideas behind its story—that Tademy's family was full of women who "were not mammy or Jezebel or Topsy, the slave images made safe and familiar in *Gone With the Wind* tradition. They were flesh-and-blood women who made hard choices, even in oppression" (xi), as the author's note informs us—this pick from June 2001 was excruciatingly poorly written. The entire book of factual genealogy dressed up as fiction suffered from flimsy, tedious writing, such as this passage, which attempts to describe the interiority of a young slave woman, forced to be a white man's mistress, on the delivery of her second unwanted child: "Doralise turned her head slowly, and her breath caught as if with pain. 'Suzette, you must be more careful. This is your second baby and you are what? Fifteen, sixteen?' Suzette pricked the bubble of bitterness before it had a chance to rise. As much as she loved Gerant, as much as she would do now to protect the new life inside her, their making had nothing to do with how careful she was allowed to be" (Tademy 54). It's only fair to mention here that Tademy is not a professional novelist, but rather—as the dust jacket explains—a former vice-president of Sun Microsystems who left the corporate world to immerse herself in tracing her family's history and writing her first book. Bearing this in mind, I read 127 pages of this amateurish effort before conceding there was no way I'd make it through the remaining 291.

In the interest of advocating a more refined cultural hierarchy—these unreadables were not wholly without value. For one thing, unlike myself, millions of other people did not find them unreadable, which would give them a high score in Levine's suggested subcategory of quantitative criteria; these books were certainly widely diffused. For another, when viewed through Levine's proposed thematic criteria, the aforementioned novels can all be said to have possessed well-intentioned messages, including racial equality, brotherly—or sisterly—love, and courage in the face of adversity. Moreover, as I stated before, this systematic analysis of the quality of the novels of OBC is entirely based on my own reasonably well-informed, yet highly personal opinion, and I realize that many readers may take serious issue with it. In fact, I hope they do.

Next, since so many people share in the perception that the majority of OBC books are bad books, I'm going to argue that only five more of them are truly awful, and describe specifically in what ways they are so. First, though, I have to point out the chief ways in which they are *not* awful, those ways being memorability and readability. For unimpressive as these books are as solid literary fiction, each one somehow manages to remain cloyingly with you long after you think you've rid yourself of it, not unlike a pop song you hate to hear, but perversely have to admire for its being so well designed as to worm its way into your brain and remain lodged there for days, weeks, even months on end. Winfrey herself says, after all, that she enjoys books whose characters stay with her, and she's not kidding. Moreover, as patently terrible as these five books really are, Alice Hoffman's *Here On Earth,* Chris Bohjalian's *Midwives,* Anita Shreve's

The Pilot's Wife, Maeve Binchy's *Tara Road,* and Elizabeth Berg's *Open House* still manage to compel you to turn their ill-conceived pages, to read them in their entirety from cover to rapidly reached cover.

I'll start chronologically with the March 1998 pick *Here on Earth* by Alice Hoffman, which was *such* a rip-off—so watered down, so dumb—of *Wuthering Heights* that I can't even stand it. E. M. Forster lists Emily Brontë among only four writers he considers to have attained the highest order of novelistic achievement—that of prophecy, or a superior tone of voice—writing: "Why should *Wuthering Heights* come into this inquiry? . . . My answer is that the emotions of Heathcliff and Catherine Earnshaw function differently to other emotions in fiction. Instead of inhabiting the characters, they surround them like thunder clouds, and generate the explosions that fill the novel" (145). Brontë, he says, "had in some ways a literal and careful mind. . . . Then why did she deliberately introduce muddle, chaos, tempest? Because in our sense of the word she was a prophetess: because what is implied is more important to her than what is said" (Forster 145–46). In other words, Brontë created a carefully crafted work of raw, sweeping, otherworldly, elemental passion, whereas Hoffman contents herself with terrible sex scenes and stuff about horses. Forster concludes his laudatory treatment of *Wuthering Heights* by observing that "it is local, like the spirits it engenders, and whereas we may meet Moby Dick in any pond, we shall only encounter them [Catherine and Heathcliff] among the harebells and limestone of their own country" (146). Forster was for a long while correct, until Hoffman came along and tried to stick them in Massachusetts.

Hoffman's novel amounts to little more than the watery tale of the obsessive and destructive reunion between March Murray (a silly middle-aged whiner who, incidentally, Catherine Earnshaw could eat for lunch)—a successful artisan living with her professor husband and teenage daughter in California—and her long-lost malevolent hearththrob Hollis. In a *New York Times* review from September 14, 1997, Karen Karbo calls *Here on Earth* a "*Wuthering Heights* for the nineties," then quickly points out that *Wuthering Heights* could never happen in the '90s, for "Unlike March, Cathy doesn't even have a telephone, much less talk shows, support groups and books about women who love too much. But it's hard to believe that March could exist within such an emotional cocoon. And so . . . her novel's premise—of doomed, fated love, submitted to without question—never becomes plausible" (Karbo 25). Moreover, Hoffman busies herself not with transcendental passion, but with pedestrian episodes of intercourse, as when, "Hollis has his hand inside her jeans now; he's pushed her down so her back is flat against the seat. She knows the way he likes it, as if love was a secret; or at least that's the way he likes it with her. . . . He doesn't stop when she tells him to, and then stops just when she's about to come" (Hoffman 127). Hoffman clearly intends such passages to shock, or at least titillate us as readers, but the work as a whole is so dull and derivative, that they come off both as boring in their own right and a total affront to the greatness of the original. And so many people's familiarity with this knock-off, it should be noted, is due to the fact that Brontë is long-dead—which is merciful inasmuch as this book would probably kill her—and thus cannot appear on a TV show.

In addition to appearing as OBC pick for October 1998, Chris Bohjalian's *Midwives* ended up appearing on TV as a Lifetime network movie starring Sissy Spacek, which I happened upon while dyeing Easter eggs in April 2001 at the apartment of a friend who owns a television, and which turned out to be no better than the woefully superficial and misguidedly narrated book itself. Promisingly, the novel is supposed to recount the tale of a middle-aged, ex-hippie midwife named Sibyl Danforth who may or may not have accidentally killed a laboring mother during an emergency Caesarian. Instead of allowing us to hear the story from Sibyl's mouth, as good authorial sense would seemingly dictate, Bohjalian opts to filter the action through the implausible and irritating voice of Sibyl's teenage daughter, a choice he attempts to justify by having the daughter explain, "Besides, I view this as my story, too, and why I believe babies became my calling as well" (21). The immediate and lasting effect of this narrative decision is that we as readers find ourselves subject to stereotypically shallow teen musings about first kisses and frivolities of that ilk. Our narrator tells us, for instance, that "at twelve (and fast approaching thirteen), I would ride or run or walk miles out of my way to watch Tom Corts . . . smoke cigarettes. Tom was the first of many sensitive smokers with whom I would fall deeply in love, and while I have never taken up the habit myself, I know well the taste of smoke on my tongue" (23–24), when what we really want hear is what's going on in the mind of the story's titular midwife.

Awful OBC pick number three—*The Pilot's Wife* by Anita Shreve, in which an absurdly clueless woman discovers that her recently deceased husband had been leading a double life not only as the patriarch of another family in Ireland, but also as an international terrorist—hit the list in March 1999. Of the damage I feel its selection caused to the reputation of the club, little more needs to be said than what Laura Jamison includes in her June 7, 1998, *New York Times* review wherein she observes that Shreve, the author of five previous novels, "writes in that genre known as 'women's fiction'—which, if her new book, *The Pilot's Wife* is at all representative, means building a story around a bourgeois romance (the subject likely to hook a large number of female book buyers) using the most generic, white-bread characters imaginable" (Jamison 37).

In short, even though *The Pilot's Wife* is in no way representative of the majority of selections for OBC, it serves as an embarrassingly opportune example for critics who find it convenient to believe that it is.

And speaking of things that give so-called popular fiction in general and "women's fiction" in particular a bad name, the OBC pick for September of the same year, *Tara Road* by Maeve Binchy, spoon-feeds readers the story of a silly cow of an Irish housewife named Ria, whose husband, Danny, is sleeping with her best friend but who passively agonizes over whether to do anything about it before the situation neatly resolves itself for the best. For even though, as the dustjacket cheerfully points out, "with each new book, Maeve Binchy continues a remarkable progression of sales and audience growth," nothing can alter the sad fact that this book is a flatly characterized, lazily written waste of valuable reading time. I wanted to present you the most representatively wince-inducing quotation from the entire 502-page affair, but I couldn't decide among: "Ria thought of Mona

McCarthy and how she had taken Barney's children every weekend to see their grandparents even though she was tired from working all week. [new paragraph, solitary sentence]. Life was hard on people" (Binchy 44) for its slack prose and obviousness; "Sit down with your own family, Ria, and look after that husband of yours. It's a miracle that you've held on to him for so long. I've always said that you were born lucky, to catch a man like Danny Lynch when all was said and done" (Binchy 149) for its shameless adherence to reductive and damaging stereotypes of gender; or this bit of dialogue between an estranged husband and wife, "'I feel so helpless out here, it's so strange, things sort of multiply in your mind.' . . . 'It'll get better, Greg.' 'I'm sorry, I sound like someone on *Oprah*.' 'Is that so bad?' 'No it's just the way I am . . .'" (Binchy 273) for its awkward self-consciousness. Thus, I give you them all.

Finally, rounding out the triple threat of alleged "women's fiction" in the OBC canon as well as the top five worst books in the history of the club, we have *Open House,* Elizabeth Berg's formulaic wish-fulfillment fantasy for the easily amused, middle-aged, divorcée set. As I've mentioned in previous chapters, part of my research for this project involved delivering letters and questionnaires to all of the OBC-selected authors. So, since I'd met Berg in the summer of 2001 at the Anderson's Bookshop reading before which I was able to interview the friendly and down-to-earth inaugural club author Jacquelyn Mitchard, I thought that Berg, like her friend, might be amenable to answering a few questions about her own Oprah experience. And she was, at first, giving me her fax number so I could send her my survey, which I did immediately since I was going out of town. Upon returning to work a week later, I entered the store in eager anticipation of her response, which a co-worker had hung on the time clock next to the punch cards. It read, in its entirety, "Dear Kathleen—Eeeeyikes! If I'd known what this interview involved, I'd never have agreed to it. This is way [underlined twice] too much work, Kathleen, and I'm afraid I'm going to have to pass. Sorry. Good luck in reaching the other authors. Elizabeth Berg" (fax to author). The implication here, of course, is that Berg is pressed for time, and after reading *Open House* I certainly wished she'd put a bit more time into making it a better book. For this novel—about a bland, middle-class woman in her mid-thirties who finds herself abruptly divorced and must then remake her life while finding a job and raising an eleven-year-old son, taking on a series of stereotypical boarders and falling in love with her hidden-in-plain-view next-door neighbor along the way—was one of the weakest, most hastily constructed things I've ever read.

Samantha, the protagonist, is thoroughly unlikable and pathetic, with an cloying voice bestowed upon her by a creator who seems not to like her own creation all that much herself, let alone care if we do. I give you Exhibit A, Samantha's deluded and insipid plan to make breakfast for her prepubescent son: "French toast he'll have today, made from scratch, cut diagonally, one piece lying artfully over the other; and I'll heat the syrup, serve it in the tiny flowered pitcher I once took from a room-service tray. I'll cut the butter pats into the shape of something. . . . I really think Travis will like this" (Berg 5).

Next, I give you Exhibit B, from the end this time, when Samantha ends up—surprise!—with her shy, retiring, diamond-in-the-rough neighbor, whose name is King but who may as well have been called Love Interest: "No one answers when I knock at his door. I try it, find it open, and put my head in. . . . I take off my coat and my boots, undress as I walk down the hall, enter the bathroom naked. . . . He picks up the soap, and I watch his big hands in front of me, lathering up, then rubbing across my breasts, my stomach" (Berg 240–241). Then, inexplicably, we receive a kind of saccharine reversion to Samantha's childhood when, "I lean in closer to King, close my eyes, and suddenly I am a little girl again," just before the book ends with the non-sequitir, "We are full of faith, blessed by it. I remember now" (241). Thus, in addition to exhibiting what Forster would call a "slackening of emotion and shallowness of judgement, and in particular that idiotic use of marriage as finale" (38), *Open House* is absolutely awash in bad writing.

All in all, my intention so far has been to prove that bad Oprah literature tends to be bad for the same reasons as bad literature in general. I've classified this combined total of ten unreadable and truly awful books as I did because each of them was blandly formulaic, blatantly derivative, gratuitously sensational, grossly sentimental, flatly characterized, terribly written, hysterical in pitch, lacking in sense of tradition, excessively earnest, oppressively didactic, shamelessly therapeutic or some combination thereof. Not unlike other bad novels drawn from across the contemporary literary field, these ten works tend to showcase not merely bad writing, but also bad authorial ideas. Their authors stack the deck with manipulatively sympathetic characters: what human being with half a heart would not feel sorry for, say, an essentially average guy whose life is made a living hell by his schizophrenic twin? In doing so, these authors commit a grievous insult to the intelligence and moral capacity of their readers. This is not to say that the authors of these books and others like them have not taken their responsibilities as novelists seriously, or that they have been in any way uncommitted to their literary tasks. Quite to the contrary, in fact, these ten novels are truly what they seem to be: boring—albeit in some cases compulsively readable—yet apparently sincere fictional explorations of such hard-hitting real-life issues as slavery, childbirth, abuse, death, disease and divorce. Oscar Wilde was right, though, when he said "all bad art is sincere." That's why, now, I want to go on to prove that the majority of Oprah literature does not suffer from this graceless, topical sincerity—that rather the picks of OBC tend to be good, and sometimes even great, and that they may be judged as such by the same standards as similarly designated literature anywhere else.

Originally, for consistency's sake, I intended to review the top five best OBC picks, but upon further consideration, I concluded that the Oprah canon simply contains too many genuinely good novels for a mere five-item list to do it justice. Thus, I decided to expand the list to the top ten. I realize that both for expediency's sake—and because you are quite capable of reading the rest of the books yourself—I should be satisfied with this number; nonetheless, I want to add that you may be reasonably certain that any of the remaining, unmentioned books would also be well worth your while.

So away we go again, in chronological order, starting with the January 1997 pick *She's Come Undone* by Wally Lamb. Lamb creates a complex and realistic world for his not-always-sympathetic, frequently self-hating, never humorless and always heroic protagonist Dolores to inhabit, and uses a smart authorial voice—complete with an implicit running criticism of television and its link to depression—to do so. He even goes so far as to open the book with the 1956 delivery of the Price family's first TV set by having the now forty-year-old Dolores recount, "In one of my earliest memories, my mother and I are on the front porch of our rented Carter Avenue house watching two delivery men carry our brand-new television set up the steps. . . . Here's the undependable part: my visual memory stubbornly insists these men are President Eisenhower and Vice President Nixon" (Lamb 3). Lamb bestows upon the book a full cast of lesser characters, all of whom are well-drawn, as well as a complete and satisfying context in recent American history and society by having Dolores encounter rape, abortion, infertility, AIDS, Parkinson's disease, and even the struggle of the whales along the course of her progress into adulthood. In the midst of all this, though, it is Dolores herself who is Lamb's real triumph.

Forster tells us that "it is only round people who are fit to perform tragically for any length of time and can move us to any feelings except humor and appropriateness" (73). Lamb has made Dolores undeniably round. It has been remarked that what's most amazing about *She's Come Undone* is that Lamb was able, as a male author, to write so believably and even humorously from the perspective of a woman. In fact, in one of the effusive blurbs on the book's back cover, *People* magazine declares "this male writes so convincingly in the voice of a female, tracing her life from 4 to 40, that you have to keep looking back at the jacket picture just to make sure." Even beyond gender, though, via this rendering of such a wry and riveting protagonist, Lamb achieves what Forster calls "the incalculability of life . . . life within the pages of a book" (78).

Now, on to book two: although it was published in 1993, Ernest J. Gaines's *A Lesson Before Dying* was already beginning to emerge on educational reading lists by the time Winfrey selected it for her own project in September 1997. In fact, I first encountered the novel as part of my winter break reading in December 1997 at the suggestion of my senior year high school English IV Honors teacher, Mrs. Linda Augustyn. In his August 8, 1993, *New York Times* review, Carl Senna wrote that "*A Lesson Before Dying,* though it suffers an occasional stylistic lapse, powerfully evokes in its understated tone the 'new wants' in the 1940s that created the revolution of the 1960s. Ernest J. Gaines has written a moving and truthful work of fiction" (Senna 21). Thus here it is again, showing up in my OBC top ten.

Continuing in this southern vein, the OBC selection for January 1999 was *Jewel* by Bret Lott, a novel that Judith Freeman describes in her *New York Times* review as a "sweeping and beautifully written book" in which Lott "has given us something unusual—an unsentimental account of the life of a woman from rural Mississippi who transcends poverty and ignorance to become part of a pioneering movement in the treatment of children with Down Syndrome" (Freeman 21). Lott is an adroit writer, cutting deftly back and forth in time presenting us not only Jewel Hilburn's contemporary management of the plight of her mentally disabled daughter Brenda Kay and the rest of her children, but also Jewel's own childhood, including the early deaths of her half-Choctaw father and sadly dependent mother, as well as her experiences at the Mississippi Industrial School for Girls, where she is sent by her vindictive grandmother. Futhermore, Lott devotes as much care and attention to his depiction of the early lives of the Hilburns in Mississippi as he does to their new ones in 1950s Los Angeles, where they transplant themselves in order to better treat Brenda Kay's condition. Last but not least, in a move that would warm Forster's round-character-loving heart, Brenda Kay's own character is every bit as rich as, if not richer than, any of the others in the book, second only to the compelling and realistic figure of Jewel herself.

The next book in the top ten lineup, May 1999's *White Oleander* by Janet Fitch, is just this side of the sensationalism that marred more than a few of the worst OBC picks, but it is precisely this walking of the line between the lyrical and the lurid that secures this novel's status as one of the best. When her imperious poet mother Ingrid ends up imprisoned for the murder of a spurning lover, *White Oleander* protagonist Astrid finds herself thrust into the miserably inadequate foster-care system of the state of California. Under the institution's auspices she ends up statutorily raped by one foster parent and shot by another, in addition to which she tries her hand at small-time prostitution, has her face ripped off by dogs, and has to fight for both her belongings and her life among her fellow wards of the state. In the middle of all this adversity, Fitch touches on the tried and true literary themes of coming-of-age and mother-daughter relationships, but as Gretchen Holbrook Gerzina writes in her *New York Times* review, "until she is 18, Astrid lives with an often disastrous series of surrogate mothers . . . each time rising from the ashes of disaster wounded and transformed . . . and her growth as a painter and sculptor parallels her growth as a vulnerable but self-aware young woman. Fitch handles this progress deftly, pulling *White Oleander* back from the brink of predictability" (Gerzina 21). Indeed, it is Fitch's rendering of the almost poetic voice of the unpredictable Astrid that makes this novel such a lonely, haunting, and ultimately beautiful one. Fitch makes Astrid's point of view startlingly complex, ironic, and discerning as when she describes a rare moment of solitude—quickly broken, of course—by saying:

> I walked toward the light, past businesses and little houses advertising childcare. . . . I rested my arms on the damp concrete railing and looked north toward the hills and the park. . . . A tall white bird fished among the rocks, standing on one leg like in a Japanese woodcut. Fifty views of the L.A. River. A horn honked and a man shouted, "Give me a piece of that" out of a car window. But it didn't matter, nobody could stop on the bridge anyway. (Fitch 274–75)

Forster says that the test of a round character is whether it is capable of surprising in a convincing way. By this definition, Fitch's Astrid is anything but flat.

The third entry on this list to fall into the category of male authors writing about female protagonists comes in the form of the January 2000 pick *Gap Creek* by Robert Morgan. Like *She's Come Undone* and *Jewel*, *Gap Creek*'s strength lies in Morgan's dedication to the voice of Julie Harmon, the young heroine of his story of the first year of a marriage in the unforgiving wilderness of turn-of-the-century Appalachia. Dwight Garner writes in his *New York Times* review, "Morgan is a voracious student of rural life in the United States during the 18th and 19th centuries. . . . You may think you couldn't care less about how to, say build a road or render lard. . . . But in Morgan's hands these details become the stuff of stern, gripping drama" (Garner 10). Thanks to Morgan's commitment to the authenticity of Julie's point of view, as well as to the description of the minutiae of her daily tasks, he achieves a highly unified, solidly good novel.

Next in line is Toni Morrison's *The Bluest Eye,* which, although it was her third induction into OBC in April 2000, is actually her first novel. In it, the eleven-year-old African American Pecola Breedlove prays ardently for blue eyes so that she too may be as beloved as she believes the white kids of America to be. Morrison gives a consistently true and poetic voice to Pecola's yearning when, for example, she writes, "It had occurred to Pecola some time ago that if her eyes, those eyes that held the pictures, and knew the sights—if those eyes of hers were different, that is to say, beautiful, she herself would be different. . . . If she looked different, beautiful. . . . Maybe they'd say, 'Why look at pretty-eyed Pecola. We mustn't do bad things in front of those pretty eyes'" (46). In short, this language—combined with the novel's evocation of a highly specific place, time, and community, its clarity of artistic purpose, and its keen awareness of tradition—make *The Bluest Eye,* in my opinion, far and away the best Toni Morrison novel in the OBC canon.

Next, as broad in its vision of social injustice as *The Bluest Eye* is focused, is the June 2000 pick, *The Poisonwood Bible,* Barbara Kingsolver's shifting, nonlinear narrative of a fervent patriarch possessed by a zeal to dedicate his and his family's lives to African missionary work in the fractious Congo of the early 1960s. Featuring a well-developed five-way point of view—in the form of the distinct voices of wife and mother Orleanna Price and her four daughters: little Ruth May Price the youngest, Leah and Adah the fraternal but almost opposite twins in the middle, and Rachel the silly, vain, self-absorbed eldest—*The Poisonwood Bible* manages not only to tell the story of the fractured Price family, but also to depict an especially contentious period in the tumultuous history of the Congo. In a style never preachy or predictable, Kingsolver addresses concerns of social justice, U.S. foreign policy, and post-colonialism while at the same time managing to allow her novel to be funny, ironic, tragic and human. Here, as with so many of her selections, Winfrey has picked a book that examines familial struggles head-on, but which—unlike some of the lesser picks—also addresses vast outlying political concerns, making for a powerful combination of personal interiority and political externality, as when Orleanna, reflecting on her experiences from a distance of many years, says:

> Fifteen years after it all happened, I sat by my radio in Atlanta listening to Senator Church and the special committee hearings on the Congo. . . . Where had I been? . . . of Lumumba's imprisonment, escape, and recapture, I recall—what? The hardships of washing and cooking in a drought. . . . Ruth May's illness, of course. . . . History didn't cross my mind. Now it does. Now I know, whatever your burdens, to hold yourself apart from the lot of powerful men is an illusion. (Kingsolver 323)

Thus, Kingsolver's acknowledgement of the interconnectivity of the public and domestic spheres is a skillful and welcome one.

Selected for the club in November of the same year, Andre Dubus III's *The House of Sand and Fog* features another highly effective multiple point of view. This time readers receive the story of three principal, and not always sympathetic, characters—the formerly powerful, now menial-job-holding Iranian immigrant Colonel Genob Sarhang Massoud Amir Behrani, looking to get into real estate; Kathy Nicolo, a homeowner whose property is wrongly seized due to a bureaucratic tax error; and Sheriff Lester Burdon, who, despite a crumbling marriage and problems of his own, becomes determined to help Kathy fight for what's hers—and their conflicting quests for the American dream. All three move through the novel's thick, well-written atmosphere seeking shelter, love and security with single-minded, selfish determination until they collide violently over one over-determined suburban bungalow, the titular *House of Sand and Fog*.

At this point, I'm going to break chronological order for the sake of passing over the September 2001 pick, *The Corrections*, and skip ahead to the remaining novel left in the top ten. I intend to come back and deal with Franzen's book more thoroughly—both because I consider it the best, most sophisticated book in the OBC canon, and because it speaks directly to this project's inextricably inter-twined concerns of taste and power and exclusion. Thus, briefly: Rohinton Mistry's *A Fine Balance,* a sweeping epic set in India during the Emergency of the 1970s, proved itself an excellent choice on Winfrey's part to follow up last fall's disinvitation dust-up. Ranking with *The Poisonwood Bible* in terms of its fully realized concerns with social justice on an international level, Mistry's novel maintained its own fine balance between its description of the era's gross human rights violations—the castrations, the sterilizations, the poverty, and the homelessness—and its depiction of its four main characters, of their interactions with each other, and of the richly evoked world in which they move. Rohinton Mistry, writes A. G. Mojtabai in her June 23, 1996, *New York Times* review, "needs no infusions of magi-cal realism to vivify the real. The real world, through his eyes, is quite magical enough" (Mojtabai 29).

Now—before moving to the tenth novel on the list—I'd like to emphasize that each and every one of the top ten best Oprah books may be identified as such based upon the same criteria that allow us to identify other good books. We may judge these ten books as good for exhibiting dexterous authorial control of voice and point of view, to the extent that they do not always rely simply on warm, sympa-thetic, reliable first-person narrators, but rather frequently allow us to hear the shifting, prickly, unreliable voices of more than one per-son; for presenting round characters, to the extent that we gain insight into several complex and fascinating consciousnesses; for cre-ating worlds that are never weak in historical or contemporary detail, to the extent that setting functions not merely as a backdrop in front of which characters perform, but rather as a richly realized entity in its own right; for possessing an informed sense of literary tradition, and, of course, for demonstrating undeniable stylistic skill and a high quality of actual writing.

Frequently, as serious readers, we—and I intend to include the readers of OBC, as well as academically trained readers under the auspices of this pronoun—crave the complex, odd, unsettling con-sciousnesses that challenging novels give us, novels in which we aren't always certain where the narrator's sympathies—or our own—are supposed to lie; we may consider these ten Oprah books good for giving us the opportunity to engage with precisely these kinds of consciousnesses. Moreover, we crave novels that allow us to feel—as when we read Kafka or Dostoevsky or Mann, for instance—that we are interacting with something new and strange, and therefore good, as opposed to something familiar and formulaic, and therefore bad. We crave ironic novels, novels with a sense of humor—for humorless novels are irrevocably doomed to be flatter than ones that, no matter how occasionally, display this added dimension—novels in which themes feel suggested and nuanced rather than stated, novels that give us the sense that much of their meaning is implied, that there's far more to them than meets the eye. In short, we crave novels with sweep, a sense of vision, a sense of fully real wholeness indicative of the author's intention and ability to include all the components and details necessary to truly capture an entire world.

That said, whether you consider it within the context of OBC or without, Jonathan Franzen's *The Corrections* is arguably such a book. On its most basic and already impressive level, the novel addresses virtually all things American—from the politics of college literary criticism classes to clinical depression, from ambivalence about the death penalty to the exploitation of developing nations, from the abuse of drugs, legal and otherwise, to the pressure to conform to a sexual identity, from the fevered and often fruitless quest for material wealth to the kinds of unique and hellish pain that only members of one's own immediate family can inflict—in a full, fearless, and complicated style. His handling of these subjects—which in the hands of a lesser writer could certainly fall into the category of mere issues—transcends simple topicality and engages in cultural truth-telling on an enormous scale. For while great ideas are certainly a necessary condition in the creation of great novels, they are not sufficient. Rather, truly great novels result not only from an author's intellectual, political, social, and cultural seriousness, but also from an author's ability to evoke a kind of enigmatic, philosophical and almost spiritual quality—an aura of unity and humanity—within their writing, to foster a truly unsettling atmosphere in their work that guarantees that it will remain with us as readers long after we've finished the act of reading.

In other words, Franzen—like virtually every author responsible for a great novel—understands the importance of intimation, which is to say the Aristotelian distinction between art and documentary, poetry and history, for where history is about a realistic and ostensibly truthful recording of discrete elements, art is about the subtle manipulation of implication. Great art, then, conveys not only the immediate truths of our present lives, but also implies the truth of what's to come; it seeks not only to explore moral and cultural conditions in a particular fixed moment, but also to explicate the effects of said moral and cultural conditions on the future. In *The Corrections,* then, Franzen approaches what Forster calls prophecy defined not "in the narrow sense of foretelling the future," but as "an accent in the novelist's voice, an accent for which the flutes and saxophones of fantasy may have prepared us. His theme is the universe, or something universal, but he is not necessarily going to 'say' anything about the universe; he proposes to sing, and the strangeness of the song arising in the halls of fiction is bound to give us a shock" (125). Prophecy, then, has as much to do with an author's tone of voice as it does with her or his cultural predictions, and Franzen's tone in *The Corrections* manages to be ironic, funny, and sharp, without becoming condescending or cartoonish. Franzen clearly loves not only the ideas behind his story, but also his frequently unloveable characters. In his writing, we may find numerous instances of what Forster calls "the implication that signifies and will filter into the turns of the novelist's phrase" (126). Clearly, I could go on and on about *The Corrections,* but—since you are all quite capable of reading it yourselves—at this point I'll just give you a couple great and/or prophetic moments from a novel that possesses quite a few of them.

Thus, I present to you Exhibit A, wherein Chip Lambert, second son of the novel's family of protagonists and an English professor at D— College, gives his intro theory class, Consuming Narratives, an arguably objectionable corporate ad campaign to analyze on the last day of the semester. During the ensuing discussion, precocious undergraduate Melissa Paquette interrupts:

"Excuse me . . . but that is just such bullshit. . . . It's one critic after another wringing their hands about the state of criticism. . . . *It is so typical and perfect that you hate those ads!* . . . Here things are getting better and better for women and people of color and gay men and lesbians, more and more integrated and open, and all you can think about is some stupid, lame problem with signifiers and signifieds. Like, the only way you can make something bad out of an ad that's great for women— which you have to do, because there has to be something wrong with everything—is to say it's evil to be rich and evil to work for a corporation, and yes, I know the bell rang." She closed her notebook. "OK," Chip said. "On that note. You've now satisfied your Cultural Studies core requirement. Have a great summer." (Franzen 44)

I've excerpted this passage first because of its development of the character of Melissa herself. In a lesser novel—even a pretty good one—she could have functioned satisfactorily as a kind of plot device: an expedient, jailbait character with whom Chip has the love affair that gets him fired so he can enter the novel in the pathetically underemployed state in which we first encounter him, thereby setting up the fly-by-night scheme which later lands him in Eastern Europe. Instead, Franzen gives Melissa a roundness—implying, for instance, that she is more than able to move on with her young life after her indiscretions with Chip—that would've done Forster proud.

Forster says of Dostoevsky, "He is a great novelist in the ordinary sense—that is to say his characters have relation to ordinary life and also live in their own surroundings, there are incidents which keep us excited, and so on; he has also the greatness of a prophet, to which our ordinary standards are inapplicable" (133). This passage and others like it throughout *The Corrections* illustrate how Forster could have said almost the same of Franzen, for the substance of this exchange between Chip and Melissa signifies far more than just itself. It echoes debates—over capitalism, political correctness, feminism, and even taste—that we as readers have no doubt heard and will continue to hear elsewhere in the culture.

In fact, the ambivalence signaled by this episode—for the class is indeed bullshit, but so is the ad campaign, thus we thrill to Melissa's vitriol, but aren't totally ready to dismiss the point Chip's trying to make—resonates even with the sense of conflictedness experienced by many readers, authors, and critics regarding OBC itself. Just as this in-class argument should not be boiled down to black and white, neither should arguments over the worth of OBC be reduced to terms of high versus low culture. In a way, it *is* so typical and perfect for critics to hate OBC, inasmuch as a significant part of their problem with the institution seems to be that it is a lucrative, profit-generating endeavor, one whose beneficiaries are, more often than not, women. By the same token, for the club's defenders to insist that there's nothing about OBC that could be done better is similarly unfair. Thus, by getting caught up in high versus low, or high versus middle diatribes, no one's really concerning themselves with what this ambivalence *means,* or what kind of cultural work is actually being accomplished by OBC.

Now, speaking of ambivalence and taste, I give you Exhibit B, wherein Denise, the only daughter of the Lambert family, and her mother, Enid, argue over their own respective preferences—in this instance, in relation to a Midwestern dinner party:

> Enid had, true enough, had fun at Dean and Trish's party. . . . "I guess there's no accounting for tastes," she said. "That's true," Denise said. "Although some tastes are better than others." . . . "That's what everybody thinks," Enid said. "Everybody thinks their taste is the best." "But most people are wrong," Denise said. . . . "Enough," Alfred said to Denise. "You'll never win." "You sound like a snob," Enid said. "Mother, you're always telling me how much you like a good home-cooked meal. Well, that's what I like, too. I think there's a kind of Disney vulgarity in a foot-tall dessert. *You* are a better cook—" "Oh, no. No." Enid interrupted. "I'm a nothing cook." (Franzen 99)

In addition to depicting convincingly a specific family dynamic, complete with miniature power struggles and intergenerational button-pushing, this excerpt, like Exhibit A, speaks to issues external to itself; it speaks, among other things, to this project. Here it is: the antagonism between highbrow and middlebrow tastes expressed in terms of a mother-daughter exchange about pyramids of shrimp and foot-tall desserts.

Here and elsewhere throughout its 568 pages, *The Corrections* seems to call attention to just how much it has to say about the far-reaching ramifications of taste of all kinds—as well as, by extension, how very unfortunate the cancellation of its televised OBC discussion segment really was. In Exhibit C, Gary, the eldest of the Lambert children, complains with misanthropic sourness that "all around him, millions of newly minted American millionaires were engaged in the identical pursuit of feeling extraordinary. . . . There were further tens of millions of young Americans who didn't have money but were nonetheless chasing the Perfect Cool. And meanwhile the sad truth was that not everyone could be extraordinary . . . because whom would that leave to be ordinary? Who would perform the thankless work of being comparatively uncool?" (Franzen 197). Shortly thereafter—exhibiting a kind of obsessive preoccupation with high versus low, coast versus center hierarchies not unlike that which Franzen himself appeared to display after his OBC selection—Gary continues that he has lately observed that:

> population was continuing to flow out of the Midwest and
> toward the cooler coasts. . . . At the same time, all the restau-
> rants in St. Jude were suddenly coming up to European speed
> . . . and shoppers at the mall near his parents' house had an air
> of entitlement offputtingly similar to his own. . . . Gary wished
> that all further migration to the coasts could be banned and all
> midwesterners encouraged to revert to eating pasty foods and
> wearing dowdy clothes and playing board games, in order that
> a strategic national reserve of cluelessness might be main-
> tained, a wilderness of taste which would enable people of
> privilege, like himself, to feel extremely civilized in perpetuity.
> (Franzen 198)

So, in a world where, as Gary notes, it's becoming harder and harder to maintain this feeling of civilized privilege, we can extrapolate how comforting it is to have something such as Winfrey's club—which, I'd like to point out, is based in Chicago, and thus in the aforementioned Midwest—to point to and say that, because of its mass-appeal, it cannot possibly be cool.

And since by now I've hopefully shown you that Winfrey recommends some damn cool stuff—*The Corrections* included—we can further extrapolate that the real-life desire of the ones who would be cool to relegate OBC and things of its ilk into the ranks of the permanently uncool can hardly be considered a sound—or in some cases even an informed—decision. As Chris Bohjalian wrote to me on a promotional postcard for his latest novel, *Tran-sister Radio*, "My sense is that when we presume that popular books cannot be good or that good books cannot be popular, we: (1) Needlessly denigrate some complex fiction simply because it sells well; (2) Fail to support solid literary work, assuming that Mainstream America will find it too challenging." The reality, he continues, "as *Cold Mountain* and *White Teeth* and *Plainsong* have shown, is that good books CAN be popular, if we give 'middlebrow' America a chance" (postcard to the author). Certainly, some tastes can be identified—as can some books—as superior to others. Nonetheless, these issues of taste deserve to be discussed intelligently and thoughtfully, not merely to be reduced to a question of the hip elite versus the lumbering masses.

A failure to do so in this case overlooks one of the most remarkable aspects of the selections of OBC, which is their astonishingly wide range in terms of quality and sheer readability. Indeed, as Striphas has pointed out, "Some critics have expressed dismay over the range of titles chosen. . . . The *Journal* was troubled . . . by the seemingly inconsistent demands Oprah's Book Club placed on participants in terms of club selections which fluctuated between arguably straightforward books . . . to more intricate, lyrical titles" (303). Yet it is this very inconsistency—a characteristic typically loaded with negative connotations—that proved to be one of the club's most powerful attractions. As Winfrey and her producers seem to have figured out, "Perhaps those who had not read books in many years were drawn to Oprah's Book Club precisely because of this apparent inconsistency" (Striphas 303).

In fact, by speaking with a number of OBC readers while standing in line outside Harpo Studios before the taping of second-to-last book club segment of the first OBC on April 4, 2002, I found most of them to be well aware of the need for this kind of discussion. Senior publicist Audrey Pass had told me in no uncertain terms that, during my attendance of this taping, I was forbidden to ask anyone affiliated with the show—except her, of course—about their opinions of the club, the workings of the program, or anything else of the kind. As it turned out, there was no one affiliated with the show waiting outside anyway, although there was a cluster of warmly dressed women standing behind me, chatting knowledgeably about both the show itself and the latest pick at the time, Ann-Marie MacDonald's *Fall On Your Knees*.

Two of the three women—Clara Carter and Heidi Adams—had come all the way from Baltimore, while one—Paula Argue—was from Chicago. When asked her opinion of OBC, Argue—for whom April 4 would be her fourth time on the show, but her first time on a book club segment—replied without missing a beat, "I think it's quite nice. It raises people's awareness of a particular book and also of reading. It makes reading a social event, and that's a new thing, and it works." Carter agreed, even though she admitted to only having read a couple of the selections. "Like Paula says, it really opens people's eyes and raises their curiosity to newer writers, and mostly to very strong writers." Adams—who told me that she, like myself, had attended the George Washington University—voiced particular enthusiasm about the latest selection, explaining that earlier on in the club's history, she had had a hard time getting into some of the OBC picks. "I've tried, but I just haven't been able to get through [them]. *Midwives* just wasn't for me, but this one I really enjoyed. It had a faster pace and the author engaged you much sooner. Some of the others have seemed too much like something you'd have to do for a homework assignment."

As appreciative as they were of Winfrey's project as a whole, Argue, Carter, and Adams were far from totally uncritical when asked their opinions of how Winfrey actually discussed the books on TV. Over the course of the impromptu interview, the women made it clear that it was in fact possible and even beneficial to understand the faults within a phenomenon they viewed for the most part as a positive one. "I like the idea of an intimate dinner with readers and the author," Adams said, "but I'm honestly not sure that the guests invited are ever really at ease to say all they want. I think it's basically good for Oprah and maybe even the authors, but the guests seem like they've been placed in their seats. It's artificial." Assenting, Argue added trenchantly, "So many of the people at the discussions seem to think that they have to cry."

Heidi's husband Ray Adams joined the interview at that point, admitting somewhat sheepishly that he too had read *Fall on Your Knees*. "Don't tell anybody," he joked when I asked him about the stereotype that Winfrey's selections were somehow only for women. "I took this as the opportunity to read a novel, which is something I hadn't done in a long, long time. After I got into it, it was very interesting, not just in terms of plot, but in terms of content. The story kept turning the corner, so just when you thought you understood what the author was trying to say, you realized that nothing in the book can be assumed." I asked whether he, as a man, felt at all alienated by Winfrey's latest female-centered selection, prompting him to reply that "this is not an agenda-oriented book. There's enough going on in it to apply to anybody, and I personally was more or less invested in how it was going to work out with the characters." Adams added, though, that "looking at this crowd today, obviously, I see very few males, and honestly it was mostly my wife's interest in the club that got me into it. Oprah's meeting her goal of getting people to read, but she could still accomplish more by getting more males involved." How could she motivate more men to participate, I wanted to know. Maybe by doing some kind of giveaway, something for the first fifty men in line, or by having more men involved in the on-the-air discussion, he answered. "The whole situation is sort of like follow the leader. If guys see more guys doing it, I think they'll want to do it, too."

As it turned out, mere hours later, Winfrey announced the cancellation of her club. Still, the readers and others like them knew all along that the institution of which they had chosen to be a part was not to be unconditionally praised. They understood that even though OBC was not perfect, even though it bore room for improvement, so too did it bear thoughtful discussion. Above all, they understood that—presuppositions and stereotypes aside—the club's novels were, for the most part, well worth engaging with.

In his October 15, 2001, *New Republic* review of *The Corrections,* James Wood—with reference to Franzen's 1996 complaint that his novel hadn't successfully engaged with the culture, that it had in effect been published in a vacuum—wonders rhetorically about the very possibility of the existence of a novel *not* published in a vacuum. A novelist's only true success, claims Wood, "is aesthetic success, and 'the culture' will never validate aesthetic success, will never 'engage' with that. And finally we will not be the judges of this success: Samuel Johnson suggested that a hundred years might be the test of a book's artistic power" (Wood 34). Moreover, continues Wood, "every great novel is published in a vacuum; it teaches the empty space around it. *Nausea* and *The Stranger* are not great novels that successfully engaged with an existential culture, but great novels that taught a culture existentialism" (34). I feel compelled to acknowledge again that everything I just did—that the assembly of my bottom ten and top ten lists—was entirely and undeniably subjective; my designations are not necessarily right or wrong, and they are certainly not infallible. They may even strike some readers as absolutely wrong, but that's the exactly kind of provocation and opportunity for debate that was conspicuously absent from Winfrey's televised discussions. My goal with these critiques, particularly in the case of the bottom ten books, was not to engage in negativity for negativity's sake, but rather to call attention to the seeming gag order placed on this kind of criticism within the televised confines of OBC.

Moreover, I hope that this critical overview of particular titles has called attention to the exceptional eclecticism, heterogeneity, and inconsistency of Winfrey's selections. I hope too that it has illustrated that:

> There was no single level, then, at which members of Oprah's Book Club read, and indeed their range of reading interests and abilities was reflected in the seemingly inconsistent profile of the titles chosen for the club. Winfrey and her producers deliberately made and timed selections to appeal strategically to a broad range of women/readers and to welcome newcomers to the club, some of whom may have felt intimidated by books

and book reading. (Striphas 305)

In other words, there was most definitely a method to what many critics dismissed as Winfrey's madness; she knew exactly what she was doing, and it worke d. For even though there were books that I have acknowledged that I found bad and/or unreadable, this hardly proves that every other OBC participant would agree with me. Certainly, none of these books bombed or flopped, and each and every one went on to become a bestseller.

That said, I have to point out, too, that even though I will not be around in another hundred years to conduct an adequate Johnsonian test of any of these books' artistic power—nor will Wood, nor anyone else—any and everyone can, should, and to a certain extent does do what I just did. We *can* read, evaluate, and rank, to the best of our abilities, the merits, aesthetic and otherwise, of these and any other extant novels. In doing so, we engage with them in the best possible way, relating them to our present moment, interpreting what they have to say about the future, and allowing them to teach us what they have to teach. Winfrey's book club, then, has provided an inviting and inclusive forum for interested parties to engage with contemporary novels in a way that can be achieved contemporarily. Thus, "the work of the Book Club consisted not just of finding good books, in other words, but more importantly books that fit—an intractable alchemy that has vexed the book industry for a century" (Striphas 311). In this sense, the books of OBC did as well as—and often times better than—many of their non-selected counterparts, in the sense that in Winfrey's hands, novels are wielded with the express purpose of teaching the surrounding culture.

To conclude this chapter, I'll cite the same concept Forster did in conclusion to his series of lectures at Cambridge, that concept being:

> Expansion. That is the idea the novelist must cling to. Not completion. Not rounding off but opening out. When the symphony is over we feel that the notes have been liberated, they have found in the rhythm of the whole their individual freedom. Cannot the novel be like that? Is not there something of

it in *War and Peace?* . . . such an untidy book. Yet, as we read it, do not great chords begin to sound behind us, and when we have finished does not every item—even the catalogue of strategies—lead a larger existence than was possible at the time? (169)

Thus, this expansive effect is one achieved by good and great novels in general, and certainly by the good and great novels of OBC. Winfrey's selections, then, are far from the problem with OBC, but rather, as they should be, the very best aspect of the club. The true problem with OBC arises later, when those books are formatted to fit your screen; their roundness gets flattened, their expansiveness gets reined in. But this will all become apparent in the next chapter.

CHAPTER FOUR

Formatted to Fit Your Screen: The Flattening Effects of Television on the Books of OBC

> "The only real criteria we have is that the author has to be alive, so that he or she can appear on the TV program."
>
> —Oprah Winfrey Show *spokeswoman,*
> Writer's Digest, *October 2000*

> "The queen of television rarely watches television herself; it 'promotes false values,' she admits. Instead she spends her evenings reading."
>
> —Marilyn Johnson, Life *magazine,*
> *September 1997*

As you may already be aware, if you were paying careful attention in the previous chapter, this is the second time that the quotation in the first epigraph appears in this book—and while I've said it before, it bears repeating. For here, in this caveat that authors must appear on the program, lies the source from which any and all truly legitimate complaints about, or criticisms of, the club have their origin. Indeed, most other objections—that the club was too commercial, for instance, or that Winfrey represented the consolidation of too much power in one person, or that we resent being "told" what to read—amount to little more than so much tangential bitching; TV itself was where the real trouble originated.

Winfrey's use of television as a vehicle for the presentation of literature was in large part what enabled her to be "the most influential promoter of books in the world," to the extent that the announcement of a book on her talk show "always results in an increase in sales of more than 500,000 copies for a selection, often of more than one million copies, and sometimes more" ("The Bookseller" 22). Simultaneously, though, Winfrey's televisual approach was responsible for the imposition of manifold intermediary and external superfluities on novels that were already complete and intended for unmediated absorption. In his essay, "Criticism and the Experience of Interiority," Geneva School phenomenological critic Georges Poulet writes, "At this moment what matters to me is to live, from the inside, in a certain identity with the work and the work alone. It could hardly be otherwise. Nothing external to the work could possibly share the extraordinary claim which the work now exerts on me" (46). And although at times Poulet's effusive writing on his desire for purity in the act of reading approaches the pitch of a religious fanatic ecstatically declaiming on his faith, his assertion here is a sound one. Indeed, Winfrey relied so obviously on the exertion of an entirely external medium upon the books themselves that the dissipation of some measure of the novels' extraordinary claims upon their readers was inevitable.

What's more, Winfrey's show strove in its book club segments to make communal and familiar that which should be an individual and unsettling experience. As Forster says, "The reader must sit down alone and struggle with the writer, and this the pseudo-scholar will not do. He would rather relate a book to the history of its time, to events in the life of its author, to the events it describes, above all to some tendency" (Forster 13–14). In other words, the true mode of reading is solitary and silent, characterized by the direct reception of a complex fictional consciousness into a thoughtful real one. Thus, Winfrey's highly historicized, autobiographied, and unapologetically issues-based televised approach to literary fiction was, to use Forster's phrase, pseudo-scholarly. Put another way, hers was an imperfect, reductive project of interpretation.

I want to emphasize here that the real problem with Oprah's Book Club originated not with the books, but rather with the competing narratives cultivated by the show on which the books were presented. As I asserted in the previous chapter, the narratives of the novels themselves were consistently worthwhile; however, when we experience these novels within the context of the televised book club, we are confronted with a slew of extraneous narratives from which the novels simply cannot be extricated. These parallel narratives include most obviously that of the show itself, which necessitated that each and every one of the books be put to didactic use as an ennobling tool for learning about and coming to terms with assorted issues in the interest of living your best life and rediscovering your spirit. Additionally, each and every one of the novels had to be woven into the fabric of Winfrey's own personal narrative of struggle against, and triumph over adversity. For not only did Winfrey tend to pick books with which she, given her own famously tumultuous coming-of-age, could easily identify, she also imposed her own narrative on the book club project at large. Even as she promoted the beneficial and enriching effects of reading in general, Winfrey used OBC to promote the beneficial and enriching effects of reading on herself in particular, thereby aggrandizing her own personality. For even when she couldn't draw a direct comparison between a fictional character's life and her own, Winfrey remained at the ready with intimate anecdotes and mini-narratives designed to fortify the quasi-cult of personality she constructed of herself as striving reader. In a September 1997 issue of *Life* magazine, for instance, she recounts:

> Not only was my mother not a reader, but I remember being in the back hallway when I was about nine—I'm going to say this without crying—and my mother threw the door open and grabbed a book out of my hand and said, "You're nothing but a something-something bookworm. Get your butt outside! You think you're better than the other kids. And I'm not taking you to no library!" I was treated as though something was wrong with me because I wanted to read all the time. (qtd. in Johnson 1)

In the midst of all this heartfelt confessionality, striving for spiritual wholeness, and shameless self-promotion, it's little wonder that disentangling the novels themselves from among the program's clashing narratives became virtually impossible.

Still, there were those, including twice-selected OBC author Wally Lamb, who would say that the OBC-selected books themselves were somehow immune to the unavoidable imposition of such extraneous trappings as the ones to which they were subjected when they were formatted to fit the *Oprah Winfrey Show*. Even though he did so "with some concern that your questions carry a negative bias, and, perhaps, some presupposed conclusions" Lamb replied via e-mail to my survey, thoughtfully addressing my queries in a lengthy single statement. Among other things, he wrote:

> Was I happy with the way my novels were presented? Sure. The format is tight and the vast audience consists of a majority of viewers who will not have read the novel. The show is what it is: a mass-market vehicle that must survive the ratings race and serve a general populace. You want erudition and in-depth textual examination? You seek other venues. The edited and televised book discussion, I think, mirrors what goes on in the thousands of living rooms across the country where book discussion groups proliferated: a general discussion during which people relate their questions, observations, and reasons why they did or didn't relate to the characters. We both filter fiction through our own lives and use it to go beyond our lives. That, in my opinion, is more purposeful than the performance of critical autopsies. (Lamb, e-mail to the author)

Ultimately, he draws the conclusion that, "bottom line: The Oprah Book Club is the medium. The novel itself is the message and must stand or fall on its own merits." While it's certainly comforting to think that this might have been the case, I am compelled here to respectfully disagree with Lamb, inasmuch as—for the various reasons I've already listed, and into which I will delve more deeply over the course of this chapter—it seems shortsighted and falsely optimistic to characterize OBC as no more than a medium.

As Lamb himself points out, the program must propagate its own mass-market message and push its own agenda—a television program must, in the most literal sense, sell itself. In doing so, the televisual component of OBC couldn't help but distort and obscure the true merits of the books it featured. Indeed, the game of ratings, approval, and popularity ensures that television will never be *just* the medium, since it must, by its nature, strive to become the message as well so that it may survive. Even after acknowledging this to be the case, Lamb suggests that books—and perhaps all forms of art with a capital A—possess some kind of transcendent quality that cannot be corrupted, whored, or deleted by the machinations and processes involved in the production of television. In doing so, he seems to willfully ignore the innately auto-promotional nature of television as medium and message, as well as the inexorably flattening and confining effect of TV on an art form that, at its best, is round and, in Forster's word, expansive.

As a forum for the discussion of literary fiction, then, TV sucks. To put a finer point on it, TV sucks and flattens: sucks away all meaning save that which it can manipulate to its own ratings-friendly advantage, and flattens novels so that they may be condensed and crammed into easily interpretable, highly salable packages. Now, since we should all know by this point that television is scarcely the most reliable, complex, or intellectually taxing of the media, I won't be citing Newton Minow or Neil Postman or any of the other TV-as-wasteland theorists. I *will* be citing David Foster Wallace, specifically Wallace from "E Unibus Pluram: Television and U.S. Fiction" (originally published in 1993 in *The Review of Contemporary Fiction* and anthologized in *A Supposedly Fun Thing I'll Never Do Again*) because in it Wallace says, as the title suggests, a number of things relevant to this chapter. Among these things is his assertion that

> It is of course undeniable that television is an example of Low Art, the sort of art that has to please people in order to get their money. Because of the economics of nationally broadcast, advertiser-subsidized entertainment, television's one goal—never denied by anybody in or around TV since RCA first authorized field tests in 1936—is to ensure as much watching as possible. TV is the epitome of Low Art in its desire to appeal to and enjoy the attention of unprecedented numbers of people. But it is not Low because it is vulgar or prurient or dumb.

> Television is often all these things, but this is a logical function
> of its need to attract and please Audience. (Wallace 37)

Wallace is quick to explain that he's not claiming that TV is vulgar and dumb because members of Audience are vulgar and dumb. Rather, he says "television is the way it is simply because people tend to be extremely similar in their vulgar, prurient, and dumb interests and wildly different in their refined and aesthetic and noble interests. It's all about syncretic diversity: neither medium nor Audience is faultable for quality" (Wallace 37). So, no matter how earnest, pure, or noble Winfrey's intentions for OBC may have been, nothing can alter the fact that, given the medium via which it had to be disseminated, OBC was never a pure institution. Each and every time Winfrey and OBC promoted a book, they simultaneously promoted themselves.

That said, as damaging as the imposition of television upon literary fiction can certainly be, the basic task Winfrey undertook—to, as the media kit I received from Harpo Productions puts it, "get the country excited about reading again!"—was an admirable one, as well as one she performed remarkably well while attempting to balance everyone's best interests. So, rather than concluding that OBC as an institution was either entirely good—as do those in the "people are reading so what could possibly be wrong?" camp—or entirely bad— as do those in the "how could anything good for serious literature possibly be accomplished by TV?" camp—the best way to conceive of the club seems to be that it was like a knife: it cut both ways. In order to apprehend that Winfrey's televisual approach to fiction was, like virtually everything else discussed in this book, neither wholly good nor wholly bad, we need to understand exactly what it was she was doing, what her critics objected to about what she was doing, and what she actually should have been criticized for doing.

Wallace observes of television criticism in general that most scholars writing about American popular culture simultaneously seem "to take TV very seriously and to suffer terrible pain over what they see. There's this well-known critical litany about television's vapidity and irrealism. The litany is often even cruder and triter than the shows the critics complain about, which I think is why most younger Americans find professional criticism of television less interesting than professional television itself" (27–28). The same tends to hold true of criticism levied against Winfrey's club. Indeed, such cultural commentators as Mary Schmich of the *Chicago Tribune,* Tom Shone of the *New York Times,* Jonathan Yardley of the *Washington Post,* and Richard Roeper of the *Chicago Sun-Times,* to name but a few, loved to lay into what they perceived to be the weaker aspects of OBC. Yet even as they did so, their criticisms received far less notice than the program in question, the popularity of which continued to hover almost effortlessly at stratospheric levels. These critics and others like them exhibited what Wallace calls a "strange mix that's been around for a few years now: weary contempt for television as a creative product and cultural force, combined with beady-eyed fascination about the actual behind-the-glass mechanics of making that product and projecting that force" (28). Certainly, objectors to OBC seemed to relish any and all opportunities to call attention to the general unworthiness of the televised club, while at the same time expressing a perverse attraction to that which they purported to abhor.

And here, reader, I must pause for clarification, lest you mistake me for another trite, anti-television alarmist quixotically determined to drag the tired, hackneyed "TV is evil" slogan kicking and screaming into the twenty-first century. That argument's been made for decades now—most famously by Jerry Mander in his 1978 *Four Arguments for the Elimination of Television* and Neil Postman in his 1985 *Amusing Ourselves to Death;* ergo, at this point, one must do more than announce that TV flattens the complexity of things (which you'd have to be a fool to deny that it does) and leave it at that. Thus, I call your attention now to a few of the more salient points of Donald Lazere's 1987 essay "Literacy and Mass Media: The Political Implications," which contains some of the sanest, scariest analysis ever written of exactly how and why television simultaneously damages the mind of the individual viewer and the very fabric of society and democracy. I don't mean to be as reductive here in my argument against television as the very medium with which I take issue, but it really is this simple:

> It is widely admitted in the media business . . . that most mass communication aimed at adults, both in television, radio, records, or film and in print, is at a literacy level not much higher than that of children's programming. In order to maximize ratings and sales of advertised products, commercial media must appeal to the largest possible market, thus to the lowest common denominator of cognitive development. Having an adult populace that is fixed in an infantile mentality also conveniently happens to prevent people from becoming very critical about either advertised products, the corporations that produce them and those that own the media, or the whole sociopolitical order in which those corporations play a central role. (Lazere 289)

So there you have it: TV is not intrinsically *evil* per se, but by dint of the intrinsically commercial ends to which it must serve as a means, its sociopolitical effects are, at their broadest, negative.

Lazere's arguments are more political than strictly literary; however, it is important to remember that the cognitive capacities to which he refers—the ones most threatened by the infantilizing influences of television—are the ones most closely linked to the process of reading actively and critically, among them the ability to concentrate for a sustained period of time on a particular situation or line of reasoning, as well as the capacity to perceive ambiguity and multiple points of view. In other words, TV kills your imagination. For:

> Perhaps the most profoundly conservative force in all of the cognitive patterns discussed here is their potential for inhibiting people from being able to imagine any social order different from the established one. The present reality is concrete and immediate, alternatives abstract and distant; ability to understand an alternative is further obstructed by lack of the sustained attention span necessary for analytic reasoning, the capacity to imagine beyond the actual to the hypothetical (which semantically entails reasoning from the literal to the figurative and symbolic), and a sense of irony necessary to question the social conditioning that endorses the status quo. (Lazere 295)

To follow this up, let me be perfectly clear that I in no way intend to suggest that a certain kind of TV-watcher—like, say, a fan of *The Oprah Winfrey Show*—is more susceptible to the televisual murder of his or her imagination than any other. Nor do I intend to suggest that there is a particular class of audience members that is especially prone to seduction by TV's pretty pictures, bright colors, and enforcedly passive behavior. No, television's insidious badness is more subtle than that, and it threatens everyone who watches it. For "to the extent that illiteracy and mass media perpetuate restricted cognitive capacities, these forces contribute to an impoverished, powerless mentality in millions of people who belong to diverse social classes by other criteria such as income level, race, and so on." (Lazere 299–300). That's what makes TV's anti-imaginative effect so frightening: no one is safe.

Really, given how hard it is to discuss imaginative literary fiction on television at all, OBC was in many respects an incredible accomplishment, one even Winfrey herself was not always convinced she could attain. "She said, 'I really wish that I could use your book but I don't use fiction on my show because it's death in the ratings. As soon as you use fiction the whole nation gets up as one person and changes the channel,'" inaugural OBC author Jacquelyn Mitchard told me of her initial interactions with Winfrey in the fall of 1996:

> I said OK and that was that . . . [but] apparently she couldn't get the book out of her mind, however, and so this was at the apex of the sort of book club formation movement, and she set her producers the task of creating a way in which they could use fiction on their show without getting people to be so bored they would turn away. And they came up with the idea of the world's biggest book club, so people on the road and people by e-mail and people on the phone and at their libraries could all be part of the book club and that they would choose the book discussion group from letters and e-mails, and so that's what they did. (interview with the author)

Indeed, in an interview with *Publishers Weekly*, Winfrey says that when her producers introduced the idea originally, "I thought we would die in the ratings. . . . I thought they had lost their minds" (Kinsella, "The Oprah Effect" 276). Past efforts to promote fiction on the air—in 1993, for instance, she hosted a show of writers she'd like to have dinner with, as a result of which book sales for those authors jumped but ratings plummeted—"just bombed" (Kinsella, "The Oprah Effect" 276).

The problem with fiction, Winfrey explains, "is that most people haven't read the book and so they can't follow the story. . . . It's the same problem when I have soap opera stars on the show; if you haven't been watching *Guiding Light,* I have to explain to everyone who the character is and what's the storyline" (Kinsella, "The Oprah Effect," 276). Moreover, in his comprehensive *New York Times Magazine* article on OBC, D. T. Max writes, "The book club, Winfrey told me, wasn't even her idea. Her producers had suggested it. At first, Winfrey feared 'horrible numbers.' But she changed her mind. 'The thing that sold me,' Winfrey said, 'was the chance to meet the authors'" (38). Given Winfrey's unabashed awe for writers, then, it's little wonder that the OBC format focused as intensely on the presence of the authors and their personalities as it did on the qualities of their novels. Thus—upon consideration of Winfrey's own concerns and interests—she and her producers invented the segmented program format allowing the host to spend as much or as little time on a topic as she felt both it and her audience could handle. And so OBC was born.

It should be noted here that Winfrey didn't *need* to add the book club segment to her program; her talk show was already doing far better than fine, and had been since it went into national syndication in 1986. "Here, finally," said peer Geraldo Rivera, host of CNBC's *Rivera Live* and *Upfront Tonight,* "was a woman—a black woman, a plus-sized woman, a woman with an attitude—holding forth. Oprah was the first host of any daytime talk show who looked and sounded like her audience" (qtd. in Farley 82). In fact, according to the press kit sent to me by senior publicist Audrey Pass in 2001, *The Oprah Winfrey Show* was in the midst of a successful sixteenth season and had been the number one talk show for the past fifteen years. Charting a domestic audience of an estimated twenty-six million viewers per week, plus a foreign distribution in 106 countries ranging from Afghanistan to Zimbabwe, the show has won every sweep since its debut in 1986, and has earned a total of thirty-four Emmy Awards, including nine Emmys for outstanding talk show and seven for outstanding talk show host. Winfrey could scarcely have gotten this far without remaining acutely attuned to the expectations of her audience. Not surprisingly, then, she selected titles for OBC with an eye for both their literary merits and their ability to go over well with an audience consisting chiefly of women between the ages of eighteen and fifty-four. Regarding OBC's first three selections, she says, "I chose these books because they are readable, poignant, thought-provoking. Our audience is predominantly female; all three books I've picked are strong stories with strong women" (qtd. in Gray 84). Moreover, explains joint-owner of Chicago's independent Women and Children First bookstore Linda Bubon, "She has made [reading] seem like something that you should really do without castigating you for not having done it in 10 years" (qtd. in Schultz 6). Clearly, Winfrey possesses an almost preternatural ability to anticipate what her audience likes to hear, and has put said ability to use with prodigious effect.

Remarking on this phenomenon, author Pearl Cleage—whose novel *What Looks Like Crazy on an Ordinary Day* became an OBC pick in September 1998—writes in the third of her meticulously itemized responses to my questionnaire:

> I think the approach Oprah takes to discussing fiction is fine. She's communicating with a mass audience via television, not teaching a college literature class. Accessibility is part of why people enjoy her show. The fiction discussions are structured to accentuate that accessibility. I think the women discussing my book on the show were a cross-section of the women who watch the show. Their questions and comments were in line with other discussions of my book at bookstores and book clubs, so I was not at all uncomfortable. (e-mail to the author)

No matter how you feel about the merits of Winfrey's approach to discussing literary fiction—an approach I'll examine in more detail later—you'd be hard pressed to argue with the results: the loyal members of *The Oprah Winfrey Show*'s television audience were watching the program, reading the novels, and delivering rock-solid ratings. Thanks to Winfrey's formidable televisual skill and savvy, Harpo Productions proudly reported that the book club segments' "ratings are consistent with other programs'" (Fitzgerald 27).

True as that was for the majority of the club's existence, it's important to remember that the good being done by OBC benefited not merely the show and its host, but also readers from all over the country, as well as the publishing industry. Certainly, the obvious good being done by the club could be, and frequently was, boiled down to slogans about the inherent nobleness of its mission, as when, for instance, Winfrey stated that, "I've always loved books. When I was growing up in Mississippi and Nashville, that's all I had. My idea is to reintroduce reading to people who've forgotten it exists" (qtd. in Gray 84), or that "books opened windows to the world for me. If I can help open them for someone else, I'm happy" (qtd. in Chin 113). Winfrey herself was hardly the only one to speak so highly, albeit vaguely, about her project. In fact, in a December 2, 1996, *People* magazine article, Toni Morrison said, "I knew there was this appetite for challenging books . . . but Oprah's being able to make people get up off the sofa and actually buy it—'phenomenon' is not a big enough word to describe that," adding later that, "She's making reading not a nerdy thing to do. Oprah is doing something important" (Nguyen 36). Morrison was correct, of course; Winfrey's project was an inarguably important one.

Still, in case you're not satisfied with this relatively touchy-feely, sloganistic, anecdotal stuff: Winfrey was honored on November 17, 1999, by the National Book Foundation with its fiftieth anniversary gold medal for her influential contribution to reading and books. According to Max, by the time an OBC segment appears, over five hundred thousand viewers have read at least part of the novel, and nearly as many buy the book in ensuing weeks (Max 36). So in concrete terms, for those of you who may have been wondering: yes, people really did read the novels. Moreover, Winfrey's efforts measurably broadened the demographic profile of the type of person who reads regularly. According to *U.S. News & World Report* on February

17, 1997, Winfrey went beyond the typical book club member profile of "mostly college-educated, white, suburban couples, particularly in the West" to include "blue-collar urban women from the South and Northeast" (Weiss 18). Aware that her authority swayed the affluent as well as those who are less so, Winfrey donated books to public libraries and other charitable institutions, and requested that all selections be made available in affordable paperback editions with the logo of OBC (Chin 113).

Not only did Winfrey encourage people of all classes, backgrounds, and ability levels to read, she also encouraged them to read good books. As early as March 23, 1998, Ingrid Chevannes observed in *Publishers Weekly* that:

> The familiar balance of spiritual solace, health, comics and computer instruction that has dominated trade paperbacks for several years has been altered by Oprah Winfrey. In the past, a literary title might be represented near the top (think *Snow Falling on Cedars, The Shipping News,* or movie tie-ins, such as *Schindler's List*). But this is the first year in decades to see so much fiction so high on the list. (56)

Continuing in her description of what she refers to as Winfrey's tender takeover of trade paperbacks, Chevannes notes, "Outside of Oprah, the trade paperback list looks very familiar, particularly in the endless ladles of chicken soup for sundry souls or absolutely anything for dummies . . . (suggested bestsellers for next year: *Chicken Soup for Dummies? The Soul for Dummies? Windows 95 for the Soul?*)" (56). In addition, she notes that Winfrey's dominion extended into mass-market fiction, as evidenced by sales of nearly two million copies of Mitchard's *The Deep End of the Ocean* in 1998.

Impressively, and perhaps somewhat surprisingly, OBC resulted in people reading books other than those selected by Winfrey. According to Bob Weitrack, director of merchandise for Barnes and Noble, not only did store managers feel that "a good percentage of shoppers coming in for Book Club titles are 'new readers,'" Barnes and Noble also discovered that "the Book Club sales often include multiple copies or other ISBN numbers. 'Seventy-five percent of the people who buy the Book Club title are buying something else, too. . . . They shop, they browse, they engage in conversations with our booksellers, and then they come back" (qtd. in Kinsella, "Is Oprah Creating New Readers?" 276). In short, by bringing thousands of new readers to literary fiction, Winfrey managed to accomplish even more than virtually anyone—including her most ardent supporters—initially believed possible. Peggy Barber, associate executive director of communications for the American Library Association in Chicago, which received ten thousand copies of each OBC pick to distribute among its members, explains, "Nobody was expecting people would be reading this much literary fiction. It's a unique phenomenon we have to attribute to Oprah" (qtd. in Fitzgerald 26). Indeed, with high schools and small community libraries receiving three copies of each selection, Winfrey's donations helped spur membership growth in the ALA, which says that high schools report book clubs sprang up among students and faculty members as a result of the program.

As all this mention of sales and distribution might suggest, the people were not the only ones experiencing the advantageous effects of OBC. Max rightly observes in his article on the club that the National Book Award's decision to give Winfrey its fiftieth anniversary gold medal was in part an acknowledgement of her contributions to literacy, and in part "a thank-you from a grateful book industry. She wasn't a force equal to Amazon.com, but she had certainly made them piles of money"(Max 39). Publishers have known for decades that television exposure moves books, but, "experience suggested that doing it successfully was a matter of getting the right author in front of an appropriate niche audience: this one on *Today* or *Good Morning America,* that one . . . on *60 Minutes.* But now Oprah had altered the equation by pushing a first novel to her massive readership" (Gray 84). Winfrey's impact on the sales of literary fiction is both quantifiably vast and consistently intense. In a September 1997 *Life* story about the club, Marilyn Johnson writes that Winfrey's project "has made her the extravagant benefactor of an ailing publishing business—the most influential individual in its history" (47). In the same piece, she goes on to quote Toni Morrison, who in 1993 became the first black writer to win the Nobel Prize for Literature, as saying of the club, "This is a revolution" (Johnson 47). Indeed, in the case of Morrison's *Song of Solomon*, the first of her four OBC picks to date, her paperback publisher—which released 360,000 copies of *Song of Solomon* between 1987 and Winfrey's selection of the novel in October 1996—immediately printed 730,000 new copies. Moreover, on the day that Morrison appeared on air with Winfrey, Barnes and Noble sold 16,070 copies of *Song of Solomon* nationwide. In short, Winfrey provided a bigger boost for Morrison's commercial clout than the 1993 Nobel Prize for Literature (Gray 84).

Winfrey's influence paid dividends not only to the Morrisons of the world, but also to such relative unknowns of the literary mid-list as A. Manette Ansay, Melinda Haynes, and Christina Schwarz. A few weeks after Chris Bohjalian received the call from Winfrey, for instance, he found himself "blinking into 'about 75 klieg lights' and TV cameras at a table where he was joined by Winfrey and four 'very smart, very thoughtful'" viewers who had traveled to Vermont for a brunch discussion of his novel *Midwives* (Fitzgerald 25). The novel—whose sales had peaked earlier at about one hundred thousand copies—catapulted onto the bestseller lists, recording sales of about 1.4 million books after the segment aired in December 1998 (Fitzgerald 25). When I asked her point blank during a telephone interview for her opinion of the value of OBC, Schwarz replied, "Everyone says how it's made so many people read who were not interested in reading before, and I know it's not an original answer, but as a writer there's nothing I'd like more. It's incredibly valuable" (interview with the author). Clearly, there's no shortage of evidence in favor of the good OBC managed to do for readers, authors, and the publishing industry.

Yet interestingly enough, all this proof of the club's overall value, much of it monetary, provided natural ammunition for some of the most vocal—and ill-founded—attacks against Winfrey's project. Winfrey's quantifiably abundant success in terms of money and authority simply made some critics almost automatically uneasy. And while spectacular selling power and book-recommending influence were not, in and of themselves, the real problem with OBC, it's easy to understand whence related anxieties about the club originated. Discussing the spaces in which symbolic hierarchies—including those based on distance from profits, those internal to each genre, and those relating to audience composition—are constructed and intersect, Bourdieu writes of "the negative relationship which, as the field increasingly imposes its own logic, is established between symbolic profit and economic profit, whereby *discredit* increases as the audience grows and its specific competence declines, together with the value of recognition implied in the act of consumption" ("Field of Cultural Production" 48). Certain commentators perceive enormous concentrations of money and popular admiration around particular works of art to be suspect, and since "the selection of a book for her club's monthly discussion can mean sales of as many as 750,000 copies; in an industry where sales of 100,000 copies can stir excitement" (Yardley, "Oprah's Bookend" C2), it's not hard to see how they might have found OBC disconcerting. That said, while I don't want to get into pointless accusations of literary snobbery on the parts of such critics, I do want to point out that this impulse to discredit OBC because of its appeal to an audience comprised largely of technically unskilled consumers is presumptuous and irrational.

Indeed, the literary industry is by definition a commercial endeavor, one which, for all intents and purposes, seeks to market and sell fiction as any other industry would any other commodity. Inasmuch as books themselves are products intended for widespread distribution and public consumption, Winfrey amassed a kind of phenomenal book-selling power the likes of which others in the industry —from authors to agents to editors—could only imagine. In fact:

> Many publishing industry executives say the TV show magnate and one of *Forbes* magazine's 400 richest Americans has single-handedly taken fiction to new commercial heights. . . . "Oprah has had a major impact on the publishing industry, and she's pushed quite a few hardcover books onto best-seller lists, giving them a longevity that would have been unlikely otherwise," says Daisy Maryles of *Publishers Weekly*. (Fitzgerald 24)

Moreover, unlike virtually anyone else involved in the business, Winfrey remained conspicuously above all this striving to turn a profit from literary works, to the extent that she herself never benefited financially from the fiction she effectively sold. Of this economic disinterestedness, Mitchard observed during our interview at Anderson's that Winfrey "is utterly independent; there's no way to buy her. No one has enough money in the world to buy her. . . . She makes selections based on her honest opinion of what she thinks is best for her audience." The fact that her influence couldn't be bought—"They may as well save their time," Winfrey has said, "this is not something a publisher can influence" (qtd. in Gray 84)—did not stop diligent publishers from trying to persuade Winfrey to hawk their projects. Still, while OBC damaged the literary fiction it promoted in a number of ways, corrupting its selections with dirty money was not one of them. Max quotes one publicist bemoaning the club's imperviousness to persuasion as saying "people tell you to write these wonderful letters, but it doesn't matter. . . . They run their show like Fort Knox. They do what they want to do" (40). Given its status as a bastion of financial independence, then, OBC remained one of the least corporate—and by extension least corrupt and impure—arbiters of literary taste out there.

Admittedly, certain of Winfrey's decisions having to do with OBC seemed—at first glance, anyway—almost patently designed to sound alarm bells in the minds of individuals concerned with the potentially damaging imposition of commerce on fiction. In 1997, for instance, OBC announced that Starbucks—a tremendously fraught locus of anxiety among the independent-minded set—would carry book club selections in most of its 1,400 stores. The prospect of an Oprah-Starbucks pairing seemed somewhat less sinister owing to the accompanying announcement that Starbucks would donate the proceeds from said books to literacy organizations. In fact, thanks to in-store sales of Mary McGarry Morris's June 1997 pick, *Songs in Ordinary Time,* Starbucks made grants of twenty thousand dollars each to Seattle's Goodwill Community Learning Center and Literacy Chicago (Angel 21). We see yet again that while OBC certainly functioned as an engine of profit generation, it managed to do so in a way that benefited literacy. If we continue to mine this rich vein of unfounded corporate fear as it relates to OBC, we realize that, as Martha Bayles of the *New York Times* suggests, "Ever since Thomas Whiteside wrote 'The Blockbuster Complex' in 1981, it has been an article of faith among literary pessimists that an increasingly conglomerated publishing industry pursues mass market success to the detriment of the so-called mid-list books that are often the lifeblood of the culture" (Bayles 35). Hasty critics falsely assumed that since OBC moved books in mass-market numbers, said books must have been little better than mass-market trash. If anything, Winfrey's club threw a wrench in this complex by selecting precisely the kind of mid-list literary fiction that Whiteside and others observed needed the most help. All in all, the literary industry publishes books for the express purpose of selling them; it seems high time for critics to get over any residual distaste for art that excels financially.

Even if that were to happen, we'd still be left with an attendantly misplaced complaint against OBC, specifically that such tremendous power to dictate literary taste should not reside within a single institution or person. Clearly, Winfrey co-opted a considerable amount of the authority once wielded almost exclusively by publishers or other industry insiders, thereby eliciting the question, "should anybody's taste be as influential as Winfrey's? 'As an industry we are both in awe and uncomfortable with someone holding so much power,' an executive at a large publishing company said, insisting on anonymity. No one could name another industry that delegates the creation of so many of its new stars to a single personality" (Max 40). To feel uncomfortable with, let alone to resent, OBC for the manifest magnitude of its cultural influence was silly for a number of reasons, the first and most obvious of which being that Winfrey managed to do single-handedly what an entire industry couldn't accomplish: she created new readers. In fact, *The Oprah Winfrey Show* "receives five letters a day from people saying that they hadn't read a book in 20 years until Winfrey made them pick one up" and Barnes and Noble reports that seventy-five percent of people "who came in for a Winfrey book bought another title as well" (Max 41).

Another, less obvious reason that discomfort with Winfrey's authority seems misplaced is that we're constantly being told by various people and institutions what to read; we just don't always realize it. Indeed, in an article entitled, "Ten People Who Decide What America Reads," (Winfrey, incidentally, weighed in alphabetically at slot ten) *Book* magazine reminds us somewhat sinisterly that:

> Unless you're still making it through a college lit curriculum, you probably thought that *you* decide what you read. Certainly there's no federal commission on recommended reading, no reading traps set up to catch you digging into Danielle Steel's latest instead of that recently purchased—but yet unopened— copy of Seamus Heaney's *Beowulf.* But there are a handful of people whose influence affects your reading choices in ways you never would've guessed. . . . The decision is yours. But you may not have known who's been influencing the process that leads up to it. (Abramson 36).

What *Book* is talking about here, in not so many words, is the cultural apparatus, a creepy, omnipresent device first identified and described by pioneering American sociologist C. Wright Mills in a 1962 essay entitled, fittingly, "The Cultural Apparatus." Mills commences his essay with the declaration:

> The first rule for understanding the human condition is that men live in second-hand worlds. They are aware of much more than they have personally experienced; and their own experience is always indirect . . . in their everyday life they do not experience a world of solid fact; their experience itself is selected by stereotyped meanings and shaped by ready-made interpretations. Their images of the world, and of themselves, are given to them by crowds of witnesses they have never met and never shall meet. (405)

Certainly, Mills makes this all sound a bit desperate and dramatic— as theorists propounding original theories tend to have to do—but his notion of preexistent structures which dictate to a greater or lesser extent our experience of the world, and that tell us, in a sense, what to read, watch, and think, holds a fair amount of truth.

In terms of literature, the cultural apparatus at work here includes, as *Book* puts it, blockbuster authors "who help support entire publishing houses, powerful literary agents who fight tooth and nail for their clients' deals, Hollywood moguls who often bring us back to the books from which they made their hits and gate-keepers you've probably never heard of" (Abramson 36). This last bit about the unknown gatekeepers is what brings the concept of the cultural apparatus into creepy, desperate, full-out Millsian worst-case-scenario territory, for the apparatus is at its most discomforting when it works as a kind of faceless, invisible, insidious force, telling you what to do whether or not you're aware of its doing so. Indeed, checking in again with Mills:

> This apparatus is composed of all the organizations and *milieux* in which artistic, intellectual and scientific work goes on, and of the means by which such work is made available to circles, publics, and the masses. In the cultural apparatus art, science and learning, entertainment, malarkey, and information are pro-duced and distributed. In terms of it, these products are distributed and consumed. It contains an elaborate set of insti-tutions: of schools and theaters, newspapers and census bureaus, studios, laboratories, museums, little magazines, radio networks. . . . Taken as a whole, the cultural apparatus is the lens of mankind through which men see. (406)

Moreover, he adds that, "the cultural apparatus not only guides experience; often as well it expropriates the very chance to have expe-rience that can rightly be called 'our own'" (Mills 407). That said, as much as Winfrey encouraged us to see the world through her lens, we still possessed the power to choose whether or not we wanted to allow her to guide experiences that should by rights be our own.

For far from being some kind of subtle, unidentifiable and there-fore unavoidable taste-dictating menace, Winfrey actually strove to be the most public and personal of cultural gatekeepers, effusively delineating her literary agenda and influence in virtually every form of media, from her show to her Web site to her magazine. If, for example, you felt you had good cause to avoid the novels Winfrey featured on her program, then—thanks to her prominently placed OBC logo—there could be no mistaking the books of which you should steer clear. Relatedly, if you felt inclined to read the novels she recommended, but didn't want your experience of them tainted by her on-the-air book discussion, no one forced you to sit down and watch. The *New York Times Book Review* and countless other book-reviewing entities, as well as such award-bestowing bodies as the Pulitzer Prize and National Book Award committees, and even the weekly bestseller lists all arrive at their recommendations by means vastly more nebulous than those of OBC, resulting in impacts upon literary taste and cultural capital that are far less easy than Winfrey's to track, or, should you so desire, to escape.

Thus, strong as Winfrey's appeals were, they remained comfortingly simple and apparent, and therefore less coercive—or at least less stealthily manipulative—than those of other producers of literary taste. I don't mean to suggest here that serious readers do, or should, possess some kind of pure desire for total autonomy of taste—that they should not, for instance, accept even the recommendation of a close friend, simply because there's no telling how said friend arrived at her or his suggestion in the first place—for such a thing seems not only impossible, but also severely limiting. I do intend to suggest that most serious readers strive for some kind of reasonable balance between taste independence and taste guidance. In doing so, they naturally privilege some sources of guidance over others, which in part explains why reactions to the cultural task Winfrey took on with OBC tend to be so strong, and frequently so strongly negative.

Situated at 1058 W. Washington in Chicago's West Loop, Harpo Studios is an unprepossessing beige brick building whose most prominent features include taut teal awnings bearing the words "The Oprah Winfrey Show" in bright white letters, an inordinate amount of cube glass, and a lengthy line comprised primarily of women snaking out the audience entrance door and extending down the block. I mention this now in the interest of dispelling the notion that the place must be some kind of dark fortress from which Winfrey plots and then dictates her literary mandates to the masses. Moreover, the women in line bore little resemblance to the sheep-like minions *Oprah* fans are frequently depicted to be by their detractors; so far as I could tell, each seemed in full possession of a mind of her own. Judging by how they were dressed—in uniformly dark colors—it was apparent that they had been told, just as I had been, that audience members are under no circumstances to wear white or beige, inasmuch as these shades look absolutely terrible on TV. Beyond this, though, it was clear—the day I was there, anyway—that their willingness to comply unskeptically with whatever orders Winfrey might give ended there. More to the point, these were people who understood that, although Winfrey's recommendations were convenient, they were far from the only way to decide what to read.

Eavesdropping as I waited to enter the studio, I found that the three women directly in front of me were carrying on a lively discussion about Ann-Marie MacDonald's techniques of characterization in *Fall on Your Knees,* as well as debating the merits of various Canadian authors and their struggles to validate themselves via success in the United States. At a lull following their comments on the green sash motif in MacDonald's novel, I jumped in and asked them to tell me what they thought of Oprah's Book Club.

Lisa Boughner of Oak Park, Illinois, spoke first, declaring right away that while she was aware of anti-Oprah sentiment, "I don't care if a bunch of snotty people in Oak Park like it or not. These people really need to get over it, and realize that if they don't like her picks they can go to other sources. I get my recommendations from a wide variety of places, but it just happens that Oprah is easy because I turn on the TV and there she is. My husband only likes to read books about the civil rights movement and baseball, which is fine for him, but I like to read a variety of things. I can like a *Bridget Jones's Diary* as much as I like *A Fine Balance.* Oprah is just one way I decide what to read."

Joanne Firby, a former bookseller, added that she, too, appreciated Winfrey's recommendations, and that even though Winfrey's discussion of fiction tended to be a bit thin, she understood that that was just the nature of the project. "I was an English and French major in college, so books just tend to fall apart neatly in my head in terms of themes and characters and symbols and plot, and you can't get into all that on a popular TV show."

And when I asked for her opinion of the overall quality of

Winfrey's selections, Rebekah Persaud said, "I don't necessarily always want a book with a message. I like to be entertained, too. And Oprah usually—not always—offers a bit of both."

Boughner, Firby and Persaud were proud to let me know that they were serious readers, committed to spending a lot of time and, when necessary, money on their passion—to the extent that when I asked Firby what other kinds of literature enjoyed, she whipped out her Palm Pilot and showed me her personal list. "I'm in other book clubs, too, so I read the reviews, I enter the titles, the number of pages, and the cost, so that if I want to recommend a book to somebody, it's all right there," she explained of her system.

Boughner said that her preferred method consists of simply going into a local bookstore and browsing the fiction shelves until she comes across something she thinks she'll like. "I love to actually be in the room with all the books, to look through them and feel them and smell them," she explained. Persaud said her favorite approach involves tearing titles out of newspaper reviews and sticking them on her fridge until she has a chance to get her hands on the books. When at last I politely extricated myself from their conversation, they continued, expertly, to name-check all manner of Oprah and non-Oprah authors, from David Sedaris to Evelyn Waugh, from Anita Diamant to Joe Queenan. By the end of the interview, all of these women had made it known that they understood the machinations of the cultural apparatus—even though none of them had mentioned it by name—and also that they were not about to put themselves under the exclusive advisement of Winfrey or any other source of literary recommendation.

Bayles observes that "the real problem is that Americans yearn for a center for cultural capital . . . but also resent the idea. So our centers (they are plural) keep forming, dissolving and forming again." She goes on to assert that, to its detractors, OBC represents "a sign of popular enthusiasm for books that gives intellectuals the willies" in that it signifies "commodification, the blockbuster mentality and the feeling that the culture either lacks a center or has surrendered its center to the wrong people" (Bayles 35). But, she adds, the thing about Winfrey is that "for all her power, she is not part of some blockbuster machine, engineering popularity in advance," and that "what is in evidence here is not some McLuhanesque gap between print and electronic culture but rather the difference between pandering to the lowest common denominator and offering people something uplifting" (Bayles 35). And while I'm hesitant to allow the word "uplifting" to be applied without comment—for it is a descriptor laden with a fairly heavy load of condescension, and not entirely appropriate for the books themselves—Bayles is, for the most part, correct.

On the most basic level, Winfrey simply used OBC to offer essentially good literature to her audience, shouldering the mantle of cultural authority as do so many other figures within the cultural apparatus. Don Imus, for instance, host of the nationally syndicated *Imus in the Morning* radio show, also uses his program to hawk books, having joined forces in 1998 with Barnes and Noble and the A&E cable network in bestowing four extremely generous book awards, three for fifty thousand dollars and one for one hundred thousand dollars. When he did so, he mounted a "pre-emptive strike against all those elitists who might knock the host of what he called a 'hideous radio program' for posing as an authority on books" (Bayles 35). As it turns out, he needn't have worried, since critical reaction to the Imus American Book Awards—promoted on more than ninety stations as well as the MSNBC network that features the show itself—have been consistently positive. Indeed, as *The Economist* good-naturedly observes "A Pulitzer prize, at $5,000, would not keep a self-respecting author in liquor for more than a few months; Mr. Imus's four prizes will be worth a total of $250,000" ("Dumbing Up," 76). Clearly, other individuals in positions of power similar to Winfrey's have opted to traffic in cultural capital on the largest scale possible, yet few people express nervousness about or resentment toward their influence. Jonathan Franzen notes:

> To the extent that the American novel still has cultural authority—an appeal beyond the academy, a presence in household conversations—it's largely the work of women. Knowledgeable booksellers estimate that 70 percent of all fiction is bought by women, and so perhaps it's no surprise that in recent years so

many crossover novels, the good books that find an audience, have been written by women. ("Perchance to Dream" 47)

Thus, since Winfrey has the eighteen-to-fifty-four-year-old female demographic locked up, her decision to apply her firmly established cultural influence to literary fiction seemed a logical one. More than that, it seemed a commendable one, for as Lazere asserts, "cultural critics and educators . . . have a responsibility . . . to help deprogram [the] public and students from the uninformed conservatism induced by illiteracy and mass media, while at the same time striving to raise American public discourse to the higher levels of unconstricted debate among all reasoned ideologies" (Lazere 301). Paradoxically, Winfrey's project to promote literacy to such enormous swaths of the population struck so many people as disconcerting in part because of its sheer size.

As was the case with related anti-OBC sentiment, though, the size of her influence itself was not the real issue. Rather, the problem originated with the medium that allowed her to wield her influence on such a grand scale. Winfrey's use of television to entertainingly sell products—in this case books—to the largest possible number of consumers should have struck no one as surprising or even offensive, inasmuch as that is fairly the medium's *raison d'etre:* to disperse advertisements and to sell, sell, sell. In fact, as Wallace points out:

> Critics like Samuel Huntington and Barbara Tuchman who try to claim that TV's lowering of our aesthetic standards is responsible for a "contemporary culture taken over by commercialism directed to the mass market and necessarily to mass taste" (Tuchman) can be refuted by observing that their Propter Hoc isn't even Post Hoc: by 1830, de Tocqueville had already diagnosed American culture as peculiarly devoted to easy sensation and mass-marketed entertainment, "spectacles vehement and untutored and rude." (36–37)

So, no, the problem with Winfrey's OBC was *not* that she used TV to cater to the mass tastes of her audience, but rather with *how* she went about doing so in ways that were inevitably inadequate for the novels themselves.

As I've already said, many of the detrimental aspects of Winfrey's approach originated in her deliberate imposition of competing narratives—her own life story, the story of her show, and so forth—onto the books. And while I'll be getting to those shortly, we need first to consider the narrative of TV itself, and how it clashes not only with those of the books, but also with those of Winfrey's own self-proclaimed mission. Early on in "E Unibus Pluram," Wallace announces that, "It will take a while, but I'm going to prove to you that the nexus where television and fiction converse and consort is self-conscious irony" (34). Suffice to say, he does prove it—and you should read the essay yourself to see how he does—but this passage's relevance is that it hits upon one of the chief ways in which the nature of Winfrey's chosen medium came into direct conflict with that of her vision. For one of the biggest beefs with *The Oprah Winfrey Show*—or one of the biggest beefs among people who actually had beefs with the show—was that it's so naively sincere, so apparently convinced of its own realness, so idiotically accepting of its own ability to be somehow genuine. Even though Winfrey knows full well that TV is a grossly untrue and distorting medium—that it "promotes false values," as she says in this chapter's epigraph—she never acknowledges on the air—as do some of the most ironic and therefore arguably the best programs, such as *The Simpsons, The Daily Show,* or *The Late Show with David Letterman*—that her medium of choice may at times be silly, shallow, and phony.

Indeed, this failure to engage in any kind of irony automatically denies the show a potential additional layer of intelligence and depth—skeptics feel that they understand more about the character of TV than Winfrey does—while simultaneously contributing to the perception that there's something sneaky, threatening, smarmy and narcissistic about Winfrey's entire endeavor. Her refusal to acknowledge TV's natural capacity for fakeness actually adds to suspicions many people feel regarding the fakeness of Oprah herself—which is to say the Oprah who wants to be all of our best friends, who wants us all to live our best lives, to rediscover our spirits, and to call her by her first name. Wallace writes:

> For Emerson, only a certain very rare species of person is fit to
> stand this gaze of millions. It is not your normal, hardworking,
> quietly desperate species of American. The man who can stand
> the megagaze is a walking imago, a certain type of transcendent
> semihuman who, in Emerson's phrase "carries the holiday in his
> eye." The Emersonian holiday that television actors' eyes carry
> is the promise of a vacation from human self-consciousness. Not
> worrying about how you come across. A total unallergy to
> gazes. It is contemporarily heroic. It is frightening and strong. It
> is also, of course, an act, for you have to be just abnormally self-
> conscious and self-controlled to appear unwatched before cam-
> eras and lenses and men with clipboards. (25)

In other words, Oprah's ability to withstand the megagaze in
conjunction with Winfrey's refusal to acknowledge at any point that
her act is both contemporarily heroic and frightening unsettles those
among us who are nonbelievers in Winfrey's desire to fulfill our various self-actualization needs.

During the book club segment taping I attended, both Winfrey
and her staff seemed to exercise a concerted refusal to believe that not
everyone in the audience was as at home with the idea of appearing
on-camera as "Oprah" so famously is. Never mind that after filing
through the metal detectors and before being herded upstairs to a kind
of pre-show holding area, each of us had been required to check in at
the reservation desk both to claim our tickets and to receive an official Program Guest and Studio Audience release.

Among the form's six provisions were Number Two, which stipu-
lated with an almost sinister suggestion of infinite regression that "you
may use and reuse forever and license others to use my name, voice,
picture, materials and/or statements made by me during the taping
of the Program including the pre-show, post-show and commercial
breaks for any use throughout the world, in all media, including promotional use for the Program. I understand that once I enter Harpo
Studios, I may be videotaped and recorded at any time." Number Six,
meanwhile, indemnified, "YOU, your officers, directors, agents, affil-

iated stations, distributors and licensees against any claims against you arising out of my appearance on the Program, the materials I supply, and/or my acts or statements off air or on the program. I HEREBY RELEASE YOU from any loss, claims or injuries I may incur arising out of my participation or appearance on the Program and/or its permitted uses."

The memory of affixing our names, addresses, social security numbers and signatures to this release fresh in our mind as we made our ways to our seats, we were confronted almost immediately by the figure of Stacey, a tall pony-tailed blonde woman in a black turtleneck, spiky heels, and black leather pants. Earlier in the afternoon, she had stalked the line outside, clipboard in hand, checking people's names and reservations. I had spoken with her briefly on the phone weeks ago and then there she was in person, appearing from backstage, miked-up and stalking the set this time, her job being to train us to be an active audience, to teach us to ask questions and to generally warm us up.

Her shtick included gesturing at the set behind her—beige, neon, and spare, with an enormous TV screen as the center backdrop—and demanding, "How many of you came here to be on TV today?" prompting half the hands in the stands to shoot up. "OK, now stand," she commanded the hand-raisers. "Now look around at everybody sitting. You know what they are? Liars. You guys sitting are all liars— look at you with your nice new outfits on and your hair all done up—you all want to be on TV." In short, her routine was both vaguely obnoxious and intimidating, but ultimately effective. By the end of about five minutes, everyone in the studio was well-versed in the rudiments of standing to pose a question and clapping enthusiastically when anything remotely amusing got said. It never once seemed to cross her mind that some of us might be weirded out by all this.

Later, after Stacey and all other staffers had removed themselves from the stage, we in the audience were given to understand that the show was beginning, because the on-set television showed us the same opening sequence that everyone in America sees each time they watch the program at home. The soundtrack, a gospel-inflected collection of breathy phonemes, played as the screen flashed shots of Winfrey entering the studio like a preacher entering a revival tent, prompting the audience to rise as one, clapping, cheering, reaching for her upraised hands and mugging ecstatically for the camera. When the real Winfrey entered I found myself, along with everyone else around me, doing the same.

According to the *Oprah Winfrey Show* fact sheet for the 2001–2 season, sent to me by Senior Publicist Audrey Pass, Winfrey says of the mission of her show that:

> I am guided by the vision of what I believe this show can be. Originally our goal was to uplift, enlighten, encourage and entertain through the medium of television. Now, our mission statement for "The Oprah Winfrey Show" is to use television to transform people's lives, to make viewers see themselves differently and to bring happiness and a sense of fulfillment into every home.

This immediately struck me as an unhealthy lot to expect from TV, and gave me cause to think that perhaps, instead of helping countless millions emerge from misery into happiness, Winfrey's program is actually part of what's making everyone so miserable in the first place. Wallace asserts that "Every lonely human I know watches way more than the average U.S. six hours a day" and that television appeals so much to such "voluntary shut-ins" because:

> The lonely . . . love one-way watching. For lonely people are usually not lonely because of hideous deformity or odor or obnoxiousness—in fact there exist today support- and social groups for persons with precisely these attributes. Lonely people tend, rather, to be lonely because they decline to bear the psychic costs of being around other humans. They are allergic to people. People affect them too strongly. (22–23).

Indeed, by trotting out a seemingly endless cavalcade of various real—and in the context of the book club, fictional—hopeless cases (fatally ill child-poet Mattie Stepanek, author of *Heartsongs,* for instance) Winfrey's program affords viewers a kind of cannibalistic pleasure in consuming the suffering of others, coercively feeding us the feeling that because we've *seen* an instance of struggling humanity, we've somehow *dealt* with it, when in reality we've done nothing of the sort; we've simply sat for an extended period in front of a piece of furniture.

Conventional wisdom tells us anecdotally that depressed, trapped-feeling people tend to watch a great deal of television. A fair number of the selections of OBC tell us the same thing. In her *A Map of the World,* twice-selected OBC author Jane Hamilton, for instance, has her embattled protagonist observe of her time in prison that "The television was on all day and into the night, and it was by osmosis that I partook of endless reruns of 'Cheers,' the 'Bob Newhart Show,' 'M*A*S*H,' 'Dobie Gillis,' and 'Star Trek.' The one happy constant in my life, however, was the 'Oprah' show at three o'clock every weekday" (287). Twice-selected OBC author Wally Lamb has his protagonist, Dolores Price, discard her television in order to signal that she intends, at long last, to take charge of her wayward life. "In the morning, I snuck behind the superette with my black-and-white portable and threw it in their dumpster. Then I called the satellite-dish company. They balked at a full refund, but I shouted them up to 75 percent," he writes of Dolores's determinedly proactive gesture (419). Even the assorted characters in OBC picks know deep in their fictive hearts that television—in spite of how medicated it can sometimes make them feel—won't help them actually deal with anything.

Harvard political scientist Robert Putnam, author of *Bowling Alone,* presents empirical evidence that regardless of what depressed people watch, television won't cure them. In fact, Putnam has found that because of the negative, grudging, and distrustful world-view fostered by TV, the more hours a person watches, the more depressed and paranoid—and the less likely to actually go out and interact with others or contend with external problems—he or she tends to become. Indeed, he says:

> There is reason to believe that deep-seated technological trends are radically "privatizing" or "individualizing" our use of leisure time and thus disrupting many opportunities for social capital formation. . . . Television has made our communities (or, rather, what we experience as our communities) wider and shallower. In the language of economics, technology enables

individual tastes to be satisfied more fully, but at the cost of the positive social externalities associated with more primitive forms of entertainment. (Putnam 75)

Not that any of this matters to the millions of *Oprah* fans who clearly just want a program that both entertains and affirms them, nor does it seem to matter to Winfrey herself. For "this is, after all, what TV *does:* it discerns, decocts, and re-presents what it thinks U.S. culture wants to see and hear about itself. No one and everyone is at fault." (Wallace 68). Even as her show's promulgation of its own transformative power continues to render Winfrey's mission unconvincing to her critics and potentially deceptive to her supporters, she keeps broadcasting and her audience keeps watching. Above all, she keeps imposing competing narratives upon the books she selects for her club, competing narratives that I am about to address, starting with that of *The Oprah Winfrey Show* itself.

Winfrey realized that, while it is remarkable that she managed to make the discussion of literary fiction viable in a televised format, the novels themselves remained the phenomenon's most remarkable element. In full awareness that TV simply can't do what books can, Winfrey even went so far as to acknowledge that, "I feel strongly that, no matter who you are, reading opens doors and provides, in your own personal sanctuary, an opportunity to explore and feel things, the way other forms of media cannot" (Kinsella, "The Oprah Effect" 277). In fact, according to *The Nation,* Winfrey "is a smart reader with a profound respect for literature. She understands that books exist to challenge and teach, provoke and disturb, and consistently chooses works that live up to that" (Simon 25). Unfortunately, Winfrey understood too that, in the interest of keeping ratings aloft, she had to structure OBC's televised discussions in such a way as to prevent the novels from achieving anything resembling these effects. Indeed, rather than giving her chosen novels free rein to provoke and disturb, Winfrey's strategy was "to make the book-club episodes resemble all her other shows. . . . She minimizes what is unfamiliar—namely, that the stories are made up" (Max 36). During a telephone interview—which, inasmuch as she was hard at work wrapping up her second novel and had just given birth to her first child, she was generous to grant—I asked Christina Schwarz, author of September 2000 OBC pick *Drowning Ruth,* how she felt about Winfrey's approach to fiction as something that really happens. She answered:

> Well, to be honest, that's not my approach to fiction. First, they do this little author profile before the show about the book. And they definitely had specific issues that they wanted me to talk about that were not the ones I thought the book was really about. But it's their show and they know what makes good television. So I think that how you approach a book is sort of a matter of personal opinion. (interview with the author)

Winfrey certainly knew that it was her program, and was not nearly as oblivious to the potentially detrimental effects of imposing the narrative of her talk show upon literary fiction as the book club segments of her show might have suggested; she simply understood that she had to do it anyway.

The majority of my time in the audience of the OBC taping passed as uneventfully and predictably as I had expected it to. In fact, we spent what had to be half the segment simply staring at the TV screen behind Winfrey, watching, among other things, the biographical background sketch about *Fall on Your Knees* author Ann-Marie MacDonald. Gamely performing the act of being an author, MacDonald delivered her personal take on Nova Scotia, while musing about happy endings, her love of stories, and of course her passion for secrets, as black-and-white and occasional color footage of Cape Breton Island—her novel's setting—drifted by. In short, we were watching TV on TV. The monotony of heavy-handed cross-fades and shots of MacDonald walking pensively along the frothing ocean were broken only by Winfrey's periodic announcements of commercial breaks and exhortations that everyone at home stay tuned.

Simply put, the narratives of OBC-selected novels are for the most part disturbing in the sense that the best fiction can be described as such, whereas the narrative of *The Oprah Winfrey Show* itself is, by comparison, simply disturbing. It is disturbing, of course, in the way that virtually all TV talk shows tend to be, a way that Christopher John Farley of *Time* magazine attributes to Winfrey's having "ushered in an age of confessional, ultrapersonal TV . . . television that cared, that wanted to know, that wanted you to spill your feelings and your guts and just forget about the 15 million people or so watching. . . . TV to explore, to empathize, to try to figure out where people were coming from" (82). Moreover, pointing to Winfrey's 1994 announcement of her intention to make her show more meaningful by adding such regular segments as "Remembering Your Spirit"—which sets its sights frankly and rather televangelically on the goal of dealing directly with viewers' souls—Farley adds:

> That is of course, what Winfrey tries to do on her talk show. In real life, such efforts can sometimes seem silly or superficial or narcissistic. "Forgiveness is something you do for yourself so you can move on," one guest told Winfrey's audience on a recent show. As the theme of a short story, perhaps that line would work. On the show it came off as self-centered and graceless. On another show last month, guest John Gray taught the audience to meditate by saying the following words "O glorious future, my heart is open to you. Come into my life." Perhaps the exercise was useful. But it sure sounded goofy. (83)

Somewhat counterintuitively, then, much of the disquieting nature of Winfrey's particular brand of TV stems directly from the best of intentions. Simply placing the books of OBC in such a pop-therapeutic context subjected them to the inescapable glow of so much extraneous touchy-feely, new-age candle lighting. And even though, as I've taken pains to prove, the books of OBC are decidedly not intended to be chicken soup for anyone's soul, *The Oprah Winfrey Show* assuredly is.

Certain especially charitable critics asserted that Winfrey should actually be praised for her willingness to shoulder the mantle of book-recommending cultural authority in spite, or perhaps even because, of her propensity to use texts as tools for personal development. Bayles, for instance, writes that Winfrey's "appeal to viewers has never been based on the exploitation of their social and emotional problems (in the manner of Jerry Springer) but on self-help: a trendy term that nonetheless subsumes older and more deeply ingrained notions of self-improvement and (yes) moral uplift" (35). The exact manner in which Winfrey exploits her guests remains debatable; however, the manner in which she exploited the books is rooted in this very dedication to moral uplift. By heaping so many expectations on the selections in terms of their use as stepping stones to a better lifestyle, Winfrey consistently interpreted the books of OBC not as literary novels, but as so many self-help texts. Winfrey damaged these complex, sophisticated narratives of her own choosing by treating them as corollaries to her program's doctrine of mindless American optimism, a doctrine that seems to suggest that via pluck and forgiveness, everything can be worked out for the best. The majority of the novels of OBC—like the majority of good novels in general—portray human suffering in all its unresolvable complexity; their characters aren't always able to simply get better. Winfrey learned, though, that the master narrative of *The Oprah Winfrey Show* simply didn't have room for any such pesky, open-ended competing subplots.

What the show *did* have room for, Winfrey discovered, were the added narratives of her audience's own lives, narratives she packaged neatly and superimposed enthusiastically on those of the books, to the extent that they effectively fostered and maintained viewer interest in fictional events. As Robert Morgan—who, when I asked him if he ever watched the show, explained "I work in the afternoons and watch little television"—says, "Oprah has found a way to focus television viewers on books. One technique is to view fiction in the way it relates to readers' lives" (e-mail to the author). Thus, book club segments typically opened with a short documentary about the author, followed by a discussion over a meal among Winfrey, the author, and a few lucky viewers who were selected based upon their written responses to the book—the show receives as many as ten thousand letters each month from people hoping to participate—as well as how much their actual lives resembled the latest selection's plot. During the discussion, they talked about "what they thought of the book and—especially and extensively—its relevance to their own lives. Could they be friends with the main character? What did the book teach them about themselves?" (Max 36). Winfrey's strategy proved so effective that she employed it again and again: at the conclusion of each OBC show, Winfrey announced the name of the latest novel she had read and admired, after which she and her staff distributed said novel to the studio audience, all the while assuring them and the at-home viewers that they would have several weeks to finish her latest assignment. This, then, "is the real innovation that allowed Winfrey to turn novels into TV. She focuses the discussion on viewer's and her response"(Max 36). Max observes:

> There's something odd about Winfrey's insistence on treating novels as springboards for self-reflection. Aren't novels about stepping outside one's experience? Yet this therapeutic approach has made Winfrey the most successful pitch person in the history of publishing. Since its debut in September 1996, Oprah's Book Club has been responsible for 28 best-sellers. It has sold more than 20 million books and made many of its authors millionaires. It has earned publishers roughly $175 million in revenue. (Winfrey and her show do not profit from the books' success.) (36-37)

Bearing these impressive outcomes in mind, there were those who asked—and who were justified in asking—what could be so wrong about Winfrey's approach?

In answer, I would accede that it's OK to generate revenue, as well as that it's far better than OK to motivate enormous groups of people to read. I would add, though, that it's less OK to actively squash genuinely good literary novels into a format that seeks to ensure that they be experienced in the most superficial way, and that brings to bear upon them the most primitive and silly of critical interpretations. Regarding Winfrey's proclivity to deal with fiction as based on issues that really exist, Anna Quindlen—author of April 1998 OBC pick *Black and Blue*—asserts in an especially Pollyannaish mode that, "I was pleased with the way the book was handled on the show, not because we discussed its literary merits, but because we garnered additional publicity for domestic violence" (e-mail to the author). I have to interrupt here to say that this is all well and good for Quindlen to suggest, inasmuch as her book's literary merits were far fewer than its topic-based ones, but her statement becomes remarkably shortsighted when applied to novels of overall superior quality. Quindlen continued in her e-mail that:

> I suppose that's one criticism of the Book Club shows, that they tend to focus on the issues the selections raise as opposed to the questions of characterization and craft; that is that an Oprah discussion of *Anna Karenina,* for instance, would likely go to the question of whether it is right or wise to leave your marriage for romantic love. I can understand the criticism but I think any mechanism that leads hundreds of thousands of people to read a literary novel is on its face a good thing. I think there are almost no negatives connected with the book club.

Excellent as her *Anna Karenina* analogy is, Quindlen manages here to sound rather unfortunately like Winfrey herself, refusing to level any actual criticism of OBC, resorting instead to reductive, optimistic boosterism and sloganeering.

For indeed, Winfrey's insistence that her selections be viewed almost exclusively through the weak lenses of readerly sentiment and real-life response was a shallow one. Musing on the question of how best to access the novel as an art form, Forster himself asks:

> How then are we to attack the novel—that spongy tract, those fictions in prose of a certain extent which extend so indeterminately? Not with any elaborate aparatus. Principles and systems may suit other forms of art, but they cannot be applicable here—or if applied their results must be subjected to reexamination. And who is the re-examiner? Well, I am afraid it will be the human heart, it will be this man-to-man business, justly suspect in its cruder forms. The final test of a novel will be our affection for it, as it is the test of our friends, and of anything else which we cannot define. Sentimentality—to some a worse demon than chronology—will lurk in the background saying, "Oh, but I like that," "Oh, but that doesn't appeal to me," and all I can promise is that sentimentality shall not speak too loudly or too soon. (23–24)

So it would seem that some kind of sentimental response to the novel is only natural, and therefore virtually inescapable. Still, as Forster makes abundantly clear, base sentiment as an exclusive mode of dealing with a text leads to the dangerous oversimplification of an elaborate art form, and is therefore to be avoided in order that the best interests of both the novel and its readers may be served.

In this respect, the framing of the standard OBC book discussion was inadequate—and by way of her own very public admission, we know that Winfrey knew this to be the case. Even before the inception of her official club, Winfrey's televised responses to fiction had never been what you might term sophisticated. Regarding her appreciation for Robert James Waller's *The Bridges of Madison County* —the tale of a lonely Midwestern farmwife who decides not to abandon her husband and family for an itinerant photographer with whom she falls in love—Winfrey says she "read *Bridges* in an afternoon. Sitting in my living room crying, and called him, Robert James Waller, on the phone. Shocked that I could get through. I know it wasn't literature, I just loved the idea of the story. Give me that, O.K? Just give me that" (qtd. in Johnson 56). As it turns out, her audience was more than willing to give her that, buying the book in droves and making *Bridges* one of the first works of fiction mentioned on *The Oprah Winfrey Show* to garner such a response. Non-viewers, too, could give Winfrey that, but had to do so while acknowledging this kind of response to be flat and undeveloped by design. In fact, referring to the story—which is to say the narrative of events arranged in their time sequence, which either makes or fails to make the audience want to know what happens next—as the lowest and simplest aspect of the novel, Forster writes:

> Yes—oh, dear, yes—the novel tells a story. That is the fundamental aspect without which it could not exist. That is the highest factor common to all novels, and I wish that it was not so, that it could be something different—melody, or perception of the truth, not this low atavistic form. For the more we look at the story . . . the more we disentangle it from the finer growths

that it supports, the less we shall find to admire. (26)

Winfrey's approach to the novel was problematic, then, in large part because she rarely bothered to examine any of these so-called finer growths, but rather contented herself with the most basic what comes next and how does it relate to me lines of interpretation.

Such a reductive and sentimentalizing approach—one which told people only that it's good to read, not necessarily that it's even better to be thoughtful about it—could hardly be expected to teach people to be careful, contemplative, discriminating readers. And indeed it didn't. As Max points out:

> Winfrey's system has leveled previous distinctions between, say, Edwidge Danticat, a delicate literary writer whose books had sold modestly, and Maeve Binchy, a commercial writer whose perky *Tara Road* was already on the best-seller list when Winfrey picked it. . . . New York's publishers treat one as art and the other as commerce; one gets prestige, the other money. But within the world of Oprah they are equals. (40)

It's one thing, and a fine one at that, to muddy the segregation between art and profitability; just because something sells well does not signify a lack of literary merit. It's yet another—and a far more harmful one—to assert that all novels are created equal and may therefore be read in exactly the same way. Winfrey's approach rendered virtually every novel a mere salable unit of story, to be understood almost exclusively in terms of how we feel about the characters and what happens to them over the course of a given plot. How, audience members were encouraged to ask, might our own stories unfold if we were placed in the same fictional situations?

Even though it contained the requisite woman who admitted that the book made her cry, as well as two real-life survivors of familial sexual abuse whose lives were literally changed by reading the book, the April 4 taping's traditional dinner with the author discussion among Winfrey, MacDonald and selected readers managed to be less than captivating. Winfrey herself looked bored during the clips, sitting in the overstuffed leather chair that had been brought onstage for her to sit in, chin in hand, staring straight ahead, commenting only occasionally on events on the screen behind her. Watching the tape later, I realized that this portion of the show was just as boring on TV as it was from in the studio, if not more so.

In other words, Winfrey's reliance on the imposition of her audience's own stories upon those of the novels failed to encourage her readers' tastes to evolve. Continuing in his analysis of story, Forster writes that:

> It is immensely old—goes back to neolithic times, perhaps paleo-lithic. Neanderthal man listened to stories, if one may judge by the shape of his skull. The primitive audience was an audience of shock-heads, gaping around the campfire, fatigued with con-tending against the mammoth or the woolly rhinoceros, and only kept awake by suspense. What would happen next? The novelist droned on, and as soon as the audience guessed what happened next, they either fell asleep or killed him. (26)

Cartoonish as they are, the appreciation Forster's cavemen harbor for only the most basic element of the novel causes them to resem-ble the type of low-effort audience Winfrey seemed to want to cul-tivate via her book club. Instead of a glowing campfire, her chosen storytellers gathered their audience around a television set, and instead of falling asleep or becoming murderous when dissatisfied, said audience simply changed the channel, turned the set off, or refused to buy the book, but the underlying principle remained dis-tressingly similar.

Moreover, like Forster's apocryphal cavemen, Winfrey's viewers were encouraged to experience the novels of OBC as part of an audi-ence, a unit, a large group of people doing the same thing at the same time. Even though Winfrey has said that "It's one thing to win an Emmy, but it's another thing to influence somebody who hasn't read a book since they were forced to in high school to read *Song of Solomon* and start thinking differently about their own life as a result of that" (Kinsella, "The Oprah Effect" 278), she did her best to ensure that this person wouldn't simply think about the novel in relation to their own life independently. Rather, she or he would be thinking about it in the way that Winfrey instructed them to, as would millions of other erstwhile non-readers who picked up a novel at Winfrey's behest. In a *Chicago Sun-Times* article on January 22, 1998, entitled "Oprah's Sheep Ready to Follow Every Whim," cultural critic Richard Roeper writes of this phenomenon:

> A front-page article in *USA Today* this week detailed Oprah's effect on the marketplace. Just a few examples: After Bill Cosby's Little Bill children's books were featured on the show in December, 1.5 million copies were sold in just three weeks. Sales of a particular line of pajama soared 200 percent after getting the Oprah seal of approval. Michael Bolton sold 250,000 copies of his latest CD after appearing on "Oprah," and Yanni sold 200,000 copies of his CD, "Reflections of Passion," after performing two songs on the show. (11)

Roeper continues—somewhat histrionically, but not altogether incorrectly—that, "It's amazing. Oprah endorses a product—and hundreds of thousands of her fans immediately put on their coats, dash out the door and purchase that item, simply because their television best friend has recommended it," adding of OBC that "Some fans of Oprah's say they went 10, 15, even 20 years without reading anything before their role model started the book club. It's wonderful they're reading again. Kind of sad, though, that it took a TV personality to nudge their minds" (Roeper 11). Roeper is being a bit harsh here, allowing television as a medium to be a source of taste anxiety, rather than addressing the real issue, which had less to do with the fact that a TV personality was promoting literacy, and more to do with the questionable methods she used to do so. Still, by the time he draws the conclusion that "here's hoping that one day she recommends the philosophy of independent thought!" (Roeper 11), it's clear while he is engaging in ostentatious op-ed page antics, his overall point is a valid one.

In fact, in his clarion call to independent thought, Roeper hits upon another set of competing narratives created by OBC, this one having to do with the tension between the intensely personal and autonomous act of reading and the extremely public and communal ideology of both the show and the club. The reading of novels is a private enthusiasm typically expressed via a kind of quiet admiration and dignified respect, and is therefore an activity that cannot compete with what television, in all its loud excess and splashy spectacle, can offer. Nor would most serious readers say they wanted it to. In this light, though, if Winfrey's massive popular influence is, as Roeper suggests, just generally disconcerting, then it is even more so when applied to something so ostensibly self-contained as the novel. Returning then to Wallace, who writes that "U.S. pop culture is just like U.S. serious culture in that its central tension has always set the nobility of individualism against the warmth of communal belonging" (54), we find that *The Oprah Winfrey Show* seems to have an especially hard time with this tension, to the point where it frequently appears to be contradicting itself. For although most Winfrey projects—OBC being no exception—claim to advance a kind of healthy individuality, one wonders how deep, or even how individual, such individuality can really be when each and every viewer is supposed to be following the same template. Speaking of Winfrey's filmic endeavors, Kate Forte of Harpo Productions explains, "We look for projects that show individuals being responsible for themselves. It's all about seeing human beings as active creators of their lives rather than as passive victims" (qtd. in Farley 83). Still, even as Winfrey and her staff deliver their message to be happy and be you, they seem to imply the caveat: as long as it's the you we tell you to be.

The superficiality and hypocrisy, as well as the attending unease, fostered by such an ideology couldn't help but taint the presentation of OBC novels. Cathy Davidson, editor of *Reading in America,* observes that "Michel de Certeau has written eloquently of 'everyday creativity,' the ways in which the very act of reading a text transforms and enhances the meaning of that text. This active intellectual and emotional engagement renders suspect any model of reading in which the reader is relegated to a merely passive, receptive role" (Davidson 16). Certainly, on an individual level, the members of the club—particularly the ones I encountered at the taping—are intellectually and emotionally active readers; their page markers and marginalia expressing points of agreement and contention with the texts themselves would do de Certeau proud. Still, such meaningful, active engagement with a text is not—and to some extent cannot be—shown on TV, for it is simply too small and quiet, and therefore too boring. Thus, when the aforementioned active readers enter the studio—or sit down to watch the show in the privacy of their own homes—they are thrust into the unquestionably passive role of "the viewers," expected to be receptive, or at least attentive, only to what their host tells them. Indeed, "psychologists confirm that the information processing involved in watching television is a passive cognitive operation compared with the active mental effort necessary to decode written language. This passivity reinforces the absence of audience interaction with broadcasters and of control over media institutions and mass-mediated politics" (Lazere 291). Despite Winfrey's best intentions and the readers' own best efforts, OBC participants' modes of experience must inevitably shift—for the duration of the book club segment at least—from one of active engagement with the text to one of passive engagement with the television, from one of struggle with the challenging nuances expressed on the page to one of acceptance of splashy opinions that play well on the small screen.

Poulet observes that when he reads, "I am aware of a rational being, of a consciousness; the consciousness of another, no different from the one I automatically assume in every human being I encounter, except that in this case the consciousness is open to me, welcomes me, lets me look deep inside itself, and even allows me, with unheard-of license, to think what it thinks and feel what it feels" (Poulet 42). Here, we may locate the reason why the clash between the individuality of the novel and the communality of *The Oprah Winfrey Show* remained so unresolvable. Poulet refers to the depth, the mystery, the interiority, and the overall humanity that are to be found within the pages of the best literary fiction, all of which are qualities that TV in general and *The Oprah Winfrey Show* specifically tend to lack. In spite of Winfrey's best efforts, it is this lack of human warmth—this sense that television is almost entirely about surfaces, and the fact that there simply is no interiority behind the images flashing on-screen—which makes TV so scary, at least to those of us who find it so. Again, this televisual vapidity and superficiality seems bound to encourage huge groups of people to risk reading rich novels in a shallow fashion, before discussing them in a way that is even more so.

We have no way of knowing for certain how thoughtful each and every participant in OBC was when she read, or how much depth she felt was conveyed by the televised book club segments. We do know that Winfrey was not asking much of her audience by way of these things, having chosen instead to concentrate on getting them to do as she said, to engage in reading and watching as unified actions undertaken by a unified group. One of the few demands she made of her audience above and beyond her most basic request that they participate was that they do so with enough vigorous and vocal enthusiasm to match her own. Indeed, in discussion, "Winfrey's own reactions tend to be the most vivid" (Max 36), and she handled everyone else's responses with an eye toward sentiment and sensibility in a manner not unlike that which might be found in an eighteenth-century ladies' novel society. Participants were expected to weep over the same sad parts, be moved by the same poignant bits, and come to the same favorable conclusions at story's end. The result was that, despite its name, OBC resembled an all-encompassing, unfailingly positive literary support group far more than it did an actual book club. Negative comments or criticisms of any type may as well have been banned from OBC under pain of death, for they were simply never made.

Also banned—as I, along with everyone else who made the mistake of bringing the April 4 selection with them, was informed at the door—were any actual books. We were required to leave all copies of *Fall on Your Knees* behind at the security checkpoint, along with our purses, cell phones, writing utensils and electronic recording devices of any kind. The imposition of such a restriction on what was ostensibly to be a discussion of said book struck me as surprising at first, but became gradually less so as Stacey made way for another miked-up staffer, this one a tall, thin, pale man with long, lank brown hair and a clipboard. His name might have been Peter, but since I wasn't allowed a pen to write it down, I can't say for sure.

Be that as it may, his job was to quiz us on how many of us had read the selection—the majority of the audience, if hand counts are to be trusted—before reviewing a few basic plot points and character names. Next, he asked us what questions or comments we had about the book. Interestingly enough, this turned out to be the part of the episode most resembling an actual literary discussion, as various audience members stood and spoke their pieces, frequently making incisive points about the narrative and approaching thoughtful debate regarding these points.

Sadly, all this took place so that the producers could pick out ringers to participate in the actual taping. Those people making the most television-friendly—which is to say vapid, sensational, and frequently only tangentially relevant—comments got their names scribbled on the clipboard for ready reference. One woman guaranteed herself camera time later in the show with the extravagant claim that she found *Fall on Your Knees* scarier than *The Exorcist*. The staffer then explained—outwardly to the whole audience, but mostly to these hand-picked few—that when it was time to talk, the microphone would move automatically in their direction, the point being that they needn't worry about their volume, but rather should concentrate on just acting natural. Under these stacked circumstances, it never once crossed my mind to bother raising my hand.

As predicted, when audience participation time rolled around, the *Exorcist* lady spoke, as did a few audience members with mostly superlative but relatively content-free comments upon the novel, which, incidentally, won the Commonwealth Writers Prize for best first book. We heard a testimonial from a woman who claimed to have been so thoroughly bowled over by the intensity of *Fall on Your Knees* that she experienced difficulty reading any other books for some time afterward. Another woman expressed shock at the revelation that James Piper, the family patriarch, was actually the father of his daughter Kathleen Piper's twins. All in all, only one woman remarked sophisticatedly upon anything beyond the novel's most superficial features: Cheryl, who admitted that she doesn't normally like period books, spoke of experiencing "two contrary motions" during her reading of the novel as a result of MacDonald's inspired stylistic decision to use whimsical, almost joyous language to write about deep despair. And even though she somehow managed to make it below the producers' radar to deliver this slightly higher-order observation, it was, like all the rest, unrelentingly positive.

Winfrey's apparent inability to make or even to allow a single critical comment about any book ever is well known, showing up even offhandedly in such places as Andrew Sullivan's "Daily Dish" Web site on March 5, 2002. In an update for his own nationwide book club, Sullivan wrote, "some of you are dismayed that I've picked a book critical of George Bush by a *New York Times* reporter, but this is not Oprah. Picking a book to read and argue about is not an endorsement or a promotional love-fest. It's an opportunity for debate" (screen 2). While I have no grounds to write about the nature of Sullivan's book club, I can say with certainty that he is correct in his assessment of Winfrey's. For whatever else it may be, OBC is a promotional lovefest, inasmuch as the mission of *The Oprah Winfrey Show*—like that of every other televised program—is to sell: both the products hawked by its various sponsors, and also, above all, itself. To this end, Winfrey displayed a kind of incredible, girlish, shrieky enthusiasm regarding each and every selection announced on OBC, prompting a friend of mine to ask with regard to the club, "Why can't we just love a book, and not want to eat it? Or marry its author?"

The answer, I feel, is that although—as Poulet tells us—novels are principally characterized by interiority, complexity, mystery, ambivalence and individual experience, that's just not what TV wants to give us. Nor is it what we typically like to get from TV. Rather, we know that TV's appeal is rooted in wild, excessive hype and the indulgence of childish enthusiasms—as when, for instance, Winfrey's fellow talk show host Rosie O'Donnell (who is a lesbian) cultivates and maintains a huge, public, schoolgirl crush on Tom Cruise. In short, we expect TV to make us feel either extremely good or extremely bad. We certainly do not expect it to cause us to feel in any way confused, contemplative, or ambivalent. Thus, since her show—as its own mission statement points out—is designed to make its audience feel extremely good, it would have served no useful purpose for Winfrey, as a concerned and caring talk show host, to select a book that could be construed as even slightly bad. Winfrey neither wanted nor needed to foster debate or to allow room for negative commentary, and that was her prerogative, just as Sullivan's desire to do the opposite is his. The problem with Winfrey's prerogative, however, was the fact that she never acknowledged that her so-called discussions were inadequate, allowing her audience to get by with the belief that, if they had read the chosen book, and listened to Winfrey and a few special audience members relate their own lives to the story, then they had thoroughly understood the novel, and could start prepping for the next episode.

In fact, the only time Winfrey approached any sense of ambivalence about a discussion remaining incomplete was when she announced that soon there wouldn't *be* a next episode. As quarter to four rolled around on the afternoon of the April 4 taping, I sat in my row thinking that this segment had been every bit as dull and facile as I had feared it might be, and had almost relegated my experience to the category of occasions where the anticipation exceeds the excitement of the actual event. I was in the process of trying to decide how best to get from the Loop back to Midway Airport, as a matter of fact, when all of a sudden we returned from a commercial break to hear Winfrey explain that we were witnessing the end of the book club as we knew it. Clutching a copy of Toni Morrison's *Sula,* she declared that the book in her hand would be the final regular selection of OBC. Suddenly, I wasn't bored anymore.

Devoid as it was of pandering or predictability, Winfrey's announcement instantly became one of those rare times when television actually managed to shock its viewers. Inured as we have grown to TV's carefully rehearsed hype and pre-packaged drama, Winfrey's cancellation of the club was one televised surprise that genuinely surprised. Still, by the time she and her staff had handed out copies of the final novel, Winfrey and others in the audience were laughing again. All thoughts of *Fall on Your Knees*—to say nothing of the fact that a tremendous blow seemed to have been delivered to literary culture in America right before our very eyes—seemed to have fallen right out of everyone's head. The so-called discussion was over.

Last but not least in the cavalcade of extraneous narratives Winfrey saw fit to parade across those of the novels themselves were the ones belonging to said novels' authors. An OBC appearance undoubtedly entitled Winfrey's chosen novelists to an especially spectacular and lucrative fifteen minutes of fame. Yet uncomfortable as it made some critics, this brief celebritization was not the chief drawback to OBC's handling of the authors themselves. For, as Max observes, "in the end, a book-club author is merely a stop on the voyage of self-discovery Winfrey leads each and every day. The author is just another guest" (41). Rather, the real problem with Winfrey's dealings with novelists had to do with how it indicated the weaknesses of having literary fiction on TV at all, inasmuch as the authors must be alive and willing to appear on-screen. In fact, explaining that she's not merely into contemporary literature, Winfrey recounts that that she spent her twenties catching up on classics she missed in school, saying, "I liked Hemingway. Steinbeck was my favorite. I remember being just absolutely struck when he did that whole chapter in *The Grapes of Wrath* about the turtle crossing the road" (qtd. in Johnson 54). Still, no matter how much Winfrey may enjoy their work, or how much she'd like to discuss the structural and artistic function of the intercalary chapters of *The Grapes of Wrath* with the late Steinbeck, neither he nor the late Hemingway would ever be able to appear on the show. And so Winfrey discussed contemporary literature in an extremely topical fashion.

Moreover, in keeping with the ideology of fiction as something that really happens, OBC tended to impose the biographies of living authors directly onto their literary creations. Sue Miller, author of May 2000 pick *While I Was Gone,* observes of this habit:

> I think Oprah is like most other public discussers of fiction in treating novels as springboards for cultural discussion. I've been interviewed on quite serious radio and television programs and only a very few, with a very elite audience (mostly small NPR stations) treat fiction in any other way. Even Terry Gross wants to know how it connects to your autobiography and to social trends. Fiction is hard to discuss in a compelling way with a wide audience. (letter to the author)

That said, Miller still comes right out and answers my questions regarding her level of satisfaction with OBC's handling of literary fiction with the reply that "no, I wasn't happy with the way it was presented. And I think the discussions are generally astonishingly reductive. But she knows her audience, and the discussions, finally, minimal as they are, are more like advertisements for the books than true discussions. At least it has helped me to think of them this way" (letter to the author). In any case, while Winfrey may not have been alone in her tendency to frame literary discussions in terms of authorial autobiography, she was certainly the only cultural gatekeeper who so frequently used her own autobiography as a framing device.

Given that so much of *The Oprah Winfrey Show*'s appeal lies in Winfrey's ability to be affably, empathetically "Oprah," it comes as no surprise that the most dominant biographical narrative she associated with the novels is her own sentimentalized, made-for-TV one. Contracted to publish her autobiography in 1993, she cancelled the project months before it was due, and says of her decision, "I am by no means a writer. . . . I would not dare kid myself. . . . I will tell you this—I feel that I'm a great communicator. That is my gift. I cannot do that with writing'" (qtd. in Johnson 60). And she's not kidding, for she has, via her program, successfully communicated her rags-to-riches life story to millions of audience members and has in the process managed to style herself not merely as some distant TV personality, but as a friendly figure who shares with her audience her deepest secrets in the interest of proving commiseratively that she has been through and therefore understands virtually everything her audience may have experienced.

By all accounts—especially her own—Winfrey's life has been one long, continuous upward progression, to the extent that it's almost irresistible to draw parallels between her story and those found in your average *bildungsroman*. Even such details as the fact that her mother would have christened her "Orpah," after the Biblical figure in the Book of Ruth, had not the "p" and the "r" gotten inadvertently transposed on the birth certificate, seem oddly literary ("Dumbing Up" 76). This being the case, Winfrey's impulse to use her tale of struggle against adversity as a means of advocating literacy seemed, at first glance, forgivable and even logical. For the most basic purpose of Winfrey's incorporation of her own life story into the project of OBC seemed to be to teach her audience that reading can be—in both an abstractly psychological and a tangibly financial sense—enriching. A photograph accompanying Marilyn Johnson's 1997 *Life* magazine profile depicts a crimson-clad Winfrey posing luxuriantly in the sumptuously appointed library of a Chicago prep school. Seated in a caramel-colored leather club chair with two glossy-furred spaniels resting obediently nearby, she holds a thick gold-stamped volume in her elegant lap. Classical, radiant, warm, and welcoming, the portrait calls invitingly to the viewer, "Come, read with me, and you too can have all this!"

Such concerted image control in conjunction with Winfrey's emphasis on certain key elements of reading's positive impact on her upbringing rendered this aspect of her application of her personal life to OBC somewhat cheaply persuasive and simplistic, but mostly harmless. A favorite anecdote from her formative years, for instance, describes "when a seventh-grade teacher noticed [Winfrey] reading during lunch, he got her a scholarship to a better school. Winfrey's talent for public performance and spontaneity in answering questions helped her win beauty-contests and get her first taste of public attention" (Tannen 196). Thus, Winfrey ensured that her audience became well-versed in the plot of her own life story, in order that they could conceive of reading as a kind of golden key that opens doors to opportunity, happiness, success and well-being. Although Winfrey's use of her life story as a paradigm for the improving nature of active literacy may have been rather transparent and manipulative, it was her use of the more lurid elements of her biography as a means of approaching the books that was truly damaging.

Almost automatically, Winfrey imposed her own sensational narrative over the narratives of the books to the point that it fairly overshadowed them, or at least characterized them as far more sensational than they actually were. For no matter how wealthy or influential she becomes, Winfrey can't forget the pain of her past, discussing said pain episode after episode. Over the course of her career as a talk show host, she's shared with the public her shameful secrets and personal struggles, including her poor and illegitimate birth in 1954 in the segregated South on a farm in Kosciusko, Mississippi, as well as her upbringing by the maternal grandmother to whom she was abandoned—and from whom she learned to read and recite Bible verses by the age of three—until the age of six when she moved to her mother's home in Milwaukee, Wisconsin. Winfrey's loyal viewers know that she was raped at the age of nine by a cousin, that she became pregnant as a teenager, that she smoked cocaine in her early twenties, and that she has eaten herself up to 237 pounds; once she went so far as to drag a cart of fat into the studio to dramatize her battles with obesity (Farley 82). These narratives, then, got in the way of the narratives of the novels themselves, giving critics of OBC impetus to assess its selections as little more than "a literary manifestation of Winfrey's own desires, fears and ghosts. Certain themes and topics are explored again and again, in book after book. Secrets. Child abuse. Physical abnormalities" (Farley 84). Thus, even though the selections of OBC were not typically among the lower orders of literary fiction, Winfrey's autobiographically candid reactions to the books were among the lower orders of reader response.

Her insistence on real autobiography as a lens to focus on fiction indicated her own questionable, immature, and possibly even unhealthy attitude toward literature, and in turn cultivated a similarly shallow, narcissistic approach to fiction on the part of her audience. During Winfrey's famously troubled teen years, especially following her pregnancy at fourteen, "books were her preferred reality. 'I went back to school after the baby died, thinking that I had been given a second chance in life. I threw myself into books. I read books about troubled women, Helen Keller and Anne Frank.' The harsher the stories, the more she liked them. She empathized with any heroine going through hard times" (Johnson 53). Such grim anecdotes lend insight into why Winfrey tended to pick certain types of books, as well as why so many critics tended to stereotype such books as more miserable than they may actually be. Still, the real problem arises not from the kinds of novels toward which she gravitated, but from her seemingly deliberate confusion of the make-believe world of fictional characters with her own reality. Time and again, Winfrey explained her affinity for reading as a sort of childish, one-for-one total identification with literary characters, as when she says of *A Tree Grows in Brooklyn,* one of her all-time favorite novels, "There was a tree outside my apartment, and I used to imagine it was the same tree. I felt like my life was like hers" (Johnson 53). Now I'm not saying that Winfrey is truly delusional in her experience of fiction, nor that her development as a reader was somehow arrested during her tumultuous adolescence; in fact, I consider Winfrey one of the most passionate, careful, contemplative readers around. What I *am* saying is that, as Oprah, she established a poor model for how other people should read. In other words, Winfrey seemed inclined to turn Oprah into the main character of each and every novel, and in doing so distracted her audience from a deeper understanding of, and appreciation for, the actual protagonists.

There is something almost studiously immature about Winfrey's manner of discussing literary fiction. Her televised responses to literature were sophomoric, in the sense that they resembled nothing so much as the reactions displayed when our sophomore English Honors class read *The Catcher in the Rye.* Until Mr. Irving Lester taught us how to interpret the text otherwise—with an eye for anything beyond our almost instinctual appreciation of a compelling protagonist similar to ourselves—our commentary ran along the severely limited lines of "Oh my god, I practically *am* Holden Caufield; I want to *be* him!," "Oh my god, I practically *am* Holden Caufield; I want to *marry* him!," or some combination of the two. Leading by example, Winfrey actually encouraged her audiences to interpret texts in the same way a bunch of mildly bookish fifteen-year-olds might, and could not, for various reasons, be bothered to espouse more complex approaches. Additionally, she was so dramatically upbeat about reading as an institution that she seemingly could not bring herself to say a single bad thing about any specific book, regardless of whether or not she included it in the official OBC canon. Instead, she made such sweeping, hyperbolic, and frequently teenagerish declarations as "getting my library card was like citizenship, it was like American citizenship" (qtd. in Johnson 48).

Although Winfrey clearly intended such behavior to evoke in her audience a similarly passionate devotion to literature, it more often than not caused her to come across as rather blindly narcissistic and obsessive. Speaking of Alice Walker's 1982 novel, *The Color Purple,* Winfrey explains:

> The first thing I do on Sundays is read *The New York Times Book Review.* And I read the review. . . . I remember getting out of bed, going up to the mall and buying every single copy that they had in stock. I read it that day. I was devastated, overwhelmed, empowered. All of that. I gave the book to everybody I knew. I couldn't have conversations with women who hadn't read *The Color Purple.* (qtd. in Johnson 54)

This anecdote seems at first to illustrate, as Winfrey means it to, how absolutely committed she is to the promotion of deeply moving literature. After only slightly more consideration, though, it becomes apparent that Winfrey is not merely expressing admirable enthusiasm about a powerful novel, but that she's doing so in a fashion that is less about the book itself, and more about what it means to her. In fact, in a kind of self-indulgent dream come true, Winfrey found herself with the opportunity to actually become one of the novel's characters. Called by Quincy Jones and Steven Spielberg—after Jones spotted her on her local Chicago talk show—to audition for the movie version of the novel, Winfrey says it was:

> "absolutely divine intervention" when she was cast as Sofia, the woman who beats up her abusive husband . . . the fact that her fictional husband was named Harpo (Oprah reversed) was further proof that this role was "part of my destiny." Her acting debut won her an Oscar nomination. Oprah also discovered herself as a mogul. After working with Spielberg, she formed her own company, Harpo Productions, took over the production of her show, negotiated a lucrative syndication deal and, with her growing fortune, began acquiring the film rights to literary properties. (Johnson 54, 56)

Thus, not only did Winfrey advise her audience to harbor infantile fantasies about becoming fictional characters, she actually indulged in the means to make herself over in said characters' images, thereby making each and every book she saw fit—Toni Morrison's *Beloved,* to name another example—effectively about her.

Perhaps the most maddening thing about Winfrey's self-important public approach to literature was how close it came to more sophisticated and therefore more beneficial ones. Poulet, for instance, writes that his own love of reading lies to a large extent in its liberating nature, for, "the greatest advantage of literature is that I am persuaded by it that I am free from my usual sense of incompatibility between my consciousness and its objects" (43). Reading, he continues, "is the act in which the subjective principle which I call *I* is modified in such a way that I no longer have the right, strictly speaking, to consider it as my *I*. I am on loan to another, and this other thinks, feels, suffers, and acts within me" (Poulet 45). In a similar vein, Winfrey declared of reading, "What a difference it makes in your world to go into some other life. It's what I love doing the most. I'm reading always to leave myself, always to leave my self behind. . . . That's what reading is. You get to leave" (qtd. in Johnson 60). Still, she managed to prove that she had just barely missed the point by turning around and saying things like, "The reason I love books is because they teach us something about ourselves" (qtd. in Max 37). Thus, she managed to overlook reading's real power to let us leave by placing us in unsettling, unfamiliar consciousnesses, resorting instead to using books as comfortingly familiar and therapeutic tools for self-improvement. Turning one more time to Poulet, we see him observe that, although it is an object, a book is wholly unlike other such material things as vases or statues in that, "A book is not shut in by its contours. . . . It asks nothing better than to exist outside itself, or to let you exist in it. In short, the extraordinary fact in the case of a book is the falling away of the barriers between you and it" (42). All this makes it especially disappointing, then, that Winfrey, in her desire to lose herself in books and to provide her fellow readers with a similarly enriching experience, not only failed to cause said barriers to fall, but instead erected all manner of new ones.

CHAPTER FIVE

Is This It?: The End of Oprah's Book Club as We Know It

"I just want to say that this is the end of the book club as we know it. Yes, yes, yes, every month for the past six years I have selected a novel and this is my last regular selection. From now on when I come across something I feel absolutely compelled to share, I will do that, but it will not be every month. The truth is, it has just become harder and harder for me to find books on a monthly basis that I really am passionate about, and I refuse—because you all have noticed that first it's a month, then it's like five weeks, then it's like six weeks, then seven weeks—and so I refuse to pick a book I have not personally read. I have to read a lot of books to get to something that I really passionately love, so I don't know when the next book will be."

> —*Oprah Winfrey, The* Oprah Winfrey Show, *April 5, 2002*

"Oprah has sparked something in America, reminding people how good reading is. If we can remind them that reading light works of fiction is also good . . . why not? This is the season for it. This is a time where people don't want reality: we want some nice, light reading!"

> —*Kelly Ripa of* Live with Regis and Kelly, *etonline, May 15, 2002*

When I sat down to write this—what I believed at the time would be the final chapter in my study of Oprah's Book Club—it was the middle of August 2002. For the first time since my rushed attendance of the second-to-last regularly scheduled segment of the original OBC, I was back in Chicago, this time on vacation and visiting my family. When last I was there, I had left town thinking—as I had following the Franzen disinvitation—that I had just witnessed an event that must certainly be good for my project, but ominous for American literary culture. Outside of the Yellow Cab I took to the airport, the temperature dropped and the weird early April snow fell harder; inside, I wrote down everything I had seen at Harpo Studios and tried to figure out what had just happened.

By August 2002, having had several months to consider Winfrey's cancellation of the club in terms of what led to the announcement in the first place, as well as the fact that the original club was, for all intents and purposes, defunct, I felt considerably better about the events of the afternoon of April 4, 2002, than I did immediately after they occurred. In fact, I came to the conclusion that Winfrey's announcement was neither as surprising nor ultimately as saddening as I initially believed. With regard to the element of surprise, certainly I—and everyone else who followed OBC with even a modicum of interest—experienced shock upon hearing of the cancellation. In hindsight, though, it appears that if anyone had been keeping an eye out for signs of the club's impending demise, they might actually have been able to see it coming. For one thing, Winfrey's selections were growing ever fewer and farther between. In 1997, for instance, eleven books were inducted into the club canon, whereas 2001 saw only six new picks. Correspondingly, the taping schedules for the discussion episodes themselves kept getting pushed back, with the segment on Rohinton Mistry's *A Fine Balance* airing late in 2001 and the one for *Fall on Your Knees* not running until spring of 2002. In retrospect, it's clear that Winfrey, for whatever reason, had been allowing the club to flag for some time.

With regard to the element of sadness, I have to admit on a purely personal level that I am always disappointed—sometimes irrationally—when anything measurably or even just mostly good comes to an end. (I became inordinately distraught, for instance, when, several years ago, in a decision that had exactly no bearing on my life whatsoever, the U.S. Navy announced that it would no longer teach sailors to navigate via the stars.) Consequently, I become especially sad when anything in which I've been heavily and subjectively invested draws to a close. And so it was—initially—with OBC. Having come to see, reluctantly at first, how much good Winfrey's institution was actually able to do, I felt that, as a promotional force for literacy, OBC could never be replicated or even approximated; I was convinced that the cultural position Winfrey had vacated so unceremoniously could never be filled. And—Winfrey being the peerlessly influential personality that she is—it can't, exactly. But I no longer want it to be. Back in 1996, at the height of America's book club formation craze, Winfrey's idea for a televised segment that loosely mimicked the workings of a private club dealing with contemporary literature was one whose time had come. By 2002, for a variety of reasons I'm about to get into, Winfrey and her producers realized that the time had come to let that idea go.

In my struggle to make sense of the death of OBC, I arrived at the conclusion that, as is the case when most of us set about making major, life-altering decisions, Winfrey's motivations for the cancellation were probably multifactorial. At the end of the segment on which she dropped the cancellation bombshell, Winfrey claimed to have known years ago that regardless of when she ended the club, *Sula* would be her final selection. "I'll wait until I really don't have anything else to choose," she said of her rationale. Thus, in the April 5 TV edit of the taping I had attended just the day before, Winfrey stood before all of America with the special Oprah edition of *Sula* clutched to her chest, and declared, "This is it. This is it from me. It's either this or go back to the classics and dead authors, which is hard to do with dead authors, because who comes to dinner? That's the problem with the book club discussion." (Little did anyone suspect that approximately fourteen months later, Winfrey would have figured out a way to circumvent that problem in order to present great books of the past via a new incarnation of OBC.) By this point, anyone with any interest in the matter knows that Winfrey went on to *say* that she quit because "It has become harder and harder to find books on a monthly basis that I feel absolutely compelled to share. I will continue featuring books on *The Oprah Winfrey Show* when I feel they merit my heartfelt recommendation" (qtd. in Conklin 1). After she issued this seemingly summary dismissal of contemporary literature, it didn't take long for people to begin to doubt whether this could possibly be what she *meant*.

Indeed, many people with a great deal of interest in the matter, including authors and others affiliated with the publishing industry, expressed reactions similar to that of Nora Rawlinson of *Publishers Weekly*, who declared, "For her to say that she can't find enough books to be passionate about is insulting, because there are so many wonderful books out there yet to be discovered" ("O, No," screen 1). Nancy Huddleston Packer, fiction jury chair for the 2002 Pulitzer Prize, said, "I don't think there was a shortage [of good books]. I've been on the Pulitzer before, and I thought this was a stronger year. . . . There were maybe 20 books I would not have been ashamed of having my name attached to as a judge" (qtd. in Keller, "Dear Oprah" 1). Packer goes on to explain that although "some of the books were marked by surface excitement . . . or 'snap, crackle, and pop' . . . she also found books that were more subtle in their effect, among them [the 2002] fiction winner, *Empire Falls* by Richard Russo, which Packer described as 'a quiet, deep, very well-done book" (Keller 8). Booksellers, too, took issue with Winfrey's assessment of the availability of compelling books. Among them was Erik Wilska, co-owner of the thirty-year-old Bookloft in Great Barrington, Massachusetts, who argued, "I think she misspoke. Clearly, there are good books out there" (Grogan, "The Future," screen 2). He went on to point out that if Winfrey required assistance locating solid book club recommendations, she need only seek the advice of independent booksellers like himself.

While it was disingenuous of Winfrey to insinuate that there are not enough high quality books out there, I personally am inclined to agree with those cultural commentators who were more charitable in their interpretations of Winfrey's remark. According to Laura Miller of salon.com, "Anyone who reads new fiction for a living can identify with this burnt-out weariness—the seemingly endless stacks of mediocre candidates to sift through as the pressure mounts to find an endorsable book" ("After Oprah," screen 2). Furthermore, as bookseller Susan Morgan, owner of the Yankee

Bookshop in Woodstock, Vermont, says, "I'm assuming [she meant that] she couldn't find the time. From all the advance copies I get, if she couldn't get something out of that, I don't know" (qtd. in Grogan, "The Future," screen 2). Far from being the only ones to question both the significance and the very wording of Winfrey's statement, Miller and Morgan join legions of readers who can't help but wonder if perhaps Winfrey meant not that there was a lack of appealing novels, but rather that the strain of OBC had become too much for her.

Still, I'm sure that Winfrey's assertion is—in her own opinion, anyway—at least partly true even when taken purely at face value. In fact, there are plenty of serious readers who sympathize with her assessment. Bret Lott—whose novel *Jewel* was an OBC pick in January 1999, and who recently considered over one hundred books for the 2002 Ernest Hemingway / PEN Faulkner Award for first work of fiction—expressed empathy with Winfrey's decision. "I'm not going to say American letters is going down the toilet, but I kind of know what she means," he told the *Chicago Tribune*. "It's hard to find quiet novels, moving, heart-felt, beautiful novels" (Keller, "Where Have all the Good Books Gone . . ." 1). Similarly, Joyce Carol Oates— whose book *We Were the Mulvaneys* was an OBC selection in January 2001—expressed sadness, but not surprise at Winfrey's discontinuation of the club. A professor of humanities at Princeton University, Oates said she understood Winfrey's decision to cut back on book club selections. "When I met her, she was saying that she found it harder to find books," Oates said. "I know that I've been teaching for years and after a while you've taught all the books you want to teach" (qtd. in Conklin 14).

Still, even those who have been affiliated with the club in the past seem to feel that far more than Winfrey's professed dissatisfaction with the literature presently available factored into her decision. Lott goes on to note that:

> There's almost an Oprah-kind of novel that's getting published now. I can't help but think there are publishers putting these out with their fingers crossed that Oprah might pick it. That's a bad thing. It's not coming from the author's vision. It's trying to

laminate a story over a perceived publishing bonanza. I can see her [Winfrey] having the kind of integrity in maybe even seeing that. (qtd. in Keller, "Dear Oprah" 8)

Whether this particular concern had anything to do with Winfrey's choice, it is reasonable to assume, as Lott does, that a number of circumstances informed her resolution. Anne Messitte, publisher of the paperback imprints Vintage Books and Anchor Books, expressed skepticism that Winfrey had run out of viable choices. Messitte, who has released several titles selected by OBC, suspects that the process of running the club had become too much of a chore. "I just think it's hard to pick one every 30 days and then put on a full program where she meets with the author or sometimes travels to where the book is set," she said (qtd. in Conklin 14). Indeed, it seems fair to suggest that Winfrey has axed the club as much out of a diminution of free time and personal passion as out of a purported lack of books about which to be passionate.

Following the taping of the cancellation show itself—somewhere in between the former English teacher's heartfelt plea on behalf of the classics (which seems now to have been wonderfully prescient) and the bestowing of the coveted snakeskin boots upon Jacquelyn Cosby —an audience member asked Winfrey something to the effect of, how on earth do you find time to read? Winfrey's revelation of her secret— that she never watches TV—evoked almost as many gasps of surprise from the crowd as did her initial announcement of the club's dissolution. Invoking the proverb about the cobbler's children wearing no shoes, she explained to us that since television is the critical component of her career, she has no inclination to make it a part of her precious leisure time. Winfrey acknowledged that, for a lot of people —including, she said, her best friend, Gayle King, who makes use of a VCR to ensure that she never misses an episode of her favorite shows—television provides a reliable means of entertainment, relaxation, and escape. For Winfrey, though, reading serves this purpose, helping her to stay refreshed, stable, and centered in the midst of all her other pursuits. This desire to reclaim reading as a kind of personal escape, she said, contributed to her decision to stop doing such a strictly scheduled book club on *The Oprah Winfrey Show*.

As part of their coverage of the motivation behind OBC's cancellation, *Time* magazine mentioned that, "A former *Oprah* associate says Oprah is a serial sharer. Having shared her emotional life, her diet, and her reading list, she is done with the book thing. 'I think she just got bored,' says an insider. 'Tired of the cycle'" (Lacayo 63). It should be noted here that, valid though they may be, not all the potential reasons for Winfrey's quitting the club require quite so much speculation as to her psychological makeup or her commitment to her personal well-being. *Time*, in fact, goes on to point out that one of *The Oprah Winfrey Show*'s producers "recently admitted that the book-club shows garner lower ratings than regular shows" (Lacayo 63). Conceding in the April issue of *Fortune* magazine that ratings go down during book club segments, the producer added, "But that doesn't matter"("O, No," screen 1). There are, of course, many people who will suggest that such things do matter a great deal after all. According to Robert Grove in *Hollywood Reporter*, "In television, if something is working well, you don't take it off the show. If you do take it off, no matter what you say, everybody knows that on analysis it wasn't working well enough" (qtd. in "O, No," screen 1).

Moreover, signs that the almost supernatural selling power evoked by the OBC seal of approval may have diminished had begun to surface by the club's conclusion. Sales of OBC picks exhibited such a downward trend that while the average number of copies sold for book club recommendations peaked at 1.5 million in 1999, it had dropped to 1.3 million in 2000 before finally bottoming out at 700,000 in 2001 (Grogan, "The Future," screen 2). Clearly, even though Winfrey told Patricia Sellers of *Fortune* magazine—in the first extensive interview she's given to a financial publication—that she doesn't think of herself as a businesswoman (Sellers, screen 1), Winfrey could never have remained the head of a multi-million dollar media empire for as long as she has without some sense of what's good for business.

Another concrete and quantifiable factor to consider in conjunction with Winfrey's removal of the club from her regular lineup is that she recently declared her intention to retire within a few years. In March 2002, Winfrey—among the highest-grossing entertainers in the world, with an estimated $150 million in earnings in 2000 alone—declared through her company, Harpo Productions, Inc., that she would leave the show at the end of the 2005-6 season ("TV's Oprah to Scale Back Book Club," screen 1). "I like even numbers," Winfrey explained when it was pointed out during the Sellers interview that she would be leaving after her twentieth year in the business of talk television (screen 2). Since then, she has reconsidered, signing a two-year contract extension with King World Productions, agreeing to keep *The Oprah Winfrey Show* on the air through the 2007-8 season. Nevertheless, this decision to hang up her microphone in the foreseeable future—in combination with the decline of both the ratings of book club segments and the sales of selections—seems to signal that Winfrey's discontinuation of the original OBC may well have been part of an overall plan to quit while she was ahead.

Like I said before, as I spent the days immediately following Winfrey's announcement considering how all these reasons, in addition to the one she herself gave, probably contributed to her decision to quit, I couldn't help thinking too, that—like last fall's Jonathan Franzen dust-up—this latest plot twist in the story of OBC was essentially excellent for my book, but bad for the nation. Now that it's over, I told myself, I can study the phenomenon from start to finish as a neatly defined whole, but this is only because America has just lost its most influential advocate for active literacy. Even though I've realized since then that the death of the original OBC did not prove nearly so detrimental to American letters as I had initially feared, I stand by another of the conclusions that I drew in April 2002. Specifically, I still believe that—even though "a spokeswoman for the show said Winfrey's decision had nothing to do with author Jonathan Franzen's less-than-thrilled reaction to having his novel 'Corrections' [sic] selected by Winfrey in September 2001" ("TV's Oprah to Scale Back," screen 1)—Franzen's disparagement of the club probably had a lot more to do with Winfrey's decision to dissolve OBC than either she or any of her staff would be willing to admit. For although the disinvitation fiasco—wherein Franzen insulted Winfrey and she, in turn, cancelled his appearance on the show—surrounding the selection of *The Corrections* played out in October 2001, I believe that it was only in April 2002 that we experienced the event's ultimate effect. For just as Winfrey seemed poised to pull her audience up to a new level of active readership, Franzen—through his concentrated vocalization of various elitist criticisms that had, up until that point, been hovering diffusely around the club—appeared to push her firmly back down.

In short, Winfrey's selection of *The Corrections*—which should have served as a tremendous asset to the club, the literary community, and the country—turned out to be a much larger liability than anyone involved could have anticipated. The affair degenerated into a disheartening battle of egos between its figureheads, and led to an attendant galvanization along the lines of high versus low culture among the population at large. Owing in no small part to this highly publicized challenge to her cultural authority, Winfrey seemed to have come to the conclusion that the club was just no longer worth it if it meant being exposed to such derision. Indeed, given that OBC required so much extra effort—both in terms of its demands on the show's ratings and on Winfrey's own time—and still resulted in Winfrey's getting publicly kicked around by the intelligentsia, one can see why she might have reached a point where she was no longer inclined to bother.

For even though it has been suggested that such a public figure as Winfrey should have displayed thicker skin than she did during the disinvitation fiasco, it's none too difficult to apprehend how the whole thing could have been taken personally. From the inception of her career as a talk show host, Winfrey has seemed determined to be loved and to be considered smart. At present, she has accomplished both, but the problem remains that she is neither loved nor considered smart by the critical class of people from whom she most desires this type of approbation. As *The Economist* observes, "The suspicion is that, like many who have successfully clambered to wealth and influence, Ms. Winfrey now craves intellectual respectability. After all, when you have $500 million to your name, you can afford a little vanity" ("Dumbing Up" 76).

Winfrey herself will be the first to tell you how deeply she admires literature and literary figures, as well as how much the prospect of being a part of literary circles means, and has always meant, to her. She tells the following story: "Once Maya Angelou had a party. It was a party for Toni [Morrison] after she received the Nobel Prize, and I went to it. I was surrounded by authors, and I felt like I was 11 years old. I felt like I could not even speak. At one point, somebody said, 'Oh, I'd like some more coffee,' and I got up to get it. Maya said, 'Sit down,' and I went 'No, I'll get it. It'd be a treat'" (qtd. in Max 38). This story is as representative an example as any of how very badly Winfrey has always wanted to serve—literally, in this case—the cause of literature in America.

Far from being atypical or childish, her impulse to share her admiration with, and in turn to be admired by, those cultural figures who have provided her with such pleasure has deep roots in both human nature and in history. According to cultural critic Lawrence Levine, "In the final year of his life, Walt Whitman . . . wrote that he 'should like well' if the contralto Marietta Alboni or the tenor Alessandro Bettini or 'the old composer' Giuseppe Verdi 'could know how much noble pleasure and happiness they gave me, and how deeply I always remember them and thank them to this day'" (Levine 86). Like Whitman's desire to express his gratitude to the performers and composers who so delighted him, Winfrey's desire to meet and thank the authors who have meant so much to her seems a very natural wish for connection and interaction—a bighearted, outwardly directed, and fundamentally human response. Thus, one suspects it must have hurt Winfrey to discover over the course of the six-year club that no matter how much she respected the world of literature, there was no guarantee that respect would be returned in kind. In short, even though OBC undoubtedly established Winfrey's position as a key arbiter of literary taste, her right to hold that position in the first place was always subject to a great deal of aggressively public doubt.

Even as the original incarnation of the club drew—with the selection of Toni Morrison's *Sula*—to an admirable close, certain circles persisted in the same petty, fearful, snobbish elitism that contributed to the club's untimely demise. Writing in *Time* magazine, Richard

Lacayo asked, "Why walk away now? Oprah's Book Club gave her status as a major arbiter of taste in the literary world." He then goes on to effectively answer his own question, declaring, "Culture snobs who thought of her as that mawkish woman who was always on a diet now think of her as that mawkish woman on a diet who has got millions of people to read Toni Morrison" (Lacayo 63). Weighing in on the matter in his *Washington Post* column, Jonathan Yardley opened his remarks with a reference to the full-page ad purchased by Random House in the *New York Times,* which read, "THANK YOU, OPRAH, for your unique and magnificent work over the past six years on behalf of books, authors and readers everywhere." With his final sentence, he proclaimed, "Yes indeed, thank you, Oprah, for what you've done— in particular, for enlarging the readership for African-American writers —but that wasn't exactly a Great Books discussion you were conducting, and it was about a mile short of 'unique and magnificent'" (Yardley, "Oprah's Bookend" C2). (Of course, poor Yardley had no way of knowing that in just a few months' time, Winfrey would begin conducting one of the most ambitious "great books" discussions of all time.)

Even worse, the commentary section of the April 11, 2002, *L.A. Times* featured a piece by Norah Vincent, clunkily entitled, "Good Riddance to Oprah's Book Club, and Her Literary Amateurism." I'll spare you the bulk of Vincent's own presumptuous and spectacularly unsound assertions, but I will cite her statement that, "Winfrey presumed where she should not have, and while her presumption may have led millions who might not otherwise have done so to read some good books. . . . I wouldn't want her sticker on my book either" (Vincent, screen 1). For starters, she needn't worry about the sticker—Winfrey is unlikely to feature the book Vincent coauthored, *The Instant Intellectual: the Quick and Easy Guide to Sounding Smart and Cultured,* on her show anytime soon—and I'm not even going to get into how damaging this, and commentary like it, is in terms of its promotion of the very arbitrary and reductive highbrow versus lowbrow labels OBC did its best to erase.

I *will* get into how unfortunate it is that other sources of cultural commentary seemed inclined to acknowledge how beneficial OBC was during its existence only after the fact of its demise. A staff editorial in the April 10, 2002, issue of the *New York Times,* for instance, declared of Winfrey's picks that, "The list has included some truly distinctive writers, like Ms. Morrison, Bernhard Schlink, and, notoriously, Jonathan Franzen. And it has included a string of sentimental works by unmemorable writers. In all fairness, Ms. Winfrey's batting average isn't notably worse than that of the Nobel Prize committee" ("Oprah Demurs"). Even more frustratingly, the editorial goes on to assert that, "After all, she represented only one woman's tastes." Clearly, they are correct insofar as Winfrey really is only one woman. Yet her taste in literature held far more sway than that of virtually anyone—man, woman or child—in literary history. In her introduction to 1989's *Reading in America: Literature and Social History,* editor Cathy Davidson wrote "So far, no one has yet been able to predict precisely which books will sell because readers do not operate according to prescribed rules" (Davidson 20). By 1996, this was simply no longer true. Each and every one of Winfrey's selections became a bestseller, and in an industry in which only a few novels sell more than thirty thousand copies, those recommended by Winfrey routinely sold a million or more ("O, No," screen 1). Moreover, in the publishing industry, "where profits are narrow, Oprah's endorsement of any title meant a minimum of 500,000 additional sales, says Jim Milliot, the business editor at *Publishers Weekly.* For the publisher, that translates to at least an additional $5 million in revenue" (Lacayo 63). Certainly, on a number of levels, not the least of which is economic, to suggest that OBC was in any way a minor or wholly replaceable phenomenon is to undervalue the entire endeavor.

Regardless of whether you were glad—Winfrey never should undertaken a book club in the first place, she should never have placed books in the context of a television talk show, she should never have tried to be an intellectual as opposed to a mere entertainer—or sorry—Winfrey could have been thicker-skinned, she could have held out four more years until her retirement from the show, she could have turned to the classics—when you received the news, the original incarnation of OBC had reached its end by 2002. None of this alters the fact that, while it lasted, Oprah's Book Club as a recommender of current literary fiction was an unquestionably encouraging phenomenon, indicative of an American impulse toward intellectual improvement and a hunger for the kind of seriousness and stimulation the best contemporay literary fiction has to offer. Even now it seems that such a story as that of Oprah's Book Club Part I should not have suffered from so weak an ending. I felt at the time and I continue to feel that Winfrey's walking away before a satisfactory conclusion could be reached represented a tremendous loss to the promotion of active readership in America.

Nonetheless, while I think it only fitting to treat the end of OBC Part I with the respect it deserves, I see no point in getting hysterical over it. In the wake of Winfrey's announcement, for instance, "Jane Friedman, CEO of HarperCollins, got a stricken e-mail. 'One of my colleagues had written to me one word: WEEP'" (Lacayo 63). Similarly, Bookloft co-owner Evelyn Wiska—wife of the aforementioned Erik—was so disappointed by the cancellation of OBC that she wrote Winfrey a letter asking her to reconsider (Grogan, "The Future," screen 2). Thousands of likeminded others did the same.

Admittedly, I share more sympathy with the members of this latter category, but I can't help suggesting that both OBC-phobes and OBC-philes would do well to remember that while there's certainly no need to tap dance on the club's grave as Vincent and others have done, neither is there any utility in continuing to hopelessly eulogize Winfrey's literary phenomenon. In fact, if I may flog this OBC as recently deceased loved one metaphor just one final time: although obviously OBC as it was originally conceived—as an agency for the promotion of contemporary, largely mid-list literary fiction—couldn't last forever, the spirit of what Winfrey created and of what it embodied lives on. Put another way, there are now so many other clubs rushing to fill the gaping O-shaped void left by Winfrey's absence, it seems silly to have ever thought that the end of OBC signified some kind of fatal strike against American literacy.

In the same April 10 staff editorial, the *New York Times* went on to conclude that "Ms. Winfrey's regular recommendations will be missed, but her contribution to reading in America and to the prosperity of publishers should not come to an end. . . . Where one Oprah demurs, a thousand Oprahs should bloom" ("Oprah Demurs"). When first I read this, I agreed that a thousand Oprahs *should* bloom, but had my doubts as to whether or not they actually *could*. After all, the cities of Chicago and New York, for instance, "launched book projects that attempted, as she did, to mobilize whole populations to read the same novel during the same month. Whole populations shrugged" (Lacayo 63). Ditto the citywide book club in Washington, D.C. Certainly, since they were run by committees, these clubs ran no risk of being over-shadowed by their founders' personalities. Yet as a result, so too did they seem to suffer from a lack of personal passion. Indeed, writing of the machinations of the Philadelphia Reads program, Tanya Barrientos of the *Philadelphia Inquirer* observed of the difficulties of selecting a book for such a large population that, "The committee has determined that the book needs to be somewhere near the 10th-grade reading level. It's got to be available in huge numbers from the pub-lisher. Readers have to be able to buy it in large print and in several languages. And there needs to be a 'logical' children's book that can serve as its companion" (Barrientos, screen 2). It's little wonder, then, that in spite of their best efforts, such clubs just can't seem to moti-vate readers to move in fervent droves the way OBC did.

Still, culture has managed to prove itself as dynamic a thing as ever, and during the brief period in which Winfrey left the field empty, the would-be Winfreys of the world rushed frantically in to fill it up again with new, different, and maybe, just maybe, even bet-ter clubs. "Suddenly," observes Little, Brown and Company public-ity manager Heather Fain, "it's like everyone has a book club, and I think it's great" (qtd. in Santich, screen 1). So here, to give you some sense of the lay of the post-OBC land, is a quick rundown of five clubs, all of which declared their intentions to feed the nation's need to read *en masse*, and all of which modeled themselves to varying degrees after the OBC prototype.

Within seventy-two hours of Winfrey's announcement, NBC's *Today Show* became the first televised entity to declare its intention to start a club of its own. Long a supporter of American letters—the program has a history of featuring scores of books per year even without the auspices of an actual club, and showcases the recom-

mendations of Pulitzer Prize-winning journalist, O[
Book of the Month Club judge Anna Quindlen—[
seems a logical contender to step into the post-OI
Indeed, according to *Today Show* spokeswoman Allis
was an idea that we had tossed around for a year or t
like why do it if Oprah is already doing it and doing i
as we heard she was bowing out, we decided to jui
Santich, screen 1). Called simply "The *Today* Book Club," the segment's official rules of engagement are as follows: each month, the
program will invite an established, best-selling author to select a book
by a lesser-known writer for the club to read. Later the same month,
they'll ask members of actual book groups—up to five per club—from
all over the nation to appear on the show for a chat with the featured
author. You can even visit the msnbc.com Web site to fill out an application for your own book club to participate in their celebration of
"America's fascination with the written word," so long as you are over
18 years of age, reside in the continental United States, and understand that you may apply only once per calendar year. Although it was
the first organization to declare its plans for a nationwide club, the
Today Show was the last to air, not taking the screen until June 24, 2002,
with John Grisham's recommendation of Stephen Carter's *The
Emperor of Ocean Park*. Carter's novel, his first, had already been widely
reviewed and had appeared on the *New York Times* online bestseller list
prior to receiving the televised tap from Grisham.

In the meantime, *USA Today* managed to kick off its own club
just six days after Winfrey's announcement of the death of OBC. In
a statement resembling the one made by the spokeswoman for the
Today Show, *USA Today* books editor Carol Memmott explained, "We
had been talking about starting [a book club for] many years. The
announcement that Oprah was scaling back made us decide that we
would waste no more time and offer a club to our readers" (qtd. in
Grogan, "The Future of Book Clubs is Today," screen 1). Admittedly,
it could be said that this club follows the OBC pattern the least
closely, inasmuch as it is not, technically, on TV. But as anyone who
has read *USA Today* and experienced its simple, colorful, screen-like
layout could tell you, it might as well be; thus, I'm including it here.

any case, the newspaper will announce a book approximately every six weeks before posting one question per week on its Web site message board during the ensuing six-week period; at the end of this time, the selected author will hold an online discussion with readers. *USA Today* debuted this system on April 11, 2002, with Richard Russo's *Empire Falls*—which, incidentally, had won the Pulitzer Prize and been released in paperback a few days earlier—and chose Laura Hillenbrand's account of famed 1930s racehorse *Seabiscuit* as a follow-up on May 15. As a result of the announcement, Hillenbrand's publisher ordered the printing of an additional 90,000 books, bringing the total in print to 340,000 (Trachtenberg, screen 2). On July 2, 2002, the paper selected Walter Moseley's *Bad Boy Brawly Brown*—a mystery set in 1960s Los Angeles, and the seventh book in Moseley's Ezekiel "Easy" Rawlins series—prompting it, too, to enjoy a spike in sales.

As part of "Read This!," its own imperatively titled new book club segment, ABC's *Good Morning America* has launched the practice of featuring one real-life American book club assigning a read to a second. Diane Sawyer described this premise as akin to handing "the book you love to a friend" (Grogan, "*Good Morning America*," screen 1). In fact, with the help of a couple of live remotes and a split screen, the segment's June 13, 2002, debut showcased the Pulpwood Queens book club of Jefferson, Texas,—founded by independent bookseller and hairdresser Kathy Patrick of the bookstore/beauty shop Beauty and the Book—recommending Anne Packer's *The Dive from Clausen's Pier* to the Mostly We Eat book club of Bernardsville, New Jersey. The club proceeded to choose a similarly literary novel, the Civil War story *Enemy Women* by Paulette Jiles as its second "Read This!" pick. Thus far, *GMA*'s program has remained in step with the trend of picking solid mid-list titles—which is to say works expected to sell in fair numbers nationally, but not necessarily to be major bestsellers—that most of these clubs seem to be following. True to form, then, when "Read This!" featured Packer's debut novel, publisher Alfred A. Knopf more than doubled the number of the book in print by running an additional 75,000 copies (Trachtenberg, screen 1).

Perhaps the darkest horse among the candidates up for the posi-

So printing after announcement...

• • •

no logo

benefits for the publisher clear; what incentives for us?

- more ads?

- boost in web traffic?

- good will from clubs?

tion of the next Oprah Winfrey was Lou Dobbs, host of CNN's *Lou Dobbs Moneyline*, although his club has since gone off the air. Sponsored by Barnes and Noble, Inc.—the nation's largest book retailer—his picks were, according to the *Wall Street Journal*, "considerably more highbrow" (Trachtenberg, screen 2) than some of the other selections offered. Dobbs' inaugural book, for example—Richard Brookhiser's *America's First Dynasty: the Adamses, 1735–1918*—offered readers 244 densely historic pages on the family of presidents John and John Quincy. Dobbs also singled out such works as *Lazy B: Growing up on a Cattle Ranch in the American Southwest* by Sandra Day O'Connor and H. Alan Day.

Since Dobbs tended to pick nonfiction and my main focus is novels, and since I just didn't see his club as being comparably influential, I'll move on now to "Reading With Ripa," *Live with Regis and Kelly* co-host Kelly Ripa's club. The club, which announced its first selection in spring 2002, featured a total of seven titles before becoming defunct in July 2003. I almost hate to say it, but among all the clubs profiled thus far, "Reading With Ripa" seems to have been the one that most resembled OBC Part I, at least in the sense that it was vastly more personality-driven than any of the other book features. Like Oprah, "Kelly"—who began her TV career in 1990 when she joined the cast of the ABC soap opera *All My Children*—urged her audience to perceive her as a trusted pal. In other words, as "Riphead" Kristen Johnson told the *Wall Street Journal* "When she recommends a book, it's like your friend is recommending a book to you"(Trachtenberg, screen 2).

Beyond this significant but superficial similarity, though, Ripa remained miles away from Winfrey, inasmuch her club was utterly and purposefully devoid of any hints of self-improvement, moral betterment, growth, knowledge, or the desire for any other form of literary edification. Among the "simple charter rules" still listed on the official *Live with Regis and Kelly* Web site are the stipulations, "Thou shalt read what Ripa recommendeth," "Said book shall haveth no message, what-so-ever. It shalleth be fun, frivolous, fast and fiction. Any hint of life-affirming message will automatically lead to disqualification from Book Club," and "Titillation is not required but is encouraged and/or hoped for." According to producer Michael Gelman,

"Our angle should be light entertainment. We aren't trying to save the world or offering a long hard read" (qtd. in Trachtenberg, screen 1). In fact, Ripa herself will be the first to tell you that hers was a club geared toward the shameless promotion of commercial fiction—or, as Regis himself preferred to call it, beach trash. She'll also be the first to provide the kind of vapid and comic commentary befitting such novels, as when she wondered of her first selection, *If Looks Could Kill*—a murder mystery by *Cosmopolitan* editor Kate White—"How unusual is it that the editor of *Cosmo* writes this book about people bumping off editors of women's magazines? You've gotta love that! There's murder; there's intrigue; there's a little bit of sex! There's chocolate!" ("The Ripa Effect," screen 1). She followed up her selection of *If Looks Could Kill*—the first sentence of which happens to read, "Cat Jones was the kind of woman who not only got everything in the world she wanted . . . but over the years also managed to get plenty of what other women wanted: like their fabulous jobs and their hot-looking husbands" (White 1)—with Adele Lang's *Bridget Jones*-esque *Confessions of a Sociopathic Social Climber*, as well as Carey Phillips's *The Bachelor*. More so than with any of the aforementioned book clubs, you can, as a serious reader, take issue with the quality—or roundly acknowledged lack thereof—of the "Reading with Ripa" selections. Still, you'd be hard-pressed to argue with the results; thanks in large part to her ringing endorsements, Ripa's first two picks became major bestsellers.

As you may already have noticed, many of these upstart clubs bear more than a passing resemblance to OBC. TV critic Lisa de Moraes points out, for instance, that the new *Today* book club segment airs after the first half-hour of the program, "by which time many male viewers have bailed" (de Moraes, screen 1). Thus, it seems only logical that their segment seems to be carrying on the OBC tradition of featuring books by and about women more often than not. Still, while these new efforts to use television in a Winfreyesque literary fashion are to be commended, it seems clear that none of these clubs enjoy the same kind of freedom, or perhaps the independence, of taste that OBC Part I once did. As Bill Tipper of BarnesandNoble.com points out, three of these five clubs— the *USA Today* club, "Read This!" and

"The *Today* Book Club"—"have been making choices that attend to the voice of the literary establishment; book reviewers in major magazines and newspapers had already singled out authors like Packer, Jiles and Carter with strong reviews" (qtd. in Tipper, screen 2). But while this attendance to the literary establishment seems mildly disappointing, it's difficult to really fault the clubs for it. For according to the *Wall Street Journal*, "All the new clubs are competing for the status and economic clout that accrue to those media outlets who can create overnight best sellers. When a TV show, or print publication can prove that its recommendations directly lead to thousands of individual sales, it sends a powerful message to potential advertisers" (Trachtenberg, screen 2). Fittingly, then, these new clubs are not trying to provide the kind of show-long, heavy coverage that OBC did, nor are they picking any backlist titles. Rather they seem to be joining forces with the rest of the literary cultural apparatus, such as it is, to make sure that everyone gets to hear about whatever's been anointed as the next big thing. They have no illusions about their purpose, no pretensions that they are anything other than televised book clubs designed to entertain you, to sell you books and—if everything goes according to plan—quite a bit of other stuff along the way.

So, this on-the-air book club phenomenon, with its relatively young hybrid of the literary and the televisual, is a venue now open thanks to Winfrey's pioneering efforts; for this all the upstarts owe her a fair debt, as they themselves will acknowledge. Still, it remains important to remember that in a sense there can be—and some people will find this a relief—only one Oprah. In the aftermath of the club's cancellation, Joyce Carol Oates declared that Winfrey was truly "an American original and such a force for literacy" (qtd. in Conklin 14). For while so far their forces combined come close to recreating Winfrey's immense literary influence, it seems unlikely that any of these clubs individually will ever meet with anything approaching the monolithic success garnered by Winfrey's original OBC. Admittedly, the works profiled by these newer clubs sell in much higher volume than if they hadn't been mentioned on television at all, but their sales figures fail to measure up to those of OBC-approved novels. As Random House spokesman Stuart Appelbaum explains, "All of the clubs are doing an excellent job," but a recommendation from Winfrey "meant hundreds of thousands of sales. With the new clubs, it's more like tens of thousands" (qtd. in DiCarlo, screen 1).

Salon.com's Laura Miller rightly observes that "It's the very consistency, the distinct Oprah sensibility of Winfrey's selections that made her club so successful" (screen 2). Indeed, the lack of this "unifying sensibility" is what ultimately will make it so difficult for any of the current clubs featuring contemporary fiction to replicate her influence. Simply put, Winfrey possessed the alchemical combination of passion and personality necessary to motivate her highly dedicated, extremely suggestible, preexisting audience in the direction of current literary fiction, and all this is what makes hers such an incredibly tough act to follow. Setting all her club's numerous shortcomings aside for a moment, we can see that Winfrey truly strove to be beholden to no one, at least in terms of OBC's selections, and it is in this effort to answer only to herself that the whole point I'm trying to make about taste as a thoughtful, discriminating, personal process really lies.

Before I wrap up this penultimate chapter, I offer you one more big observation about the original manifestation of OBC. I said earlier that the tensions over OBC were just one more battle in an ongoing high versus low cultural war, but now I'm not so sure that I chose the right metaphor. Given the kind of cultural diversity and variety of opinion in this country, it now strikes me as weird that so many people made so very much of Winfrey's creation of a televised book club showcasing contemporary fiction. In fact, before OBC came along, America seemed to be enjoying a period of relative cultural peace. Few people complain very audibly about, say, Disney, even though many of them consider it as facile and bourgeois an institution as ever there was. Instead, individuals who dislike it simply choose not to go to their World, to shop in their Store, or to watch their feature films; virtually no one (not even the authors of the incisive critique *Inside the Mouse*, for instance) bothers to suggest in print or on the air that the Disney empire represents a pernicious threat to good taste and rational thought in America, and should therefore be shut completely down.

More to the point, no one at present is sniveling in literary sup-

Is This It?

plements about the new televised book clubs, and I have neither spotted anyone sporting T-shirts defaming said clubs nor heard anyone comment disparagingly about them on National Public Radio. Even Kelly Ripa's club, by far the easiest target among them, seemed to go about its business relatively unscathed. (Aside, that is, from a couple of derogatory remarks about "Reading With Ripa" in the review section of the Amazon.com Web site, in which one reader wrote, "I won't be taking Kelly's suggestions anymore," prompting another to ask, "Are people so obsessed with Kelly Ripa they cannot judge a STUPID book when they read one?" [qtd. in Trachtenberg, screen 2]. But really, Kelly had to have seen this coming). In any case, now that Winfrey's prototype is dead, we seem to be at cultural peace once again; even the June 2003 resurrection of OBC with its focus on great books has drawn surprisingly little fire from the defenders of highbrow literature. In this light, the clash over the original OBC seems to be the cultural analog to the Battle of New Orleans, an American naval victory in the War of 1812, the only problem with which was that it was fought a good three weeks after the war ended. During the aforementioned time of cultural peace, Winfrey managed to unearth attitudes and opinions about taste that the American public seemed, temporarily, to have forgotten they held. The creation and continued existence of Winfrey's book club caused many of us to revert almost instinctively to the kind of high versus low binaries we had for a while acknowledged to be more or less archaic, or which we had come to simply ignore altogether.

Now that the battle is over and the smoke has cleared, we have the opportunity to consider just what it was about the first version of OBC that made so many of us so uncomfortable. I've tried in this book to explore some of the reasons behind the cultural unrest surrounding this mother of all book groups. Hopefully, in doing so, I've helped you realize that, love it or hate it, Oprah's Book Club (1996-2002) was a truly remarkable institution while it lasted, and that even though it is no more, it still has a lot to teach us about taste—specifically that it behooves us to try to understand why we, as individuals, experience such powerful inclinations to embrace certain artistic and cultural phenomena while rejecting others.

CHAPTER SIX

Everything Old is New Again:
Oprah's Book Club Returns with the Classics

"The book club is back and I am on a mission. My mission is to make this the biggest book club in the world and get people reading again. Not just reading, but reading great books!"

—*Oprah Winfrey Log-in screen
for Oprah's Book Club*

"Winfrey's first selection arched some eyebrows in academe. The literati do not hold Steinbeck's *East of Eden* in particularly high esteem—an opinion that begs some thorny questions that have occupied literary critics and English professors for more than a decade: What is a 'classic' anyway? Who gets to decide?"

—*Mark Coomes, Olympian,
August 24, 2003*

Having worked several summer vacations at Anderson's Book Shop in Chicago's western suburbs, I'm all-too versed in the frantic drill of high school summer reading: June, July, and the better part of August laze humidly by as the small yet solid "classics" section toward the back of the store goes relatively untouched in favor of paperback beach books, travel guides, and magazines suitable for reading on the airplane or in the family car. Then, T-minus-ten or so days before the scheduled start of classes, it hits: the inexorable tidal wave of kids, accompanied in many cases by harried parents, all urgently purchasing the time-honored texts that they should have

185

started reading weeks ago. It struck me as fitting, then, that Oprah Winfrey—in many ways one of the nation's most prominent, albeit self-styled, educators—chose Anderson's as the site of the segment in which she announced what amounted to her own massive summer reading assignment. On Monday, June 16, 2003, Winfrey herself appeared in the downtown Naperville store to hand-deliver crates of the mystery selection that had compelled her to bring her hugely influential book club back after a fourteen-month hiatus, a selection that would be revealed at the taping of the June 18 show to be John Steinbeck's *East of Eden*.

Personally, I was delighted with the almost novelistic circularity with which my own project had come back to where it started—the store with the anti-Oprah university press poster on the wall of the employee bathroom. The poster, I noticed, was still hanging during my July visit to the store to interview employees about their brush with massive fame. Thank goodness Winfrey didn't ask to use the restroom during her visit. And thank goodness the super-fandom and avid love of books of my former co-worker Johanna Monteith inspired Winfrey to visit the store in the first place. "I'm just kind of possessed by her," Monteith explained. "I've watched her forever, and I just really like what she has to say. I joke with my family that I'm going to be her girlfriend some day, and I'm getting closer." This candid affinity for all things Oprah prompted Monteith to e-mail the producers of *The Oprah Winfrey Show* almost immediately upon Winfrey's February announcement of OBC's impending revival. After writing to them about Anderson's itself and the multiple specialty book clubs that operate through the store, as well as her own book group, Monteith received a message back expressing producerly interest. Meanwhile, Anderson's owner Tres Anderson received a call on June 13 informing him that "someone from the show" would be arriving the following Monday around noon. "Of course, we never dreamed it would be Oprah herself," said employee Carol Katsoulis. But of course it was, and just like that, Oprah's Book Club was back.

Although it was that simple for Anderson's to be thrust into the limelight, the cultural ramifications of Winfrey's revival of OBC are—as with everything else surrounding the club—complex indeed.

For with this entirely new focus on the great books, Winfrey seems to be instating an entirely new—for her anyway—borderline-academic, close-reading approach to literature as a whole. Indeed, this more honest scholarly positioning of herself as a teacher of great novels was both foreshadowed and underscored by her eloquent remarks in a speech on February 26, 2003, at the annual meeting of the Association of American Publishers. Accepting an award honoring her for her unique contribution to American literary life, Winfrey declared, "Our society values, for some reason, swiftness of experience. I ask, can the slow art of reading—the slow, sensual art of reading—and its difficult pleasures survive?" (qtd. in M. Mills, screen 1). Winfrey's answer, obviously, is yes, it most certainly can, and statistically speaking there's no mistaking that Winfrey's still got what it takes to help see that it does.

In an article entitled "Ye Oprah Book Club Returneth" in the February 2003 issue of *Forbes*, Lisa DiCarlo speculated that Winfrey's impact on the sales of classics could be greater than that of Hollywood, pointing out that *Mrs. Dalloway*, published in 1925, jumped to number eleven on the *New York Times* bestseller list after Michael Cunningham's Pulitzer Prize-winning novel, *The Hours*, was made into movie (DiCarlo, screen 2). Sure enough, she was right; Winfrey beat Hollywood hands down. Within twenty-four hours of her televised June 18 announcement, *East of Eden* rocketed from 2,356 to number two (second only to J. K. Rowling's *Harry Potter and the Order of the Phoenix*) on the Amazon.com sales list (Coomes, screen 1). Meanwhile, Penguin, which usually sells about forty thousand to fifty thousand copies of *Eden* a year, has shipped out more than 1.5 million since then (Sharma-Jensen, screen 1). The sixteen-dollar trade paperback became the top-selling softcover book in the country in the early weeks of July 2003 (Gillin 1), prompting Susan Petersen Kennedy, president of Penguin Group USA—which owns exclusive rights to John Steinbeck's novels—to say, "When Oprah first broke the news that she was re-launching her book club with a focus on classics, we were ecstatic. Penguin Group is committed to writers and readers. We felt this program would be good for books in general and especially the classics. We are grateful to Oprah for her passion for books and her unwavering commitment to literacy" (qtd. in "Oprah Revives Book Club with Steinbeck," screen 1). Moreover, fifty-one years after its original publication, *East of Eden* rose to the number one slot in the August 3 paperback fiction division of the *New York Times* bestseller list (Coomes, screen 3).

Thus, over the course of the summer months, any doubts as to whether or not Winfrey still possessed her alchemical ability to turn literary lead into gold—or as journalist Mark Coomes would have it, whether "a billionaire populist has the chops to upgrade the intellectual reputation of any old book she pleases—starting with John Steinbeck's oft-maligned 1952 novel" (screen 1)—were laid to rest. "'First day sales of the Oprah edition of *East of Eden* were among the strongest of all Oprah's selections," Bill Nasshan, senior vice president of trade books at Borders Group, told several newspapers. "We expect the new book club choice will drive traffic to our stores and revive interest in the classics" (Gillin, screen 1). Nasshan is hardly alone in placing his renewed faith in Oprah's Midas touch. David Ebershoff, publishing director of the Random House classics imprint Modern Library, believes that regardless of whether Winfrey's classics book club results in sales as stratospheric as those of her previous selections, her new focus is still of enormous significance to the publishing industry and to the books themselves. "Her bringing attention to the classics is going to have a deep impact on what America's reading," he explains. "I'm not just talking about the one book she's focusing on. If she's bringing attention to Hawthorne or Eudora Welty, more people are going to think about browsing the classics section and not just the front of the bookstore" (qtd. in M. Mills, screen 1). One could take Ebershoff's argument a step further and add that not only will Winfrey's new focus impact *which* classics Americans read, it will also impact *how* they read them, how they think about them—and, in turn, how cultural critics will think about their thinking about them.

Given OBC's track record as an almost accidental locus of anxiety in the ever-raging struggle between high and low culture, it should come as no surprise that the club's latest incarnation has been the target of many a skeptical potshot since its June 2003 renaissance.

Rumblings from the groves of darkest academe and in the op-ed pages of the nation's major and minor newspapers have attempted to call into question the wisdom and validity of Winfrey's turn from the literary present to the past. University of Louisville English professor Dale Billingsley has gone so far as to warn Winfrey, "I hope you know that you are stepping into the middle of what the '90s called the campus 'culture wars'"(qtd. in Coomes, screen 2). Yet, when situated in a broader cultural and economic context, Winfrey's turn appears both very wise and very valid after all. As journalist Geeta Sharma-Jensen points out, "Even *sans* Oprah, the classics have been a nice, stable deal for publishing houses for years, akin to a CD in the investment market" (screen 1). William Murphy, a Random House senior editor of the paperback line of the Modern Library classics, agrees. "I think if you know what you're doing, and are committed to publishing the classics in a vigorous way, people will respond," he explains. "In these uncertain times, it *is* a stable market" (qtd. in Sharma-Jensen, screen 1). In fact, recent evidence seems to indicate that not only are the classics a stable market, they may even be a burgeoning one. According to Beth Gillin of the *Philadelphia Inquirer*:

> Market leader Penguin Classics saw its sales rise 13 percent last year over 2001. Penguin is now face-lifting its entire 1,300-book library, slapping snazzy new covers on works of authors from Charles Dickens to Jack Kerouac. Publishers and retailers are pushing classics because they are cheap to produce—no need to pay an author, much less organize an expensive book tour— but also because they've recently discovered just how well these babies sell. Last year *Pride and Prejudice*, first published in 1813 and now available in at least 130 editions, sold 110,000 copies, according to Nielsen Book Scan, which began tracking sales at cash registers in 2001. In other words, Jane Austen outperformed perennial chart-topper Mary Higgins Clark, whose *Mount Vernon Love Story* sold 108,000 copies. (screen 1)

Thus, if Jane Austen can handily outperform Mary Higgins Clark, then Oprah Winfrey and John Steinbeck can certainly hold their own against, say, Kelly Ripa and Carole Matthews.

For what it's worth, Winfrey hardly stands alone in the field of contemporary recommenders of great books. Yet, as usual, she remains the only figure at whom critical stones are being thrown. Many a classic can be located at Great Books Online at www.bartleby.com and Project Gutenberg at www.gutenberg.net. Meanwhile, Rep. Ike Skelton, a Democrat from Missouri and a senior member of the House Armed Services Committee, compiled and posted a "National Security Book List" in June 2003 at http://www.house.gov/skelton (Gillin, screen 1). Here, readers can browse a list of books ranging from Sun Tzu's *The Art of War* to Edward Shepherd Creasy's *Fifteen Decisive Battles of the World: From Marathon to Waterloo,* all of which Skelton strongly recommends to anyone interested in national defense. Moreover, in May 2003, New Leaf Press released a book entitled *A Philistine's Journal—An Average Guy Tackles the Classics.* Thus, rounding out this army of self-appointed compilers of classical canons, we have author Wayne Turmel chronicling his adventures as a forty-year-old suburbanite who finally decides to read—in one year!—all the books he should have read in school. Bearing this rather motley classics-pushing crew in mind, then, one can't help but wonder: why take Winfrey to task for her own impulse to preach the power of great literature to the people?

Heartening for anyone with an interest in seeing an end to the knee-jerk categorization of each and every cultural enterprise beneath banners emblazoned either "high" or "low," is that the answer seems to be that far fewer people rushed to condemn Winfrey's efforts in 2003 than in 1996. Certainly, there was a smattering of the usual gripes against OBC and its selections such as those uttered on Slate.com by the snarky Christopher Suellentrop:

> If Oprah wanted to get pats on the back from literary types for introducing viewers to the American canon she chose a curious way to do it. Not only is Steinbeck the canonical American writer most likely to have his work dismissed by critics as sentimental (Oprah-like?) pap, but *East of Eden* just might be his most controversial book. In fact, Steinbeck has more reason to worry about his literary reputation being sullied—at least in the short run—by association with Oprah than Jonathan Franzen ever did. (screen 1)

For starters, garnering patronizing pats on the back hardly seems to have been Winfrey's intention at all. If anything, she seems to have learned from the Franzen dust-up during OBC Part I that she needn't court the approval of those who will never accept the validity of her efforts regardless of how she frames them.

To her immense credit this time around, Winfrey actually acknowledges potential critical complaints with grace and intelligence. Suellentrop goes on in his drubbing of Winfrey's inaugural author to declare that "during last year's Steinbeck centennial, Harold Bloom decreed to the *New York Times* that the John Ford movie version [of *The Grapes of Wrath*] was the greater artistic accomplishment, and that Steinbeck didn't belong in the American canon (even though Bloom included *Grapes* in the 'canonical prophecy' section of his book *The Western Canon*)" (Suellentrop 1). In canny anticipation of just such an attack, Winfrey's Web site featured an extensive section entitled "Steinbeck Versus the Critics: Why Was *East of Eden* a Book Critics Loved to Hate?" Here, in this freely accessible public space, she encouraged her readers to discover the answer to the question, "Though it quickly made its way into the public's heart, what did the literary elite *really* have to say?" as well as to "get a glimpse of Steinbeck's thoughts on criticism and reviews—straight from the mouths of the critics!" Via the provision of such a format for candid extratextual deliberation and debate, OBC Part II exhibits marked improvement over the insularity, defensiveness, and self-imposed isolation of OBC Part I.

In light of such progress, even Suellentrop must concede—albeit somewhat backhandedly—that "while [Steinbeck] has his flaws—to name only one, his characters are often closer to symbols than people, his women always monsters or saints—it's unfair to criticize him for not writing in the modern style of his superior contemporaries Hemingway, Faulkner, and Fitzgerald, or because his books are too easy to understand," adding that "even if Steinbeck's critics are right that he is overrated, that he's a regional writer and a minor novelist, it's hard to question Oprah's selection of him as the writer to launch a book club on the American masters" (screen 2). Again, Winfrey seems to understand the importance of preparing herself for debate over Steinbeck's literary superiority or lack thereof. At the time of the announcement of the club's revival, she openly admitted that Steinbeck is "not like Shakespeare, or even Faulkner; it's reader friendly. I want to lead people down this path without them thinking they're back in school. When you read something that's good and juicy and it's called literature, then you're not closed to the idea of it" (qtd. in "Oprah Revives," screen 2). Here, then, is a woman who knows exactly what she's doing, and this time she's not going to stand quietly by while anyone tells her otherwise. In the end, even an extremely grudging Suellentrop has to accept Steinbeck's "power as a gateway drug—something you pass out to people to get them interested in the hard stuff. Oprah wants to create a few addicts. Good for her" (screen 2).

I've had to rely rather heavily on Suellentrop's complaints in order to flesh out the concerns behind the elite criticism of this latest manifestation of Oprah's Book Club because the majority of Winfrey's usual detractors—both in the media and in the academy—seem unable to find much to complain about. If anything, Winfrey's new and improved incarnation of OBC has provided not only the impetus for your average lay readers to engage with the classics, but also the impetus for your trained literary professionals—critics and columnists and seasoned academics—to reassess, reevaluate, and reexamine their own approaches to literature, the canon, and what exactly constitutes a classic in the first place. Regarding the periodic need for a radical change in perspective or direction, Rilke writes in his "Archaic Torso of Apollo": "you must change your life" (238). And while Winfrey's no visionary poet, she is providing a much-needed catalyst for dramatic transformation: she is providing an opportunity for reading individuals everywhere to change their literary lives.

The responses of belletristic "professionals" to OBC this time around have remained far more in the realm of sincere curiosity than self-righteous condescension. In the weeks immediately following Winfrey's announcement of her new focus on the classics, Indiana University Southeast Dean of Education Gloria Murray observed, "It's a pretty ambitious undertaking. Can she create her own classics and sell a mass market on great literature? Even with her power, I don't know" (qtd. in Coomes, screen 1). Now that the sales figures have begun to roll in, the answer is clear; yes, Winfrey can sell a mass market on great literature, and she has. Commercial success aside, though, anecdotal evidence at least suggests that Winfrey's most recent version of OBC is achieving some measure of critical success, as well—at least to the extent that those who self-consciously count themselves among a specialist class of literary elites are discussing Winfrey's endeavor with a seriousness that is both uncharacteristic and refreshing.

In other words, many of Winfrey's erstwhile detractors now wonder with genuine interest which classics she will select and how the club itself will work. According to former Colorado congress-woman Pat Schroeder, current president of the Association of American Publishers, "No one's quite sure what she means by 'clas-sics.' Does she mean things we would call backlist, the oldies but goodies like *To Kill a Mockingbird* or the Hemingway stories? Or does she mean the Greeks and the Romans and Shakespeare?" (qtd. in M. Mills, screen 2). Thus far, Winfrey's interest seems to lie with the former rather than the latter, but OBC Part II is still so incipient, one must not discount any possibilities. Speculating in the *Halifax Herald Limited*, critic Nicholas Wapshott writes, "By 'classics' she does not mean Pliny, Euripides, Aeschylus and the ancients, but the sort of books the BBC makes into starchy costume dramas which eventually turn up here on public television, introduced by Alistair Cooke. Which begs the question: which classics will America's first black bil-lionaire recommend to the nation?" (screen 1). After tossing around a short-list of possible classical Winfrey authors—including such heavyweights as Mark Twain, Louisa May Alcott, George Eliot, Marcel Proust and Leo Tolstoy, who Oprah did select (but more on that later)—he goes on to suggest that even though Winfrey has demonstrated "little time for white males" (Wapshott 1), she may be willing to look in their direction for her definition of what consti-tutes a classic. In the beginning he was right. With her announce-ment of Alan Paton's novel of South African racism, struggle, and reconciliation, *Cry, the Beloved Country*, Winfrey put her record at two for two in terms of white male authors, though these picks were followed by *One Hundred Years of Solitude* by Colombian-born Gabriel García Márquez and *The Heart is a Lonely Hunter* by Carson McCullers.

Critics as well as fans of OBC have good reason to pay close attention to the titles Winfrey selects over the coming months, for these books draw attention not only to Winfrey's opinion that more people should be reading the classics, but also to the entire concept of "classic" itself, including what exactly it means and who gets to say so. For while the books Winfrey has selected so far are undeniably older, their status as "great books"—whatever you take that to mean—is hardly indisputable. Winfrey herself openly acknowledges the trickiness of this issue, saying, "There are some who would argue that [*East of Eden*] is not really a 'classic' . . . and I realized that that was a conversation that would come up over and over again. . . . I just want to read great books without it becoming controversial" ("Oprah Revives," screen 1). Once again, Winfrey has put herself in the position of straddling the high versus pop cultural divide. For even though Steinbeck's book was a bestseller at the time of its 1952 publication, conventional wisdom holds that the novel's ponderous, unwieldy quality ranks it well below, say, *Of Mice and Men*. Thus, regardless of whether she intends to court or to avoid controversy, Winfrey's decision to call her latest recommendations great books "will soon show the world whether her clout extends beyond the cash register to the court of critical opinion. 'Never underestimate the power of Oprah,' says Purdue University professor John Duvall, editor of *Modern Fiction Studies,* an academic journal. 'I think she has the potential to broaden the horizon of what a classic means.'" At issue, then, "is the right of any group, no matter how learned, to decide which novels constitute the canon, the scholarly term for the small collection of works recognized as the acme of English prose" (Coomes, screen 2).

In his book *Highbrow/Lowbrow,* cultural critic Lawrence Levine points out that in the past, there has been a:

> sense that culture is something created by the few for the few,
> threatened by the many, and imperiled by democracy; the con-

viction that culture cannot come from the young, the inexperienced, the untutored, the marginal; the belief that culture is
finite and fixed, defined and measured, complex and difficult
of access, recognizable only by those trained to recognize it,
comprehensible only to those qualified to comprehend it. (252)

Not so, says Winfrey, and Levine likely would be glad to hear her say
it. For her decision to present great books via mass market television to an audience of relatively untrained millions suggests a passionate conviction that culture—literary culture anyway—is in fact
accessible to anyone, including the inexperienced and the marginal,
as well as the conviction that, far from being fixed and immutable,
culture is fluid and flexible, with the potential to reach—and to be
reached by—virtually everyone.

Winfrey is far from alone in her desire to expand the audience
for classic literature. According to Michael Millman, an editor at
Penguin Classics, "Publishers are constantly looking to expand their
titles. . . . I think we are expanding the definition of the canon . . .
and what we are doing with Penguin Classics is not only including
the classics of literature, but also of philosophy and the social sci-
ences'" (qtd. in Sharma-Jensen, screen 1). Thus, Winfrey is positioning herself squarely alongside contemporary critics with more
democratic mindsets. By acknowledging that the decision to desig-
nate a work as "great" is an enormously subjective one—influenced
by gender, economics, race, and countless other concerns not necessarily related to a particular work's inherent value—Winfrey stands
poised to usher in a new era of critical, canonical honesty, candor,
and dynamism. Even though she has not bothered to outline her official criteria of what constitutes a "classic"—nor is she likely to do
so—we can arrive at an ostensive definition of what it is she looks
for in a "great book." Indeed we can infer that her standards for the
qualities a true classic must possess are fairly—well, classical. For on
the most basic level, Winfrey tends—like Horace in his own classic,
The Art of Poetry—to favor those works that take it upon themselves
to simultaneously delight and instruct.

As has been mentioned previously, *East of Eden*—along with the

---

oeuvres of other social novelists such as Dos Passos, Dreiser, and Sinclair—has long since fallen out of favor in English departments across the nation. Even Steinbeck biographer Jay Parini has gone so far as to describe the novel as "a magnificent failure" albeit "quite readable" ("Oprah Revives," screen 1). Thus, Winfrey is making a bold intellectual move by even suggesting that *East of Eden* is a "great" or "classic" book, for in doing so, she makes the tacit assertion that readability and enjoyability (delight!), as well as appeal to the reader's moral imagination (instruction!) are components of great literature. All in all, Winfrey's selections of Steinbeck, Paton, García Márquez, McCullers, and Tolstoy remain consistent with the values implied by her previous selections, and anyone concerned with the relevance and role of literature in contemporary culture should be pleased with this fact. The novels balance strong populist appeal with acknowledged literary quality. Winfrey should be commended for her decision to pick such little-read, but relatively well-regarded novels as Steinbeck's *East of Eden* alongside standard canonical fare such as *Anna Karenina*, for this choice articulates a real desire on her part to encourage an active readership—and not merely the appearance of readership—in America.

In a thoughtful opinion piece that ran in the *Chicago Tribune* on June 23, 2003,—mere days after Winfrey unveiled her new version of OBC with the announcement of *East of Eden*—Heidi Stevens addressed the groundless concerns of various high priests of high culture that Winfrey's selection of such a great novel (and by extension her future selection of others like it) would inevitably result in a sacrilegious desecration of the sacred cows of the Western canon. "The bottomline," she concludes, "is thousands of people have just been turned on to a classic piece of literature that will introduce them to a collection of characters and ideas they didn't know existed," so:

> Why does it matter who turned them on to it? Will that alter the plot and character development? Is it somehow more appropriate to read a book when a tenured professor you're paying to learn from tells you to, rather than a TV personality who enters millions of homes a day for free? Are we better off as a society if the classics are reserved for those who received

a liberal arts education at a four-year university? Will the book become less poignant if the person sitting next to you at Jiffy Lube is reading it? (Stevens, screen 1)

Stevens adds that if Winfrey were planning to "dumb down" the classics, "that would be a different story." Yet, if anything, Winfrey's approach to said classics seems to be to smarten them up. Thus far, Winfrey has used OBC Part II to encourage her readers—through all manner of prompts, hints, tips, study guides and question-and-answer pages on the Web site as well as on the show—to approach the classics in a scholarly fashion.

In a moment, I'd like to analyze this landmark move toward serious scholarship of the classics in some detail. But first—and here's the big surprise, the suspenseful plot twist in this chapter of OBC—I'd like to point out that, yes, Winfrey has turned tens of thousands of eager readers onto various works of classic literature, but (brace yourself): *she herself is not referring to these works as "classics."* And although no one else, to my knowledge, has pointed this out—perhaps since they're all too busy either simply reading the books, or deliberating about the nature of a true classic—the significance of Winfrey's choice of vocabulary cannot be overstated. Her decision not to refer to the books in question as "classics" even as virtually everyone else— publishers, editors, critics, and, of course, readers—applies the term with tremendous vigor seems immensely consequential. For the names and labels one chooses to apply to one's enterprises—cultural or otherwise—are never accidental or value-free, nor have they ever been. Describing critic Matthew Arnold's dominion over the creation of the nineteenth-century categories that sway our ways of thinking about art even now, Levine writes that:

> "High," "low," "rude," "lesser," "higher," "lower," "beautiful," "modern," "legitimate," "vulgar," "popular," "true," "pure" . . . were applied to such nouns as "arts" or "culture" almost *ad infinitum.* Though plentiful, the adjectives were not random. They clustered around a congeries of values, a set of categories that defined and distinguished culture vertically, that created hierarchies which were to remain meaningful for much of this century.

> That they are categories which to this day we have difficulty
> defining with any precision does not negate their influence. (224)

Levine goes on to point out that, naturally, certain audiences reacted
with hostility toward this implicit ascendancy of high culture, turning their backs on—if not thumbing their noses at—the classic works
of art and letters that had been demarcated so clearly as beyond their
ken. And, naturally, scholars and other self-appointed members of the
cultural elite have been hasty to misunderstand this response, "labeling it simple Philistinism or anti-intellectualism" (Levine 240), when
in reality the situation is far more complex. Thus, by refusing to resort
to the handy—albeit loaded—label of "classic" in relation to her book
club (although it's worth noting that the URL for the online version
of the club reads, sneakily, http://www.oprah.com/obc_*classic*/
login/obc_login_intro.jhtml), Winfrey has decided to give her audience an opportunity to reclaim a culture that has long been presented
as off-putting if not entirely off limits.

Lest Winfrey's avoidance of the term "classic" be attributed to
mere happenstance or oversight, I feel compelled to emphasize that
her decision is, in fact, a considered one. Originally, Winfrey intended
to title her revived club "Traveling With the Classics," but as the time
to relaunch the project drew near, she decided to pick up where she
left off by calling it "Oprah's Book Club," exactly as she had before.
Winfrey claimed that this choice was made in order to "avoid 'the
self-imposed box' in which she found herself: the fewer expectations,
the better. She will not make monthly picks, but three to five choices
a year. She will focus on authors of the past, but doesn't rule out living ones" as evidenced by her selection of García Márquez ("Oprah
Revives," screen 1). Thus, Winfrey has alleviated much of the stress
she had admitted to feeling regarding book selection prior to OBC's
fourteen-month hiatus. For by turning to authors of the past while
scrupulously avoiding the term "classic," Winfrey has given herself
far more works to pick from; she may revisit her old favorites, while
still permitting herself to toss in the occasional book by, say, Toni
Morrison, as she sees fit. But more than merely allowing herself
greater freedom of choice in terms of book selection, Winfrey's

omission of the word "classic" from her latest literary project deflects many a potential complaint about her cultural authority, or lack thereof.

For by stepping back and watching others struggle with the concept of what exactly constitutes a classic, Winfrey has given herself space to accomplish her project of promoting the active readership of great books in relative peace. For even as Winfrey declines to do so, others—in the press, in the academy, and in the public at large—have rushed to identify her selections so far as classics (or at least to debate whether or not they deserve that rare appellation). That *East of Eden, Cry, the Beloved Country, One Hundred Years of Solitude, The Heart is a Lonely Hunter, Anna Karenina* and all the as yet unnamed works she will select in the future are "great books," Winfrey will admit, and the idea that they are therefore "classics" is, of course, implicit. Yet Winfrey's decision to let other people make this leap in categorization is terribly clever. By encouraging others to do the hierarchical heavy lifting for her, she has delegated for major cultural work to be done, acting as its administrator and catalyst, while allowing it to play out within the culture as a whole.

Thanks to OBC Part II, the appropriate question is no longer, "Who does Oprah think she is?" but rather, "Who do we think we are?" She has pushed those among us who concern ourselves with such things to wonder: what do *we* consider the classics to be? Where does *our* authority come from? How do *we* decide what works are worthy of inclusion in the canon? Thus, with her simultaneous turn toward the classics but away from the term itself, Winfrey has managed to make OBC more inclusive than ever before. Not only has she motivated her fans to pore eagerly over the words of great writers of the past, she has also compelled her critics and potential detractors to ponder how great these writers are in the first place. In short, Winfrey continues her quest to bring about cultural change and improvement while avoiding the accusations that assailed her before, among them that she pushed so-called middlebrow literature with a facile and condescending attitude under the pretense of unearned expertise. She has figured out how to prompt a healthy cultural exchange without situating herself too squarely in the middle of it, and as a result, she appears more savvy and less self-righteous that she did during OBC Part I.

Moreover, she appears less egotistical and authoritarian, not to mention less conservative and misogynistic, than such established literary experts as Harold Bloom, who declared ominously in 2003 that:

> In the early 1950s and 1960s, it was understood that the great English romantic poets were Percy Bysshe Shelley, William Wordsworth, Lord Byron, John Keats, William Blake, Samuel Taylor Coleridge. But today they are Felicia Hemans, Charlotte Smith, Mary Tighe, Laetitia Landon and others who just can't write. A fourth-rate playwright like Aphra Behn is being taught instead of Shakespeare in many curriculums across the country. (Bloom, screen 1)

Unlike many critics within the academy, Winfrey has nothing to fear and nothing to prove. She happily allows women and people of color into her informal canon alongside writers of an Anglo-Saxon male persuasion without giving any group preferential treatment. By refusing to adhere to the belief that there exists an inflexible, time-honored template to define who can or cannot write—whose works are worth reading and whose are fourth-rate—Winfrey has given herself the freedom to promote books she considers truly great, regardless of who wrote them or when. Thus, the new OBC, with its catholic taste, its ability to look beyond the automatically accepted "classics" of the Western canon, and its willingness to distribute critical authority among all its participants, stands poised to accomplish all the beneficial cultural work of the first, if not more, without leaving the bad taste of questionable means and authority in the mouths of her critics.

In order to better understand how Winfrey has positioned this latest incarnation of OBC to break down even more anachronistic hierarchical barriers, we must understand the new—and notably more scholarly—protocols by which she has chosen to have the club operate. In keeping with her stated mission of making OBC "the biggest book club in the world," anyone with access to a computer may sign up to join Oprah's Online Book Club, the sumptuously appointed

Web supplement to OBC. You can have a firsthand look of your own at her approach to the classics at http://www.oprah.com. Having already been on the mailing list for OBC Part I, I joined the Web community surrounding OBC Part II at the first possible opportunity, going so far as to set up a somewhat ridiculously named Hotmail account for this purpose. If you do sign up for updates yourself, I strongly encourage you to consider doing the same, because believe me, once you join, you will soon be the proud recipient of a heck of a lot of OBC-related e-mail. And I don't mean spam. I don't mean junk mail or advertisements or exhortations to watch *Oprah* every single weekday or anything of that nefarious sort, oh no. I mean step-by-step, section-by-section study guides pertaining specifically, edifyingly, excitingly to the great books at hand.

Like a tech-savvy college professor making use of the class listserv, Winfrey has arranged to have online members of OBC receive what amount to strikingly syllabus-style assignments on a regular basis. All participants receive—as I did on October 3, 2003, for instance—periodic bulletins under the subject line "Start Reading the Next Book," whose breathless yet authoritative text advises, "so—if you haven't already—pick up a copy and start reading the first five chapters of book one. And check Oprah.com for reader discussions, study guides (coming soon!) and all kinds of features, insights and fascinating details about *Cry, the Beloved Country* and its author, Alan Paton—it's a journey that will sweep you away . . ." Also included in such mailings are links to every extra-textual resource imaginable. The series of messages and postings leading up to the September 29, 2003, screening of the segment on *East of Eden* included—but was hardly limited to—links to the 1952 bestseller list; links to Dr. Susan Shillinglaw, professor of English and director of the Center for Steinbeck Studies at San José State University (a Steinbeck scholar who served as an editor and contributing writer for coverage of the novel on the Web site); links to the elaborate real-life and fictional family trees of Steinbeck's own ancestors and the characters in the novel respectively; links to the biblical story of Cain and Abel; and last, but hardly least, a concise, well-sourced explanation of the novel's main theme as centered upon the Hebrew word *timshel*. This latter cites evidence from both *The New Jerusalem Bible* and "the authoritative Orthodox Jewish translation from *The Chumash: The Stone Edition,*" and arrives at the conclusion that, "like all of us, Cain had free will to decide between good and evil. In this semi-autobiographical work, Steinbeck does not envision a virginal Eden as our birthright. As much as we inherit Cain's curse, we also inherit his ability to redeem himself." Certainly, this analysis, with its emphasis on struggle, self-improvement, and redemption, can be seen as very Oprah, yet so too must it be seen as an inarguably strong reading of the classic in question.

Just in case all this scholarship isn't enough to satisfy the most thorough readers—to say nothing of the toughest critics—that she's serious about getting the most out of the classics, Winfrey has decided to actually bring in a professional critic to field questions pertaining to each of the great books selected. Pulitzer Prize–winning critic Margo Jefferson, for instance, served as the gifted go-to woman for *East of Eden*. During her tenure as resident Steinbeck expert, Jefferson fielded such questions from OBC members as the historical, "What new meanings can be read into this book that weren't possible when it was published?" the sociological, "Why can't people just read for the sake of a story?" and the multicultural, "What is the reason for Steinbeck's harsh description of non-white groups in the book?" Dr. Rita Barnard, who has a Ph.D. from Duke University, is associate professor of English and Director of the Comparative Literature Program at the University of Pennsylvania in Philadelphia, and who has a book forthcoming from Oxford University Press on the subject of South African literature, filled the position of resident literary guide for *Cry, the Beloved Country*. *One Hundred Years of Solitude, Anna Karenina,* and *The Heart is a Lonely Hunter* received similar attention. Not unlike an educator bringing in a guest lecturer, Winfrey has added even more scholarly clout to her project by inviting so-called experts to help explicate the meanings of the chosen texts. This can't be taken to mean that she feels herself inexpert on the subject of classic literature, nor that she feels her readers are too, say, lowbrow to "get" the works on their own—it just means she knows that there are multiple ways to approach any text, and that the more voices brought into discussion on a particular book, the richer the insight and edification. As might be the case in a graduate school seminar-style literature class, everyone's invited to speak up, ask their questions, do their research, and offer their answers.

Thus, OBC Part II seems a deliberately far cry from OBC Part I, when updates were fewer and farther between, and an even farther cry from your average small-potatoes, non-televised neighborhood book club, which typically picks a book and asks only that you have it read by—and maybe bring some cookies or something to—the next meeting at whomever's house. (OBC Online also offers means of improvement to even the most humble of traditional book clubs, featuring links to assorted clubs from all over the nation, and ideas of how to make get-togethers fancier and more ambitious.)

Still, as ostentatiously new and improved as OBC Part II is, it has not gone so far as to jettison the techniques that made OBC Part I— whatever its weaknesses—such a phenomenally popular success. In other words, while Winfrey may have covered her intellectual bases more thoroughly, her approach to the classics is still indefatigably Oprah: effusive, inclusive, enthusiastic, hellbent on personal betterment, and fun, fun, fun. Even after a fourteen-month interruption, Winfrey's canny ability to market a particular read to her target audience proved undiminished. In the typical hyperbolic style she adopts whenever she speaks of her latest literary passion, Winfrey billed *East of Eden* as "the book that brought the book club back!" proclaiming, "I *love* this book! It's the perfect book for summer. It's a saga . . . it's *so* good! You won't be able to turn the pages fast enough. I brought the book club back to share this jewel of a novel. I was turning every page thinking, 'Oh my *goodness!*' You just don't want it to end!" And if that weren't enough, her Web site gushed that the 602-pager "has it all! Sex, murder, suicide, infidelity, greed, blackmail, nasty manipulation: no subject is taboo." Having read the book myself on Winfrey's recommendation, I can verify that regardless of whether one considers the book a classic, it is undeniably a page-turner. And while I wouldn't go so far as to announce, as Winfrey did, that *"East of Eden* might be the best novel she had ever read" ("Oprah Heads 'East of Eden,'" screen 1), I had a good time reading both it and the online supplemental material.

Clearly Winfrey's proclivity for the generous use of superlative and drama abides. Her approach—by necessity designed to play well in the sweeping, stylized, superficial realm of the televisual—remains as flashy as ever. Her application of such techniques to the alleged classics will undoubtedly irk some of the same self-proclaimed "high" cultural detractors so eager to find fault with her club before. Yet how else compel thousands of people who may have ignored these books and others like them in high school and college to pay attention to them now? For by being her usual effusive self—and by promising plenty of literary sex, secrets, and scandal—Winfrey has proven that she is capable of achieving her stated goal of drawing thousands of readers to her club—a club, which, as has been previously stated, supplements its sometimes lurid sales pitches and subject matter with genuine scholarship.

Even as OBC Part II becomes more scholarly, the feel-good attitude toward active literacy that characterized OBC Part I remains intact. During her announcement of the selection of *East of Eden*, for instance, Winfrey proclaimed, "John Steinbeck—wherever he is in the spirit world—is very happy today!" And while this statement may be taken quite rightly as more than a bit presumptuous, extravagant, and perhaps even improvident, the woman has a point. According to Thomas Steinbeck (who appeared, along with Jane Seymour and Kelsey Grammer, on the California road-trip segment featuring his father's book):

> John kept his Nobel Prize for literature in the closet and used his Pulitzer for a paperweight. But having . . . *East of Eden* designated, "the book that brought Oprah's Book Club back" would have delighted him. "My father would have been very much tickled." His father was known for his interest in working people rather than the literati. "He would have loved that this incredibly savvy black woman who has broken ceiling after ceiling has put him on top of the best-seller list." (Donahue, screen 1)

Thus, it is, as University of Louisville English professor Matthew Biberman says, "very hard to say Oprah is wrong. She seems to be reinventing the notion of a classic" (qtd. in Coomes, screen 3). More than that, she seems to be reinventing the way in which we should interact with the classics based on the principle that they can delight and entertain us, in addition to educating us and exercising our moral imaginations.

In case all these innovations and additions to the club weren't enough, over Memorial Day weekend 2004, Winfrey took her great books project farther into uncharted territory by announcing not only that Leo Tolstoy's *Anna Karenina* would be the summer selection, but also that—like, presumably, the majority of club members—she herself had never read the 838-page Russian classic. Announcing her selection of the 126-year-old saga of the aristocratic Anna's adulterous affair, Winfrey declared, "I've never, ever chosen a novel that I had not personally read," (Wyatt, screen 1), adding on her Web site that "This book has been on my 'must read' list for years, but I was scared of it. Let's not be scared of it. I'm going to team up with all of you, and we'll read it together. It's one of the greatest love stories of all-time . . . one of the greatest books of all-time." (oprah.com, Oprah's Book Club login screen). Thus, while Winfrey's approach to literature in this second incarnation of the club certainly has been more thorough and scholarly than it ever was in OBC Part I, her tactic for Tolstoy has emerged as the most refreshingly experimental and egalitarian one so far.

I have suggested throughout this chapter that Winfrey's position in the current version of the club is an almost professorial one, yet with this summer selection, one has to ask oneself: what traditional teacher or academic professional would admit to, let alone proudly trumpet, his or her having not yet read the assigned reading? With her resolution to soldier through this sprawling Russian saga along with her readers—with her vow to "finish every page" of *Anna Karenina* and to send "emails all summer long to keep you posted on how I'm doing and hopefully give you encouragement, because I believe we can do this. We can read the real literature of the world" (Blais, screen 1)—Winfrey has proven yet again that there exists more than one appropriate way to deal with literature; she has set out to further the sense of community that is one of the secrets to the OBC's success by joining the community herself, as an almost-equal.

In doing so, Winfrey has exhibited a shrewd understanding of how to manage and master one of the most fundamental pedagogical issues of higher education: the sometimes daunting balance of power between teacher and student. In my own Teaching Freshmen Writing class in graduate school—and, I'm sure, in many such classes across the nation—this delicate equilibrium was boiled down to a cheesy but apt saying about the need to know when to be "a guide on the side" as opposed to "a sage on the stage." Winfrey has certainly been both a guide and a sage at various points in her book-recommending career, but it seems a particular stroke of book-clubbing genius for her to have realized the benefits of presenting herself as both a model and a colleague in order to persuade hundreds of thousands of Americans to haul their way eagerly through what amounts to a highly atypical beach read.

As a result of Winfrey's careful positioning of herself as both the challenger, establishing the instructions and keeping the project productive, and one of the challenged, faithfully adhering to her own reading schedule, Winfrey has persuaded hundreds of thousands of readers to pick up their own copies of *Anna Karenina* and "train for reading greatness" as the Web site would have it. Realizing the importance of having all her readers on the same literal and proverbial page—as well as the value of dealing with the clearest available translation of a work not originally written in English—Winfrey explicitly selected the PEN/Book-of-the-Month Club Translation Prize-winning edition by the husband-and-wife team of Richard Pevear and Larissa Volokhonsky, intoning, "First of all, get this edition. You see the one with the little flowers on the cover, and it'll have the little banner? Look for the Oprah's Book Club little sticker there because there's lots of different editions. This is an award-winning translation, so you're really going to get scared if it's not translated well, O.K.?" (Wyatt screen 1). Subsequent to Winfrey's announcement, the Pevear and Volokhonsky translation rocketed to the top of Amazon.com's bestseller list, as well as Barnes and Noble's online list. Additionally, Penguin returned to press twice to print nine hundred thousand copies since being notified secretly of the pending selection on May 5, compared with about sixty thousand copies since the book's original U.S. release in 2001 (Wyatt, screen 2). Also thanks to Winfrey's ringing endorsement, the edition, bearing the label "Oprah's Book Club Summer Selection," has shot to the top of *USA Today*'s bestseller list, as well as the lists of *Publishers Weekly* and *The New York Times* (Colford, screen 1).

According to Tolstoy's obituary in *The New York Times*, *Anna Karenina* "provoked discussion throughout the whole civilized world" (Blais, screen 1). Now, it can again. For as extraordinary as Winfrey's having managed to get this enormously intimidating brick of a book to fly off the shelves and into the hands of eager readers inarguably is, even more extraordinary is the way in which she encouraged them to discuss it. As has been the case with previously selected great books, Winfrey has made use of both her Web site and regular e-mail updates to provide copious supplementary material, including a historical overview of Tolstoy's own tumultuous turns of fortune within Russian society and quotations from the novel itself. In addition, owing to her self-imposed status as a fellow first-time reader, Winfrey has been able to use these electronic outlets to disseminate an impressive variety of resources to help her readers maintain their motivation throughout the novel's eight parts. Her initial announcement, for instance, came accompanied by a wealth of read-along-with-Winfrey materials at Oprah.com, including a reading calendar and character guide that can be printed out in bookmark form. And an e-mail entitled "From Oprah 'Anna Karenina' Part One," contained an informative letter from Winfrey to book clubbers (complete with the encouraging send-off: "I'm headed outdoors right now to sit under the trees and see what further rules will be broken. Which ideals will stand—family and honor, or the heat of the heart? Let's keep reading, y'all!"), as well as an invitation to "Take the Quiz" for Part One "to know how well you're doing," plus "10 questions guaranteed to spark your discussion."

Not only has *Anna Karenina* provided more of a sense of camaraderie with Winfrey herself than ever before, it has also allowed room for criticism as well as praise of the book itself and of the reading experience in general. "Send Us Your Video Journal!" the Oprah's Online Book Club Web site exclaims, continuing:

> Oprah sends you her thoughts over e-mail, now she wants to see what you think of *Anna Karenina*! Whether you're reading our big summer selection solo or with your book club, produce a video diary of your reading experience! Let us know the good and the bad—but most of all, have fun! Tell us how you're going to make it past the finish line with Oprah!" (oprah.com)

Winfrey should be praised for this unprecedented invitation to express readerly dissatisfaction and frustration alongside satisfaction and gratification, for by permitting a more complex range of reader responses to her project, she promotes a more sophisticated model of reading itself. Clearly, you're still expected to arrive at the conclusion that Winfrey does in her Part One letter, that "19th century Russia can be mastered" (and why not?), but you're permitted to consider the occasional unpleasant aspects of reading as well as the excitement and joy of the activity. All in all, while Winfrey has taken the opportunity with *Anna Karenina* to do "something she's never done before—she's reading the book with you!" (oprah.com), she has nevertheless remained indefatigably "Oprah," downplaying the difficulty of the work involved in tackling such a novel, while still conveying the sense that "cross[ing] the finish line by September" is a significant and worthwhile accomplishment.

Among the few complaints that may be legitimately leveled against the "classics" embodiment of OBC is the concern that Winfrey is once again commodifying the books in question, surrounding them with commercial trappings and complementary products. Oprah's Book Club Boutique is among the online club's most prominent features, and, unlike the materials pertaining directly to the books, one needn't be an official member to shop there, no special log-in screen bars one from browsing the logo-embroidered ball caps, bucket hats, and T-shirts. Before getting too terribly annoyed, though, one must bear in mind that this set-up scarcely differs from the way books are commodifed virtually everywhere else as well. You'd be hard-pressed to walk into your average bookstore—even a venerable independent one—without being assailed by chocolate bars and specialty coffees, booklights and magnifiers, and all manner of other assorted, vaguely literary accessories. So if buying a pastel pink canvas beach tote emblazoned with the official insignia of OBC helps Winfrey's readers keep sand off their Steinbeck, fine. The point is, they're buying—and reading—the Steinbeck. As Cathy Davidson points out, "Americans still do not read many books in the course of a year and certainly cannot be accused of consuming books as frequently (or as programmatically) as they do, say, tubes of toothpaste or television shows" (17). Thus, if anything, Winfrey's doing more than her fair share to help even up those numbers. Plus all profits from the boutique go to Winfrey's Angel Network charity, which is more than can be said for the profits at, say, Amazon.com.

Even though the complaint about the commodification of literature by OBC turns out to be a fairly minor one, it reminds us again of the issue of consumption as it relates to literature—which has less to with the fact that books are obviously a commodity, and more to do with the complicated issue of who owns/reads which books and why. Nicholas Latimer, director of publicity at Knopf, explains that, "In this here-today, gone-tomorrow era of immediate gratification via the Internet, what a luxury to own a copy of a bonafide classic, to hold it in your hands, turn the pages, realize all the work that went into its production, and enjoy the actual experience of reading for pleasure—all at a relatively inexpensive price" (qtd. in Sharma-Jensen, screen 1).

Publishers have long understood the benefits of producing various editions of the classics aimed at various audiences. This means that:

> Readers can therefore find Herman Melville or Charles Dickens or Fyodor Doestoyevsky or F. Scott Fitzgerald or Dante Alighieri at many price points: in upscale hardcover editions costing $30 and more, nice-looking paperbacks between $7 and $14, or even simple Barnes & Noble editions for around $5. (The retailer's recent edition of Charles Dickens' *Great Expectations* was priced at $4.95.) (Sharma-Jensen, screen 1)

To her credit, then, via OBC with its inclusive invitation for everyone at every level of the socioeconomic spectrum to obtain and read the selection at hand, Winfrey keeps her readers—the more affluent ones, anyway—from becoming an army of Gatsbys, acquiring beautiful, costly libraries full of elegant books that remain dusty, unopened, their pages uncut.

Historically speaking, though, not all readers have been considered as valuable as others. Observing this trend, Davidson wonders, "Do books really decrease in value as they become more accessible? Books have always been available to the wealthy but did not suffer thereby—witness the common aristocratic valuing of a good library. Why, then, are books somehow diminished when they come more and more into the hands of middle-class or even poor citizens?" (16). Winfrey would answer that they shouldn't be. For while participants are encouraged to purchase the official OBC editions of selected titles, they are in no way required to do so. A less moneyed member would never be disinvited from the club, or kicked off the e-mail list, or even remotely looked down upon if her copy of a particular classic happened to come from a used-book store or library. As far as OBC is concerned, it doesn't matter what your books cost, where they come from, or how they look—the point is, and always has been, above all to simply read them, and read them club members do, with tremendous aplomb.

———

Over the course of the years I have spent working on this project, my opinions of, and approaches to, Oprah's Book Club have evolved and changed. So, for that matter, have Winfrey's. As Winfrey has taken the club in a more scholarly direction, many of her critics—myself among them—have come to take the institution more seriously as the embodiment of an inclusive pro-literacy sentiment that bodes well for the culture at large. If I've managed to convince you of nothing else, hopefully I've helped you see that OBC has always stood for far more than just itself, in the sense that Winfrey, by entering into the highbrow versus lowbrow fray, managed to take what had been a relatively cold war and make it hot again. For the dueling camps of taste seem to have been at a standstill of sorts, characterized by a lingering animosity and a pervasive knowledge of who exactly was on which side and why. Via OBC as it existed from 1996-2002, and especially as it exists in its current incarnation, Winfrey has provided everyone concerned with literary culture—and culture in general—with an opportunity to look closely at the construction of taste, thereby exploring what we value, what we disparage, and how we differentiate between the two.

In a *Boston Globe* piece lamenting the National Book Foundation's decision in 2003 to give its annual Medal for Distinguished Contribution to American Letters to Stephen King, Harold Bloom declared, "Our society and our literature and our culture are being dumbed down, and the causes are very complex. I'm 73 years old. In a lifetime of teaching English, I've seen the study of literature debased. There's very little authentic study of the humanities remaining" (Bloom, screen 1). Clearly, there's a lot to take issue with in this rather egregious denouncement of Stephen King as the recipient of an award Winfrey herself earned in 1999. For now, I just want to point out that Winfrey has done more than virtually anyone else, Bloom included, to remedy the problem of declining readership in America. Not only has Winfrey not contributed to any sort of cultural "dumbing down," she has also actively cultivated a widespread literary "smarting up." By encouraging America's discussion of the humanities to become more polyvocal and inclusive, as well as more intense and authentic, she has shown us that there are many ways, not just one, to approach the great texts of our time and times past.

Thus, rather than merely signifying another temporary intensification of hostilities in America's ongoing battle of the brows, Oprah's Book Club Parts I and II prove that "evidence of what appears to be a growing cultural eclecticism and flexibility is everywhere at hand" (Levine 243). Readers from all backgrounds have been given a new source of literary recommendations, literary experts have been given the chance to reconsider the literary canon itself, and both have been given the impetus to realize that active debate and discussion about issues of taste are vastly superior to passive closed-mindedness and the thoughtless acceptance of handed down hierarchical categories.

For even if you were among those who hated the club in its original incarnation (and it certainly possessed its share of frustrating characteristics), or if you continue to hate OBC as it exists now (and it still possesses its share of annoyances, although they are far less serious) you absolutely cannot deny Winfrey's power as an arbiter of taste, and as a champion of the quiet, personal, contemplative pleasures of reading in a culture that at times seems determined to speed past or even erase such pleasures altogether. As Davidson observes, "aesthetic criteria, as book historians frequently note, change radically form one period to another and one century's bestseller—Jean-Jacques Rousseau's *Julie, ou la nouvelle Heloise,* Susanna Rownson's *Charlotte Temple,* or T. S. Arthur's *Ten Nights in a Barroom*—can be unread or even unreadable in another era" (3). Thus, we may never know how Winfrey's picks, contemporary or classic, will bear up under the weight of time, nor can we say for sure how much it matters whether or not they do. All we can be sure of is that the selections of Winfrey's institution have indelibly altered the literary landscape of our present moment, promoting not only literature, but also a healthy discussion of the role literature and its attendant, value-laden categories and hierarchies play in shaping this landscape.

Regardless of whether people still read *White Oleander* or *East of Eden* a hundred years hence, Winfrey has secured her place as a major cultural, literary figure in the here and now. She has provided us all with a working example of the fluidity of culture—a near-perfect illustration of what Lawrence Levine means when he declares that, "Culture is a process, not a fixed condition; it is the product of unremitting interaction between the past and the present" (249). Oprah's Book Club has long represented, and continues to represent, an opportunity for everyone—even, and perhaps especially, non-participants—to understand the reductivity, damage, and general silliness wrought upon culture of all kinds by rigid, anachronistic hierarchies of taste. The inalterable fact remains that the influence of Oprah's Book Club as an emblem of culture as a dynamic process stands to extend long after Winfrey herself, and all the rest of us, have read our last.

CHAPTER 7

Based on a True Story: Oprah's Foray into the Risky Field of Creative Nonfiction

"The symmetry of form attainable in pure fiction cannot so readily be achieved in a narration essentially having less to do with fable than with fact."
—*Herman Melville*, Billy Budd, *1924*

"A disturbing question lurks behind the literary scandal that won't die: Does authenticity still matter? It is a quality that most people say they admire and value—revere, even—in people, in products and in information. And it is something to which media brands and marketers alike pay homage, with adjectives like 'real,' 'genuine' and 'trusted.' Yet as a business model, authenticity seems to be an increasingly tough way to make a living."
—*Richard Siklos*, New York Times, *February 5, 2006*

Late January 2006. A collection of young novelists and short story writers perch atop mismatched pieces of raggedy furniture around the communal big-screen television in the lounge of the Fine Arts Work Center in Provincetown, Massachusetts. They are the 2005–06 Fiction Fellows, authors at the early stages of what promise to be exceptional careers in the field of letters. I am married to one of them—in other words, I am what is known as a Bed Fellow—so I am here, too.

From the way we are screaming, groaning, pumping the air with our fists, you'd think we were watching the Super Bowl, or at least something like it, and in a way, you wouldn't be far off the mark. Because what we are watching is literary bloodsport. What we are watching could be termed our Super Bowl, or better yet, a prizefight for the title of Champion of the World, where the victor earns the right to say whether or not it matters to tell the truth. What we are watching is Oprah Winfrey take James Frey out to what critic Virginia Heffernan called "the televised woodshed" for a serious whipping because of the rampant falsehoods in his so-called memoir *A Million Little Pieces* (Heffernan, screen 1).

The spectacle is breathtaking to behold, "just like back in the days when her guests were abusers and sexual deviants," when Winfrey "came for vengeance ... on behalf of the poor, the voiceless and the women above all, who get conned and defrauded and violated by men who think they're so bad" (screen 1).

And James Frey, the man who wrote, "I am an Alcoholic and a Drug Addict and a Criminal" (57, passim) countless times over the course of his bloated, posturing 432-page book, has certainly been acting like he thinks he's among the baddest.

In a now-notorious *New York Observer* interview prior to the book's initial release in 2003, Frey proclaimed, "I don't give a fuck what Jonathan Safran whatever-his-name does or what David Foster Wallace does. I don't give a fuck what any of those people do. I don't hang out with them, I'm not friends with them, I'm not part of the literati." Of Dave Eggers's best-selling memoir *A Heartbreaking Work of Staggering Genius,* he declared, "A book that I thought was mediocre was being hailed as the best book written by the best writer of my generation. Fuck that. And fuck him and fuck anybody who says that. I don't give a fuck what they think about me. I'm going to try to write the best book of my generation and I'm going to try to be the best writer" (Bayard, screen 1).

Frey also revealed that "the message in front of his iMac reads: 'A page a day. Anything less is unacceptable you punk-ass-bitch-motherfucker. Anything less is unacceptable,'" and that "his wife calls him a savage 'because I eat with my hands. Because my best friends are my dogs. And I like pit bulls. And N.W.A. And I love boxing. Writers aren't like that anymore. They're all these guys who have fucking master's degrees and are so 'sophisticated' and 'educated' and . . . well, I'm not a guy with a master's degree . . . I can write big fat books, but I'm not an effete little guy'" (screen 1).

As for the book itself, reviews were mixed, with David Kamp writing in the *New York Times Book Review* that it "exudes the poseur scuzziness of bad indie films and MTV's 'Jackass'" (Garner "Inside the List," screen 1).

Naturally, it is a schadenfreude-filled rush to watch this self-proclaimed savage having his self-proclaimed badass calmly, thoughtfully, righteously handed to him on national television.

We watch him squirm as Winfrey interrogates him on one of the book's more sensational scenes, in which he describes undergoing a root canal with no anesthetic since, as a recovering addict, he must not permit drugs of any kind to enter his ravaged body.

"You say, 'My face is on fire and the veins in my neck are exploding and my brain is white,' and you describe the white, white hot pain. . . . And when I first saw you, that's the first thing I asked you about: 'That's unbelievable!' You said that that was true. Would you say that today?" Winfrey asks the petulant, nasal-voiced man on her beige studio sofa.

"I . . . I wrote it from memory. . . . I had medical documents that supported it. . . . About nine months after the book was released, I was speaking to somebody from the facility. They said that they doubted it happened that way, but that there was a chance that it did—that cases like that are reviewed on an individual basis," Frey backpedals.

"This is what I don't get," Oprah proceeds. "Because when you were here before, you said that there were about 400 pages of documents. You said you kept a journal. You kept pages. That there were documents and reports of everything that you did. Because I said, 'How can you remember such detail?' And that's how you explained it to me. I don't know how you remember all the detail and you forget Novocain. So what was true about the dentist and what wasn't? You did go to the dentist?"

"Absolutely."

"You went to the dentist. What's true about the dentist?"

"I mean, I went to the dentist. I had my front four teeth repaired . . . as I remember it."

"With Novocain?" she prompts.

"I honestly have no idea."

"Well then why did you say you didn't have Novocain? Because, you know, the last time I went to the dentist, my dentist said that could not have happened. And I said, 'Oh no. It happened. He told me it happened.' . . . So, why did you do that?" Winfrey asks.

"I mean, once I talked to the person at the facility about it, you know, the book had been out for nine months. We'd already done a lot of interviews about it. . . . Since that time I've struggled with the idea of it" he hems.

"No, the *lie* of it. That's a lie. It's not an idea, James. That's a lie."

The studio audience cheers (Oprah.com).

We are all red-faced, shouting to each other our opinions of the events on screen, but our friend Peter Short's blood pressure appears to be racing higher than all of ours, higher even than mine. He doesn't know Frey personally, but they attended the same alma mater, Denison University in Granville, Ohio, and Peter is livid at the deceit his fellow alum has perpetrated not only on Winfrey and the nation, but also at the crime he's committed against an entire genre of literature. As far as Peter is concerned, James Frey has essentially forsaken fiction.

When Winfrey selected Frey's memoir in September of 2005, her imprimatur helped the book to sell more than two million copies that year, making it the second-highest-selling book of 2005, behind only *Harry Potter and the Half-Blood Prince,* and helped *A Million Little Pieces* top the *New York Times* paperback bestseller list at the same time as his follow-up *My Friend Leonard* topped the hardcover list (Wyatt "Best-selling memoir draws scrutiny," screen 1).

A Million Little Pieces made the list as non-fiction, when in reality, it was a novel that Frey and his agent had been unable to sell as a novel. Thus, even though he had "repeatedly stated that his book is true" (screen 1), Frey had bowed to market pressure to bill the book as a memoir. In an interview with the *New York Times* in December 2005, Frey said "that he originally envisioned *A Million Little Pieces* not as a memoir but as a novel." According to Frey, "We were in discussions after we sold it as to whether to publish it as fiction or as nonfiction." Yet when "Doubleday decided to publish the book as nonfiction, Mr. Frey said, he did not have to change anything. 'It was written exactly as it was published,' he said" (screen 1).

This disregard for genre, and more importantly for honesty, made Peter—and a lot of us in the lounge, and across the country—feel disappointed and betrayed.

It made us feel, as Hillary Frey (no relation) wrote presciently way back when the book was first selected, that "His story might be shocking, but it isn't art" (Frey 3). Here was someone who couldn't hack it as a novelist flouting genre distinctions—and, some would say, anything resembling respect for his readers—and selling his lurid, derivative, amateurish prose to the highest bidder with no apparent concern that he'd ever be caught in his lies.

And now Oprah Winfrey was calling him—and his publisher—out. Senior vice president of Doubleday Nan Talese herself seemed to fare only slightly better on Winfrey's couch than her mendacious author did.

"We asked if you, your company, stood behind James's book as a work of nonfiction at the time. And they said, absolutely. And they were also asked if their legal department had checked out the book. And they said yes. So in a press release sent out for the book in 2004, by your company, the book was described as 'brutally honest and an altering look at addiction.' So how can you say that if you haven't checked it to be sure?" Winfrey demands.

"You know, Oprah," Talese replies, "I mean, I think this whole experience is very sad. It's very sad for you. It's very sad for us."

"It's not sad for me. It's embarrassing and disappointing for me."

"I do not know how you get inside another person's mind," says Talese.

"Well, this is my point, Nan. Otherwise then anybody can just walk in off the street with whatever story they have and say this is my story."

"This is absolutely true . . ."

"That needs to change," Winfrey persists.

"No, you cannot stop people from making up stories. We learn by stories," Talese says.

"You can if you call it a memoir. You can make up stories and call them novels. People have done it for years," Winfrey says.

"A novel is something different than a memoir. And a memoir is different from an autobiography. A memoir is an author's remembrance of a certain period in his life. Now, the responsibility, as far as I am concerned, is does it strike me as valid? Does it strike me as authentic? I mean, I'm sent things all the time and I think they're not real. I don't think they're authentic. I don't think they're good. I don't believe them. In this instance, I absolutely believed what I read," says Talese.

"So did I," says Winfrey (Oprah.com).

"That is such bullshit. That is BULLSHIT," Peter shouts, springing from his seat.

And he is right. And Peter may not know it now, but he's hit on the reason that what James Frey did was so serious and what Winfrey did in response was—in addition to being a move of prudent self-preservation—arguably heroic. Eyes flashing, nostrils flaring, the picture of poised, intelligent, yet barely controlled moral outrage in her velvety cadet blue blazer and honest gray slacks, Winfrey struck a blow for truth. More importantly, she struck a blow against bullshit.

What exactly is bullshit? According to Harry G. Frankfurt, author of the Princeton University Press bestseller *On Bullshit*, it is a "lack of connection to a concern with truth . . . [an] indifference to how things really are—that I regard as the essence of bullshit" (Frankfurt 33–34). In other words, Frankfurt asserts that bullshit can be, as Timothy Noah observes in an article on Salon.com, "substantively true, and still *be bullshit*" (Noah, screen 1). According to Frankfurt, bullshit is not merely as damaging as an all-out lie; it's insidiously more so:

> Both in lying and in telling the truth people are guided by their beliefs concerning the way things are. These guide them as they endeavor either to describe the world correctly or to describe it deceitfully. For this reason, telling lies does not tend to unfit a person for telling the truth in the same way that bull-

shitting tends to. . . . The bullshitter ignores these demands altogether. He does not reject the authority of the truth, as the liar does, and oppose himself to it. He pays no attention to it at all. By virtue of this, bullshit is a greater enemy of the truth than lies are. (Frankfurt 59–61)

Frey, for his part, seemed to be operating neither in the service of truth nor of lies, but rather of something else entirely, and this definition of bullshit seems apt to describe that something.

Winfrey confronted him on that January 26 broadcast, saying, "I acted in defense of you, and as I said, my judgment was clouded because so many people seemed to have gotten so much out of it. But now I feel that you conned us all. Do you?" Frey replied like a consummate bullshitter: "I don't feel like I conned everyone." Prodded further, he continued lamely, "Because I still think the book is about drug addiction and alcoholism and nobody's disputing that I was a drug addict and an alcoholic. And it's about the battle to overcome that" (Oprah.com).

Frey's getting taken to task by Winfrey for his shameless bullshittery proves to be especially ironic insofar as Frey appears to be in it so deeply that he doesn't even really know what it is, or realize when he's perpetrating it himself. In the aforementioned vitriolic *Observer* interview, for instance, he revealed that the initials "FTBSITTTD" tattooed on his left arm stand for "Fuck the Bullshit It's Time to Throw Down" (Bayard, screen 1). Unless, perhaps, what he really meant was time to throw down more bullshit?

In any event, immediately following the web report on The Smoking Gun that broke the story of the falsehoods in his memoir in the first place, Frey posted on his blog, "So let the haters hate, let the doubters doubt, I stand by my book, and my life, and I won't dignify this bullshit with any sort of further response."

So the air in Harpo Studios that bleak, late January day was thick with bullshit from Frey and his publisher, but the air in America was thick with other varieties of it as well. As Frank Rich, *New York Times* columnist and author of *The Greatest Story Ever Sold: The Decline and Fall of Truth from 9/11 to Katrina,* pointed out, we currently live in an era of "truthiness." As one of a panel of half a dozen writers, journalists, and critics invited to participate in the James Frey segment, Rich said:

> We live in this word now where this is just sort of the tip of the iceberg, this memoir, where anyone can sort of put out something that sort of looks true, smells a little bit like truth but, in fact, is in some way fictionalized. You look at anything from Enron fooling people and creating this aura of a great business making huge profits when it was an empty shell, or people in the government telling us that mushroom clouds are going to come our way if we don't invade Iraq for months when it was on faulty and possibly suspect intelligence. Or even things we label "reality" in entertainment like reality television. It's cast. It's somewhat scripted. You see Jessica Simpson and Nick Lachey as happy newlyweds. The reality show is over, they get divorced and split the profits. (oprah.com)

By drawing connections from the Frey debacle to the socio-political and cultural climate of the world at large, Rich elevated the discourse on a show where it was already operating at a fairly high level. And I want to spend more time discussing, as he does, the broader significance of what it means to live in a "truthy" culture, as well as the different values promoted through the reading of fiction and nonfiction.

But first, I want to fully explore why what Winfrey did that day was so significant to her book club. The very presence of Rich—and the five other reporter-critics—on the show struck a blow for truth, certainly, but also for OBC. Her handling of the Frey situation—her decision to engage in public self-analysis of the book club's choices and operations—caused this dust-up to result in a more satisfying conclusion, and far better TV, than her handling of the Jonathan Franzen contretemps roughly three years earlier. In short, I want to look at how exactly she ended up sitting on that sofa and making James Frey own up to what he'd done, thereby making an example not merely of Frey, but also—in an unprecedented way—of herself.

To do that, we have to go way back to the summer of 2005, when no one was reading William Faulkner. OK, I suppose "no one" is a bit of an exaggeration. Within a week of Winfrey's early June 2005 announcement, Vintage had shipped five hundred thousand copies and ordered a further one hundred thousand of the $29.95 box of three novels by the long-dead Nobel Prize-winning southerner (Abbott, screen 1). A lot of those copies got read, certainly more than if Winfrey hadn't recommended them, but a lot of them wound up going unpurchased and largely ignored.

Even though, as Charlotte Abbott of *Publishers Weekly* observed, "the summer pick has become the main event for the club, typically selling more copies than titles selected at other times" (screen 1), Faulkner did not enjoy the same bounce that previously picked classic authors had. The 2004 summer pick *Anna Karenina,* for instance, sold more than 900,000 copies, compared to 740,000 copies of the fall 2004 selection, Pearl S. Buck's *The Good Earth,* and 735,000 copies of the spring 2004 selection, Carson McCullers's *The Heart Is a Lonely Hunter* (screen 1). There was no spring 2005 OBC selection, so perhaps Winfrey was hoping to make up for that through her so-called "Summer of Faulkner," wherein readers were expected to eschew their usual tawdry beach reads in favor of not one, but three novels, totaling over one thousand pages: the prickly triumverate of *As I Lay Dying, The Sound and the Fury,* and *Light in August.* As it turned out, many people found the latter too heavy for August (sorry, I couldn't help myself). Meanwhile, Winfrey broke with tradition, making the unusual decision not to air a televised segment on the Faulkner selections at all, choosing instead to let readers content themselves with extensive study guides and background information on the novels on her website.

At the time of Winfrey's announcement of her Faulkner selection, Richard Howarth, the mayor of Faulkner's hometown of Oxford, Mississippi—and also the proprietor of that town's legendary independent bookstore, Square Books—expressed serious doubt that most of Winfrey's audience would be able to complete their assignment. "With a good reading-group leader, they'll make it through *As I Lay Dying.* And they'll make it through *Light in August.* But they're going to start *The Sound and the Fury* and say, 'What is this?'" he said, as he mimed throwing a book over his shoulder. By late summer, it was hard to say if this precise prophecy had come to pass, but underwhelming sales figures and piles of remaindered boxed sets seemed to suggest he hadn't been entirely incorrect.

Lest I sound like I'm laying too much blame at Faulkner's door, it should be noted that the popularity of Winfrey's classics incarnation of OBC, though admirable, had been on the decline almost from the moment it began. Sales for OBC Part II were highest the year that Winfrey kicked it off, with the first pick, John Steinbeck's *East of Eden* selling over 1.2 million copies (screen 1). And Winfrey, ever the savvy book recommender, may have been partially able to achieve this success through timing her pick just one year after the centennial celebration of Steinbeck's birth.

In any event, by the time the "Summer of Faulkner" weighed hot and oppressive on Winfrey's readers, many followers of the club had begun to feel that something had to change. One group in particular was especially vocal on that point, and had been so prior to even the tepid reception of the Faulkner boxed set. Word of Mouth, a group of mostly female authors, circulated and sent a petition to Winfrey on April 20, 2005 asking that she return to her promotion of contemporary fiction, "citing evidence that sales of fiction began to drop about the time her book club went on hiatus in 2002" (Wyatt "Oprah's Book Club to Add Contemporary Writers," screen 2). The more than 150 signatories included bestsellers and prize-winners, among them Francine Prose, Jennifer Egan, A. M. Homes, Amy Tan, Kathryn Harrison, Laura Hillenbrand, and the early OBC-selected author Sue Miller.

The letter warned:

> The American literary landscape is in distress. Sales of contemporary fiction are still falling, and so are the numbers of people who are reading. Readers complain that, although daunting numbers of new books are published, too few of them are brought to the public's attention in a meaningful way. Readers have trouble finding contemporary books they'll like. They, the readers, need you. And we, the writers, need you. America needs a strong voice that addresses everyone who can

read, a voice that will say, "Let's explore the books that are coming out today. Let's see what moves us, what delights us, what speaks to us in a way that only fiction does." (WordofMouthWriters.org)

By the end of the summer, it felt as though a change—maybe a change of the type the Word-of-Mouthers had politely requested?—must have been on the way. Winfrey hadn't announced a book in months, and those of us who keep an eye on OBC could fairly feel the shift coming. And come it did on September 22, 2005, when Winfrey announced that she would expand her club "to include the works of contemporary authors, reversing a policy of choosing only classic novels and once again offering authors and their publishers the hope of huge sales resulting from her picks" (Wyatt "Oprah's Book Club," screen 1).

On their website, under the heading "Thank You, Oprah," the Word-of-Mouthers seem to interpret Winfrey's next move as a direct answer to their plea. They write, "On September 23, 2005, Oprah Winfrey told the *New York Times* that she had been 'moved' by our letter, and she announced that her book club would recommence featuring contemporary writers." This is, strictly speaking, true. But, independent as ever, Winfrey did not say she would begin recommending contemporary writers of *fiction*. In a move that we can only imagine how she feels about in hindsight, she chose nonfiction. She chose so-called memoirist James Frey. And while the Word-of-Mouthers opted to take this choice as a full-fledged victory, I'm going to argue that it wasn't. Rather, if it can be seen as a victory at all, it was a bit of a Pyrrhic one, for nonfiction, though it moves us, does not do so in the way that "only fiction does." In many ways, even though Winfrey's decision to bring back contemporary writers was exciting, her accompanying initial decision to turn to nonfiction was disappointing, and not just because, as fate would have it, her first selection turned out to have been written by a liar.

At first, Frey's selection for the club—although it stood out insofar as it was nonfiction—followed the customary script of a Winfrey-selected author's experience fairly closely. Frey reported the typical reaction when he received The Call: "I was shocked and thrilled and had this sort of amazing and surreal moment" (Wyatt "Oprah's Book Club," screen 1). And his original appearance on the show had only slightly more slick, maudlin corniness than was characteristic of a standard book club feature. Frey and Winfrey "conspired to have Mr. Frey's mother, who he said had given him copies of many of Ms. Winfrey's picks in the past, in the audience" when Winfrey made her momentous announcement, so that "when Ms. Winfrey started talking about her son's book, the author's mother started to scream, 'That's my son!'" (Wyatt "Oprah's Book Club," screen 2).

Despite his previous bad-boy antics and interview cantankerousness, Frey proved in the announcement's aftermath that he knew to whom he should kowtow and when. He told his hometown newspaper, the *Cleveland Plain Dealer,* "I'm happy, I'm humbled, I'm honored by this" (Garner, screen 1). Winfrey, for her part, hyped the book with her inimitable, contagious hyperbole, declaring, "I'm going bold, people, bold, bold, bold. It's bold. It's bold and it's great. It's kept me up nights. It's great, great, great, great. I promise, I promise, I promise," on the September 22 show (screen 1).

Winfrey also explained the rationale behind her bold new move a bit more than she usually did the actions of OBC, a promising development suggesting that maybe some aspects of the already great club were going to change for the better, even if she had turned from fiction to nonfiction. "I wanted to open the door and broaden the field," Winfrey explained. "That allows me the opportunity to do what I like to do most, which is sit and talk to authors about their work. It's kind of hard to do that when they're dead" (Wyatt "Oprah's Book Club," screen 1). She also explained that she planned to branch out into the selection of works from nonfiction's various subgenres, including history and biography, "to give herself more room to follow her instincts about what makes a positive reading experience" (screen 1). "For six years, I couldn't really read any nonfiction or biography because I thought I was wasting my time" since those books did not qualify for consideration for the club. But "Now, when I read something really interesting or promising, I can find a way to introduce it to the public" (screen 1).

In the interest of full disclosure, I should mention here that I am quoting from a *New York Times* article for which I was interviewed. And though I am only quoted on how her Faulkner selection exhibited a lack of the "widespread enthusiasm that was evident when she was picking contemporary fiction and nonfiction," I was a) thrilled to be quoted in the *New York Times*, and b) not quoted as voicing an opinion that I held at the time that Winfrey's decision to turn to nonfiction was actually a timely and even a smart or beneficial move.

My own initial reaction was that, as usual, Winfrey had her finger on the pulse of publishing. For years now, publishers have been riding high on the waves created by the flood of memoirs unleashed throughout the 1990s and on into the twenty-first century. It only made sense that the reigning moderator of the world's biggest book club should jump in, too. The classic club, though respectable, had fallen into decline, and while recommending memoir in the confines of OBC itself would be a new venture for Winfrey, it was not an entirely untested one. She had already included two memoirs in the original incarnation of OBC: Maya Angelou's *The Heart of a Woman* in May of 1997, and Malika Oufkir's *Stolen Lives: Twenty Years in a Desert Jail* in May of 2001. And in the many years of *The Oprah Winfrey Show*'s existence before OBC was created in 1996, even though her talk show had no official club component, she'd proven herself an avid inviter of guests with book tie-ins. Even now that OBC does exist, she still has authors on when the topics of their books relate to the topics of her broadcasts. In January 2005, for instance, the month when the James Frey bullshit hit the proverbial fan, Winfrey also had *Future Jihad* author Walid Phares and *Something for Nothing: Shoplifting Addiction and Recovery* author Terrence Daryl Shulman on her show. According to the book sales tracking program Nielsen Book Scan, "whose figures account for 60 percent to 75 percent of the total marketplace," Phares's and Shulman's books "sold 6,000 and 700 copies respectively" (Thomas 2). Clearly, it's the book club that really helps an author move units, and it made sense to me that Winfrey should want to move some nonfiction ones.

Move is exactly what *A Million Little Pieces* did the instant Winfrey recommended it. Frey's book had already been doing well before

Winfrey made her announcement, making the hardcover bestseller list of the *New York Times* for one week in 2003 (Garner, screen 1), and earning "applause from Bret Easton Ellis and Gus van Sant, and reviews that labeled the memoir 'turbo-charged,' 'compulsive,' and 'unflinchingly honest'" (Barton, screen 1). Winfrey went on to make the paperback version of the book not merely a bestseller that swiftly rose to the slot of "No 1 paperback non-fiction book on the *New York Times* bestseller list for 15 weeks, as well as the No 1 seller on Amazon, and was published in 22 languages worldwide," (screen 1), but also made James Frey the single best-selling American author of 2005 (Wyatt "Writer says he made up some details," screen 1). In fact, in the three months following her selection of *A Million Little Pieces* "more than two million copies were sold, making it the fastest-selling book in the club's 10-year history" (Wyatt "Live on 'Oprah,' a Memoirist gets kicked out of the book club," screen 1).

Winfrey, as usual, had tapped into a desire that existed in the read-ing populace—in this case, a desire for a page-turning memoir of addiction and recovery—and managed to channel that desire to enor-mous effect. In the fall of 2005 it made sense to me, too, that Winfrey would want to turn her attention back to contemporary authors, and specifically to ones she could invite to appear on the show to discuss their books. As I have mentioned in earlier chapters, one of my few major criticisms of earlier incarnations of the club was that Winfrey tended to insist too heavily upon dealing with fiction as something that Could Really Happen, at the expense of discussing elements of style and craft. When she had Frey appear as a guest on her October 26, 2005, show titled "The Man Who Kept Oprah Awake at Night," it occurred to me that perhaps this problem had been effectively cir-cumvented by discussing books about something that Did Really Happen.

Since then I have revised my opinion, not unlike Winfrey herself in some ways. Even after it began to come out that—as Frey states in an author's note that the whole disaster obliged him to write, and that will appear in all subsequent editions—"I wanted the stories in the book to ebb and flow, to have dramatic arcs, to have the tension that all great stories require," and that "I altered events all the way through the book" (Wyatt "Frey says falsehood improved his tale," screen 1), Winfrey at first wanted to cling to the idea that Frey's book was basically true, as did millions of others.

In addition to The Smoking Gun's report that Frey had "wholly fabricated or wildly embellished details of his purported criminal career, jail terms and status as an outlaw 'wanted in three states'" (Smoking Gun.com), counselors from the treatment facility at which the majority of the so-called memoir is set began to come forward to question his tale. "'His description of treatment at Hazelden is almost entirely false,' said Ms. [Debra] Jay, who trained as an addiction counselor at Hazelden's operations in Minnesota and who is the co-author of two guides to treating addiction published by the Hazelden Foundation," where Frey made claims of "being physically abused by other residents of the treatment center, of being left to sleep on the floor of a common room overnight after an altercation, of regularly vomiting blood and of having his nose rebroken and set by a doctor" (Wyatt "Treatment Description in Memoir Disputed," screen 1). According to Jay, "He describes a level of medical care that would not occur at Hazelden. He would have been taken to an emergency room, and any violent behavior would have been met with a discharge" (screen 1).

Even in the face of such damning evidence, Doubleday, via their parent company Random House, "would not comment on The Smoking Gun article but issued a statement saying, 'We stand in support of our author, James Frey, and his book which has touched the lives of millions of readers'"(Wyatt "Best-selling memoir," screen 1). And on January 11, 2006, when Frey appeared alongside his mother on CNN's Larry King Live to address these allegations of falsehood, Winfrey herself phoned in to voice support of the supposed memoirist. "I am disappointed by this controversy," she said, "because I rely on the publishers to define the category that a book falls within, and also the authenticity of the work" (cnn.com, screen 1). "But the underlying message of redemption in James Frey's memoir still resonates with me, and I know it resonates with millions of other people who have read this book," she continued. "What is relevant is that he was a drug addict who spent years in turmoil from the time he was 10 years old drinking and tormenting himself and his parents, and stepped out of that history to be the man that he is today and to take that message to save other people and allow them to save themselves." She added that, "To me, it seems to be much ado about nothing," (screen 1).

Being something of an Oprahologist, I followed the entire trajectory of the Frey scandal from start to finish, and I'd grown rapidly disappointed with the club's new incarnation fairly early on. For starters, I thought *A Million Little Pieces* was an atrociously written book. I'd begun to agree with Hillary Frey, who had asked of Frey's stilted, tortured, macho antistyle way back in October of 2005, "Is this even writing?" and who had written that "too often the horror of his reality is made unreal by his posturing, by his aggressive toughness, by the monotonous rhythm of the way he writes. If Frey's story is powerful at all it's for the facts—the sickness, the hurt, the fatigue of withdrawal—not for his rendition of them" (Frey salon.com). But Winfrey's call to Larry King in defense of this supposed nonfiction writer seemed to me a new low in the history of an institution I'd heretofore admired, and a false move on the part of Winfrey, who, as I have written, I'd come to respect as one of America's most powerful public intellectual figures.

I was upset by the naïveté with which she seemed to be training her readers to consume memoir as pure truth, as opposed to a story shaped and told through a particular, and understandably limited and prejudiced, consciousness. Around the time the scandal was coming to a head, Randy Kennedy wondered in his *New York Times* magazine "Ideas and Trends" column:

> Does anyone care anymore about the ratio of fact to fiction in the memoir? . . . Whoever assumed, for example, that Casanova filled a dozen volumes by being as passionate about accuracy as he was about jumping into bed? Who held Benvenuto Cellini, the master Florentine sculptor and self-mythologizer, to account after reading his rollicking autobiography, or for that matter Benjamin Franklin or Mark Twain, whose tales often read like tall ones? Closer to the case of Mr. Frey and his descriptions of life under the influence, did anyone care whether the original drug addict of English letters,

Thomas De Quincey, could really remember in such poetic detail all those opium-fueled hallucinations about kissing crocodiles and wandering through Oriental palaces? Even when trying to stick to the truth, the earliest memoirists warned that it was hardest to do when writing about one's own recollections. (Kennedy, screen 1)

Kennedy makes a sensible point, but my problem was that neither Winfrey nor her readers—nor Frey's agent, editor, or publisher— seemed to be acknowledging the liberties taken with memoirs in general, or the idea that there were some lines between truth and falsehood that—even in memoir—couldn't be crossed, or at least couldn't be crossed and then blithely passed off and eagerly accepted as the honest-to-god truth.

I agree with Gay Talese, husband of the aforementioned Nan, that "Nonfiction takes no liberty with the facts, and it should not. . . . I think all writers should be held accountable. The trouble with book publishers is that they don't have the staff or they don't want to have the staff to ensure the veracity of a writer. You could argue that they had better, or they're going to have more stories like this one. My wife is going to hate me for this, but that is what I believe" (Wyatt "Writer says he made up," screen 1). But I also agree with poet and autobiographer Andrew Hudgins, who reminds us that not only must we expect to trust the writers we read, we must also expect them to trust us as readers. "The trust I bring to reading an autobiography is a reader's trust in a convincingly told tale," Hudgins writes, "not the trust I bring to reading the *New York Times* or a history of Assyria, in which aesthetics are secondary to accuracy. The autobiography dances on the shifting middle ground between fact and fiction, reportage and imagination, actuality and art; and different writers will draw their lines on that ground in different places" (Hudgins 195–196). Winfrey— and her book club members, readers everywhere, and the entire publishing and media industries, with the apparent exception of The Smoking Gun—failed from the outset to address that shifting middle ground.

Hence my newfound disappointment with Winfrey's handling of nonfiction on her show. She seemed to be encouraging wide-eyed acceptance and total credulity instead of thoughtful questioning and concern with the collision of craft and confessionality. Just as I asserted that she sometimes risked doing with fiction—through her insistence on discussing it through the lens of something that could exist in reality—Winfrey seemed once again to be flattening out the book she was presenting. She seemed to be reducing her argument for the book's worth to the single quality of its being "a gut-wrenching memoir that is raw and it's so real" (Wyatt "Best-selling memoir," screen 1).

This idea that memoir should be consumed with little to no concern for the praiseworthy artfulness or the condemnable deceit that an author might have undertaken in the course of its production seemed to be driven home even further considering how closely the format of OBC now resembled the format of the show at large. OBC used to be an oasis of difference, an island of alternative ways of seeing compared to the rest of the program, but now it had become frustratingly similar. As Hillary Frey was quicker than anyone else to realize, "The problem isn't that Frey's book is a memoir per se; it's that it's a memoir of addiction, of recovery—and a bad one at that. The books in her club—especially during the 'classics' years—were markedly different from much of the rest of Winfrey's show, which already covers this terrain. With James Frey, the book club is losing its identity as a literary feature, morphing into yet another vehicle for self-help" (Frey 3). Elsewhere in this weirdly prescient article on why *A Million Little Pieces* was "bad news for her viewers and her show," Hillary Frey points out that not only do obsessions with (what turn out to be fabricated) identities and the self-mythologization of the author raise issues of the integrity of the resulting texts (is this good, or do we just like it because it's "real"?), but they also promote damaging and kind of disgusting reading habits. Which is to say they train us to read things in unimaginative, prurient, and indulgent ways.

Hillary Frey rightly observes that:

> A discussion of Frey's work, then, amounts to a discussion of James Frey. On the show—and in their own homes, as they finish their weekly assignments—book clubbers will pick apart

the causes of Frey's addiction and analyze his parents and what they may or may not have done to contribute to his problems . . . Oprah's fans—who have become careful, close readers of literature—will in the end rely on their skills in pop psychology as they try to make something of this memoir. *In other words, the conversation with, or about, James Frey will likely not be about creation, or books or literature,* but about destruction—of Frey's and his friends' and family members' lives. There is something inherently creepy about a million-odd people discussing—over a series of weeks, online and at home—how and why James Frey became a drug addict. And there is something frustrating in that *these debates will take place under the guise of a discussion about a piece of writing.* (Frey, screen 3).

The italics are mine, and I think they emphasize how literary fakery of the type in which James Frey engaged—when it is exposed—points up not only the dishonesty of the supposed "memoirist," but also of us as readers. We say we like something because it's a piece of quality writing, but really we're rubbernecking: our interest is not in the creative product, but just in the supposed fact that the producer of the product suffered and survived some grotesque and horrific ordeal. It's an icky reading practice, and it's especially icky when so many people seem unaware that it's a reading practice at all—like it's so widespread that this is just how people read.

Even worse than this rubbernecking that was apparent at the outset was the way Winfrey seemed—at least temporarily—to be arguing as the scandal went on that truth, the kind we know in our minds, is irrelevant as a lens through which to view, think about, and engage with the world. Readers—even Winfrey herself—suspected with their heads that Frey's story simply could not be true, and perhaps in their brains knew it simply was not that good of a book. One reader, Jody Tressider, left a comment on the *Ploughshares* blog that provided a useful analogy to understand the quality of *A Million Little Pieces,* or lack thereof:

> imagine watching a short confessional film of someone you are plausibly told committed suicide shortly afterwards. You compassionately excuse—of course—everything that's technically

wrong with the film, the lack of focus, the bum-numbing repe-
tition of the visuals, the clichéd infelicities of the auteur—
THAT'S how it felt to read JF before you knew the truth. You
allowed him enormous dispensation from the normal rules just
to endure his prose. I've tried to reread *AMLP*—knowing what I
do now. There is simply nothing to see. (pshares.blogspot.com)

Yet even as these readers' minds told them that Frey's story was probably not entirely true and not entirely artistically worthwhile, in their
hearts they wanted it to be both, believed that it was, and then became
upset when their brains turned out to have been correct in the first
place. The book was not true, and on top of that, it was awful.

Frey himself would likely agree that the life of the mind doesn't
interest him, and that instead the heart—or perhaps the gut—does.
Even though he said at the end of the now famous January 26 show
that, "If I come out of this experience with anything, it's being a better person and learning from my mistakes and making sure that I
don't repeat them,"(Oprah.com) Frey seems still not to get it, and
seems still to be making at least some of the same mistakes. In a
September 2005 interview with the *Guardian*—the first one he'd
given since the fallout—he said, once again harping on his dispro-
portionate disdain for the work of brainy writers Dave Eggers and
David Foster Wallace:

> I mean, it just wasn't relevant, y'know? I think writers and artists
> in general come in two forms: there are thinkers, and feelers.
> And I think those guys are thinkers, their work is about the intel-
> lect. The intellectual gamesmanship, it was all about irony and
> postmodernism and it was very clever. And none of those things
> were things I care about. I care about what I feel and how I feel
> it. So I actually set out to do absolutely the opposite. Strip every-
> thing away. Make it not about intellectualism at all, make it about
> emotional heart. It's like they were making conceptual art, and
> I'm making expressionistic art. (Barton, screen 1)

This brain-heart distinction brings us back to the ideas of bullshit and
truthiness, as well as to why what Winfrey did—essentially declaring
that we cannot blindly accept either one—was so important.

It's important here to pause and make sure we understand fully what "truthiness" is, and therefore why Winfrey's effective censure of it was so admirable and unparalleled. Truthiness as a concept was introduced on the premiere episode of the *Daily Show* spin-off *The Colbert Report* on October 17, 2005. The word means "the quality by which a person claims to know something intuitively, instinctively, or 'from the gut' without regard to evidence, logic, intellectual examination, or actual facts" (wikipedia.com). In other words, "by using the term as part of his satirical routine, Stephen Colbert sought to critique the tendency to rely upon truthiness and its use as an appeal to emotion and tool of rhetoric in contemporary socio-political discourse."

On that inaugural episode of *The Colbert Report,* Colbert actually raised the issue of where books fit into the scheme of the perpetration of truthiness, saying, "I don't trust books. They're all fact, no heart. And that's exactly what's pulling our country apart today. 'Cause face it, folks; we are a divided nation. Not between Democrats and Republicans, or conservatives and liberals, or tops and bottoms. No, we are divided between those who think with their head, and those who *know* with their *heart.*" Colbert went on to use a contemporary example of how this head-heart distinction plays itself out in politics. "Consider Harriet Miers. If you 'think' about Harriet Miers, of course her nomination's absurd. But the president didn't say he 'thought' about his selection." Colbert then played a video clip of Bush declaring, "I know her heart," before continuing, "Notice how he said nothing about her brain? He didn't have to. He 'feels' the truth about Harriet Miers." Finally, Colbert extrapolated on another major recent application of truthiness, asking, "And what about Iraq? If you 'think' about it, maybe there are a few missing pieces to the rationale for war. But doesn't taking Saddam out 'feel' like the right thing?" (wikipedia.com).

Colbert's satire sounds eerily similar to the distinctions made by Frey, no? Only Colbert is being smart and satirical, and Frey appears to be quite serious. These similarities are why I believe that one of the problems with memoir in general and memoir as it was initially presented on *The Oprah Winfrey Show* in particular is that nonfiction, or at least credulously consumed memoir, can be a great validator for people who just want to *know,* and who do not want to *think*—which is a dangerous reading pratice, but also a catastrophically devastating worldview and way to behave as a geopolitical superpower.

For as full of bullshit as Frey was and apparently continues to be, he gets something right, saying in the aforementioned interview that in America, "there are a lot of issues related to truth that are at the forefront of our culture right now because of what happened [in Iraq]," and he feels that some of the furor over his deception stemmed in part from these feelings (Barton, screen 1). And this strikes me as absolutely on target: many of us are having a great deal of anxiety about the truth right now, because our government consistently manipulates, fabricates, and distorts it.

As Ron Suskind wrote in a now oft-quoted article for the *New York Times Magazine* in October of 2004, in the summer of 2002, he had a meeting with an unnamed senior White House adviser who:

> told me something that at the time I didn't fully comprehend—but which I now believe gets to the very heart of the Bush presidency. The aide said that guys like me were "in what we call the reality-based community," which he defined as people who "believe that solutions emerge from your judicious study of discernible reality." I nodded and murmured something about enlightenment principles and empiricism. He cut me off. "That's not the way the world really works anymore," he continued. "We're an empire now, and when we act, we create our own reality. And while you're studying that reality—judiciously, as you will—we'll act again, creating other new realities, which you can study too, and that's how things will sort out. We're history's actors . . . and you, all of you, will be left to just study what we do." (Suskind, screen 1)

After 9/11, the Bush administration seemed to collectively disregard, or worse, to manufacture truth, and this was and continues to be highly alarming.

Comparably disturbing is the way in which a significant proportion of the public has largely gone along with this disregard. We say we want truth, but we expect it to come in a particular package. We say we want honesty, but instead we are given—and in a disquieting number of cases, we accept or at least expect—bullshit. The reading public and the publishing industry crave nonfiction now, and I believe this craving to be at least in part a product of post-9/11 anxieties. After 9/11, we as a nation did not want—and were not encouraged—to think. We did not want, collectively, to engage with a complex other consciousness such as the forces that attacked us, a kind of engagement that I have written elsewhere is encouraged and promulgated by the reading of fiction. We did not want to think in ambiguities or complexities in the way that the best fiction urges us to think. We did not want to think, we wanted to *know*. We wanted to figure out who had done this, find them, and hit them back even harder, which we (sort of) proceeded to do: we hit someone, never mind if it was the people who'd hit us. We wanted to know, as memoir makes some of us feel that we can know. Creative nonfiction— to the nondiscriminating reader, or to the reader who fully trusts his or her genre distinctions (which may or may not be a rather naïve reader, depending on the circumstance)—is a label that tells you that you don't have to worry about novelists who use their pesky creative license to drive you to intricate thought. The label *memoir* signals to some people that they just get to *know* that what they are hearing is true, or is at least "based on a true story" as so many books and films are now advertised, and therefore familiar and comforting instead of provocative and complicated.

Timothy Noah answers the question, "Why should bullshit be so prevalent now?" similarly:

> The obvious answer is the communications revolution. Cable television and the Internet have created an unending demand for information, and there simply isn't enough truth to go around. So, we get bullshit instead. Indeed, there are some troubling signs that the consumer has come to *prefer* bullshit. In choosing guests to appear on cable news, bookers will almost always choose a glib ignoramus over an expert who can't talk in clipped sentences. (Noah, screen 1)

Noah suggests that the Bush administration is far more deeply immersed in bullshit than any previous administration, and asserts that Michael Kinsley, the founding editor of *Slate,* correctly identified the Bush administration's unique brand of lying, or bullshitting, several years ago, explaining that the administration's "lies are often so laughably obvious that you wonder why they bother. Until you realize: They haven't bothered" (screen 1). He adds that, according to bullshit expert Harry Frankfurt's standards, "what Bush does isn't lying at all. It's bullshitting. Whatever you choose to call it, Bush's indifference to the truth is indeed more troubling, in many ways, than what Frankfurt calls 'lying' would be. Richard Nixon *knew* he was bombing Cambodia. Does George W. Bush have a clue that his Social Security arithmetic fails to add up? How can he know if he doesn't care?" (screen 1).

Little wonder then, that in an editorial published on January 27, 2006, the *New York Times* declared, "In a remarkable moment of television, Ms. Winfrey did what we have so often waited for public figures to do: she admitted openly that she had made a mistake in supporting Mr. Frey. Then she did her best to force him, and Ms. Talese, to admit the extent of his deception and the publisher's failure," concluding correctly that, "One expects the language of soft psychology from Ms. Winfrey. That is what we got, instead, from Ms. Talese. Ms. Winfrey gave the audience, including us, what it was hoping for: a demand to hear the truth" (*New York Times* editorial Screen 1). Their assessment of Winfrey's actions is right on target. On January 26, 2006, Winfrey appeared on her own show and presented—honestly, candidly, and humbly—unprecedented exposure of her own vacillations and changes of heart and mind, the workings of her brain and the workings of her book club, as well as the admirable ability to admit her errors and try to correct them. This self-analysis, self-assessment, and self-effacement—for Winfrey looked directly into the cameras and apologized for having "left the impression that the truth does not matter" (Heffernan, screen 1)—made me want to stand up and cheer right there in the TV lounge of the Fine Arts Work Center.

In an interview with Nathan Rabin for *The Onion A.V. Club* on January 25, 2006, Colbert explained, "It used to be, everyone was entitled to their own opinion, but not their own facts. But that's not the case anymore. Facts matter not at all. Perception is everything. It's certainty. People love the President because he's certain of his choices as a leader, even if the facts that back him up don't seem to exist. It's the fact that he's certain that is very appealing to a certain section of the country. I really feel a dichotomy in the American populace. What is important? What you want to be true, or what is true?" (Rabin). Winfrey—admittedly after some deliberation—answered that question in favor of the latter. In doing so, and in doing so in such a public fashion, she raised the level of discourse within the book club and the publishing community, as well as in the broader community at large.

In the disclaimer that Frey was required to compose, which ended up being a three-page essay called "a note to the reader," Frey admits, among other things, that his depiction of himself in *A Million Little Pieces* is of a person "I created in my mind to help me cope" with drug addiction, and that the story, particularly the fabrications, presented "me in ways that made me tougher and more daring and more aggressive than in reality I was, or I am." He adds that, "I sincerely apologize to those readers who have been disappointed by my actions" (Trachtenberg, screen 2).

Evidently, some readers felt so defrauded by Frey's lies that this apology was not enough for them, and in a rather outrageous development in September 2006, it was announced that a lawsuit brought by such readers against Frey and Random House had been resolved. According to the agreement reached, anyone who purchased *A Million Little Pieces* "on or before January 26, the day Frey and his publisher acknowledged that he had made up parts of the book, would be eligible for a refund of the full suggested retail price, regardless of discounts or special sales" (cnn.com "James Frey, publisher settle lawsuit" screen 1). In order to receive these refunds—$23.95 for the hardcover, $14.95 for paperback—"consumers will have to submit a receipt or some other proof of purchase: for the hardcover, page 163; for the paperback, the front cover. They will also need to sign a sworn statement that they bought the book because they believed it was a memoir" (screen 1).

This large-scale payback seems ridiculous, and also somewhat beside the bigger point that Winfrey was trying to convey, which was not that she wanted to make someone pay, but rather that she wanted to make it known that bullshit and truthiness are unacceptable ways in which to view the world. As Winfrey said on the January 26 show, "I read this quote in *The New York Times* from Michiko Kakutani, who said it best, I think. She says, 'This is not about truth in labeling or the misrepresentation of one author. . . . It is a case about how much value contemporary culture places on the very idea of truth.' And I believe that the truth matters" (oprah.com).

The dust from the Frey dust-up appears for the most part to have settled, and Winfrey has—as she always manages to do—moved on. A few days after her now-retracted call to Larry King on Frey's behalf, she picked *Night* by Elie Wiesel as her next OBC book, and thereby reminded her audience of the power of memoir that is honestly and conscientiously rendered. In her announcement of the selection, made on Martin Luther King Jr. Day, she said, "Like Dr. King, I have a dream of my own, too, that the powerful message of this little book would be engraved on every human heart and will never be forgotten again. That you who read this book will feel as I do that these 120 pages should be required reading for all humanity" (oprah.com).

Like countless other followers of OBC, I was pleased when she picked this truly powerful work of nonfiction as a followup to her initial faux-powerful work of quote-unquote nonfiction. Elie Wiesel is a humanitarian, an intellectual force to be reckoned with, and a class act; James Frey is something else entirely. Normally I'd be a member of the try-to-separate-the-artist-from-the-art camp, but in memoir, that's ultimately not possible—which is part of the reason I'd prefer that Winfrey's apparent decision in 2007 to go back to recommending fiction is a permanent one. If she does continue to select memoirs, I hope that Winfrey can find more class acts. People who can do as Wiesel does on Winfrey's website, when he "lends insight to his emotions by making an important distinction. 'The anger here is in me—hate is not,' he says. 'I write and I teach and therefore, I believe anger must be a catalyst'" (oprah.com).

On the televised *Night* segment, which originally aired on May 24, 2006, Winfrey and Wiesel went to Auschwitz together. The section of oprah.com devoted to *Night* explains that, "For Professor Wiesel, this will most likely be his final trip to Auschwitz. 'The death of one child makes no sense,' he says. 'The death of millions—what sense could it make? Except for here, now we *know*. Whenever people could try to conduct such experiments against another people, we must be there to shout and say, 'No, we remember'" (oprah.com).

I agree with both Wiesel and Winfrey that it is important to remember and to learn from the past, and that good memoir can be one of the most effective tools in helping us do so. Yet I nevertheless wish that Winfrey would continue her renewed emphasis on fiction, because that genre helps us remember too, perhaps even more compellingly. Fiction helps us remember not just one life, or one event, but all kinds of themes and proofs of our own humanity. In this way, fiction can operate as the lie that tells the truth. The stories are not true, per se, but the truths they make us consider certainly can be.

In an essay entitled "*Shadowboxing*: An Open Letter to My Students About Captain Violin, Saul Bellow, the War, and the Art of Fiction," Askold Melnyczuk writes that "serious readers" who have "developed the empathic capacity fiction helps cultivate" are essentially more capable of making sense of their own places in the world, and of their places in relation to others who may or may not be incredibly different from them (Melnyczuk). So my argument in favor of Oprah's Book Club returning to its focus on fiction is that in doing so, OBC can maintain and add new life to a culture of fiction reading in the United States. With this culture of fiction reading comes a culture of acknowledging and appreciating the value of the lives of others, and of the value of the practices involved in being an avid appreciator of literature. Some of these practices, I would argue, are analysis, empathy, and the apprehension of the gray areas of life, the situations where things cannot be boiled down to Us versus Them, Good versus Evil. In other words, I agree with what the Word-of-Mouthers wrote in their letter to Winfrey: that fiction can move us in ways few other things can.

At the time of this writing, Winfrey has gone on to select one more memoir—Sidney Poitier's "spiritual autobiography" *The Measure of a Man*—followed by two novels by Cormac McCarthy and Jeffrey

Eugenides respectively. She seems to have renewed her commitment to fiction, a commitment that will be analyzed further in the epilogue. But Winfrey moves in mysterious ways, and as I have remarked throughout the book, her decisions regarding OBC cannot be swayed. I cannot predict what Winfrey's next pick will be, nor can I predict whether she will permanently return to fiction, or whether her next pick might reflect her taste for memoir. Regardless of what she chooses, I remain heartened to know that Winfrey is out there, and that OBC, in whatever shape it shifts to next, is still fighting the good fight for a culture of active readership in a country where the making of meaning has been largely, somewhat scarily, given over to images instead of words.

Doomed World War I poet Wilfred Owen wrote, "All the poet can do is warn." I'm not calling Winfrey a poet, but I am saying that she has managed, throughout the club's more than ten years of existence, to warn us time and again that reading matters. She has reminded us over and over of what good literature—and in some cases bad literature—can make us think and feel and see and do. And in this instance, she has warned us, too, that truth matters, and that without truth and without the act of reading itself, we as a free, humane, democratic society risk suffering an incalculable loss.

EPILOGUE

Gimme Fiction: Oprah Renews Her Interest in the Novel

> "Do you want me to tell you a story?
> No.
> Why not?
> The boy looked at him and looked away.
> Why not?
> Those stories are not true.
> They don't have to be true. They're stories."
>
> —*Cormac McCarthy*, The Road, 2006

> "From an early age they knew what little value the world placed in books, and so didn't waste their time with them. Whereas I, even now, persist in believing that these black marks on white paper bear the greatest significance."
>
> —*Jeffrey Eugenides*, Middlesex, 2002

Technically, I was in Tacoma, Washington, when I learned about Oprah Winfrey's unexpected return to fiction. But in another sense, I was nowhere. And everywhere.

I'm not being coy. I was just on the Internet.

Specifically, I was reading the latest entry on the blog of the Boston-based literary journal *Ploughshares*, a blog of which I am one of the editors. And although I contribute frequently to the blog, and although I am supposed to be an Oprah expert, I must confess that I had allowed my attention on the activities of Oprah's Book Club to wander.

It had been ages since Winfrey had announced her selection of Sidney Poitier's "spiritual autobiography" *The Measure of a Man*. Now, in late March of 2007, I was learning about her new pick not by watching her show, reading a newspaper, or listening to the radio, but rather by mucking around on the Internet, no doubt procrastinating some other task. But there it was, Laura van den Berg's post. Entitled "Oprah Strikes Again," it read:

> No dead authors or fabricated memoirs this time around. Oprah has selected Cormac McCarthy's *The Road* for her book club. This story of a father and son struggling through a post-apocalyptic landscape is brutal, enigmatic, and stunning. Despite having a large readership—*All the Pretty Horses* was immortalized on the screen by Matt Damon and Penélope Cruz—McCarthy is notoriously reclusive, although he has said through his publisher, Knopf, that he will appear on a future episode of Oprah, which will reportedly be his first television interview. While I wonder if some people will complain about McCarthy selling out and going mainstream, I think the exposure this book is getting is great. McCarthy is a wonderful writer and *The Road* deserves as many readers as possible. And now he will get many more than he would have otherwise. The real question is if Oprah's readers will know what the fish mean at the end. (van den Berg, screen 1)

My first reaction to Winfrey's latest selection was, "Cormac McCarthy? In Oprah's Book Club?! No way."

My disbelief was not because I thought that her readers couldn't handle his grim apocalyptic novel, with its roving bands of cannibals, its suicides, its raping, its looting, and its child sex slaves. (Though I have to admit, even I was deeply disturbed to learn, thanks to this book, the meaning of the rightly sinister-sounding word "catamite.") No, after almost sixty OBC selections, there is virtually no subject too off-putting for the more than one million readers who describe themselves as members of Winfrey's online club, not to mention the hundreds of thousands nononline members who simply read and watch (Runyon, screen 1).

I will concede that, at a few points, *The Road* does go a bit over the top in its madness and mayhem, its death and despair, and its unrelenting bleakness of both content and style. In a couple of passages, McCarthy seems to dip perilously close to self-parody, such as:

> They scrabbled through the charred ruins of houses they would not have entered before. A corpse floating in the black water of a basement among the trash and rusting ductwork. He stood in a livingroom partly burned and open to the sky. The waterbuckled boards sloping away into the yard. Soggy volumes in a bookcase. He took one down and opened it and then put it back. Everything damp. Rotting. In a drawer he found a candle. No way to light it. He put it in his pocket. He walked out in the gray light and stood and he saw for a brief moment the absolute truth of the world. The cold relentless circling of the intestate earth. Darkness implacable. The blind dogs of the sun in their running. The crushing black vacuum of the universe. And somewhere two hunted animals trembling like groundfoxes in their cover. Borrowed time and borrowed world and borrowed eyes with which to sorrow it. (McCarthy 130)

But all in all, the book is a quick and compelling read, and McCarthy's command of the sounds and rhythms of language make clear both why Winfrey is drawn to his work and why Harold Bloom considers him to be among the four greatest living American writers, along with Don DeLillo, Phillip Roth, and Thomas Pynchon—all male, of course (Reichgott "Oprah Picks Cormac McCarthy's 'The Road,'" screen 1).

It's no surprise, then, that even with its disconcerting focus on the catastrophic breakdown of civilization as we know it and the potential end of human life on Earth, *The Road* enjoyed the usual post-OBC-selection spike in sales as readers bought and read McCarthy's wonderful downer. Prior to Winfrey's announcement, *The Road* had already spent several weeks on multiple best-seller lists, and according to Nielsen Book Scan, a system that tracks about 70 percent of industry sales, it had sold 138,000 copies in hardcover. According to the Associated Press article on the subject, a paperback hadn't been planned until September 2007, but Vintage bumped up the softcover edition in response to Winfrey's selection "with a massive first printing of 950,000 copies" (screen 1).

Nor did I think that *The Road* didn't fit among the other books on her list, which are, as I have written previously, a diverse and varied lineup of serious literary works in a much wider array of styles and on a much vaster number of subjects than many critics—early ones especially—seem willing to acknowledge. Winfrey herself said at the time of her announcement that *The Road,* a finalist for the National Book Critics Circle Award and eventual Pulitzer winner, was "unlike anything I've ever chosen as a book club selection before because it's post-apocalyptic. [It is] very unusual for me to select this book, but it's fascinating" (screen 1). Yet other critics, National Book Award finalist Jennifer Egan among them, suggest that perhaps *The Road* is not such a departure for OBC as it might initially appear. "Beyond the immediate struggle for survival," Egan writes in a review originally published in Slate.com in 2006, "the deep struggle explored in *The Road* is that of raising a child in a world without hope; and for the boy, the complementary challenge of assuming the responsibilities of manhood in such a world" (Egan, Screen 1). So perceptive was her review that *Slate* ran the piece again immediately following Winfrey's March 2007 announcement, with a new introduction noting that, "Although it's set in a man's world—and is part of a masculine literary tradition— *The Road* is essentially a domestic novel. . . . Sounds right up Oprah's alley." (Egan/Slate, screen 1).

I hesitate to go so far as to say that all of Winfrey's selections are inherently domestic, since her canon has more range than that. But I agree that many of her picks do deal thoughtfully with domestic concerns, and I agree with Egan that *The Road* is among those that do. Beyond its domestic focus, the stylishness and dark subject matter of *The Road* are in keeping with numerous other Winfrey selections, perhaps none more so those of William Faulkner, an author to whom many consider McCarthy a literary heir. Fortunately for McCarthy, Winfrey, and OBC, it should be noted that sales figures for *The Road* were considerably more robust than those for Faulkner were during Winfrey's somewhat anemic "Summer of Faulkner" in 2005.

I should also note that while I respectfully disagree with Winfrey's statement that *The Road* is a particularly unusual pick, I could not agree more with her declaration that "I promise you you'll be thinking about it long after you finish the final page" (Reichgott "Oprah book club's latest pick," screen 1). The novel has a haunting zombie-movie quality, and I love it for that, as well as for its myriad finely rendered details, jolting, unexpected, yet also perfectly appropriate, like the detail about the motorcycle mirror the man attaches to his shopping cart full of scavenged goods in order to watch his back as he and his small son make their way down the eponymous road. The overall effect is gripping, making *The Road* one of many unforgettable and moving books among the more than sixty Winfrey has selected as of the time of this writing.

So the source of my shock at Laura's blog post stemmed not from Winfrey's interest in the book, but rather from the willing participation of its author, owing to McCarthy's notorious aforementioned status as a diehard literary recluse. Sitting before my laptop in Tacoma, I was amazed at Winfrey's ability to track down the man himself in spite of his gruff, taciturn persona, and what a *New York Times* interviewer described as his inclination to prefer talking "about rattlesnakes, molecular computers, country music, Wittgenstein—anything—other than himself or his books" (Woodward, screen 1). Major media appearances of Cormac McCarthy are as rare as sightings of Bigfoot. He's only done two print interviews over the course of his forty-plus-year career, one in the *New York Times* in 1992 and one in *Vanity Fair* in 2005. Even the famously media-shy Thomas Pynchon has lent his voice to an episode of *The Simpsons;* perhaps the only choice more surprising than McCarthy would have been the literary loner to end all literary loners, J. D. Salinger.

Then again, Winfrey does have a modest but impressive track record of getting hermetic geniuses to cooperate with her in the interest of promoting quality literature. Back in June of 2006, she persuaded *To Kill a Mockingbird* author Harper Lee to make a rare print appearance in *O, The Oprah Magazine* with a piece recounting her experiences reading as a child. Not only was Winfrey able to call McCarthy up after reading *The Road,* she was also able, as the eventual televised segment explained, to permit him only a forty-eight-hour window for a response. Exactly two days after she made her request— and because, according to his publicist Paul Bogaards, "Mr. McCarthy respects her work, admires what she has accomplished, has an awareness of her book club, and thought it would be interesting to participate in a conversation with Oprah" (Reichgott "Oprah book club's," screen 1)—McCarthy committed to appearing on her show. On TV. Something he had never done before. Ever. "I went straight to New Mexico before he could change his mind," Winfrey said in the televised piece that aired June 5, 2007.

I'll get into the interview soon. First, I want to quickly touch on my subsequent reactions to the blog post. My next response was less surprised and more pleased, for Winfrey's announcement of *The Road* signified not only that she would be conversing with a literary recluse, but also that they would be conversing about fiction.

As I discuss in depth in the preceding chapter, fiction is important for the ways in which it—more, perhaps, than any other genre— fosters our imaginations and builds our empathic capacities. All too often, memoirs—or at least the kind of victim-narrative tell-alls being promoted by the big trade publishing houses today—sacrifice good writing for the sake of outrageous stories. So too do they sacrifice honesty for the same reason. As the next OBC-selected fiction writer, Jeffrey Eugenides, has his protagonist Calliope Stephanides observe, very often, "real life doesn't live up to writing about it" (Eugenides 189). Due to tremendous pressure from agents, editors, and publishers—over all of whom market forces hold sway—many memoirists find themselves at least tacitly encouraged to fabricate their tales for the sake of salability.

This creepy desire in the world of trade publishing for ostensibly true work—especially for lurid, confessional sob stories about disability and abuse and eating disorders and depression and so forth—is a dangerous drift. Often, these memoirs are hailed in blurbs and reviews for their honesty and fearlessness, as if the authors are noble for having written the books, just as the readers are noble for reading them. But there is something vampiric about this trend, as if audience members are being encouraged to feast ickily but self-righteously on the outsized sufferings of others. Also, this preference seems to suggest that if one hasn't experienced these colossal landmarks of suffering—if, for instance, one's life is more nuanced, complex, and subtle—it's somehow not interesting or serious.

Fiction, on the other hand, at least the kind of fiction Winfrey has shown herself to favor, allows for just such complexity and nuance, and permits its readers to be more sympathetic and less cannibalistic in their responses to the experiences of their fellow human beings. *Middlesex,* for instance, Winfrey's second pick since OBC's apparent return to fiction, even contains a refutation of the idea of memoiristic writing as serving an automatically brave or therapeutic function. Calliope Stephanides, the intersexual protagonist, remarks, "It occurred to me today that I'm not as far along as I thought. Writing my story isn't the courageous act of liberation I had hoped it would be. Writing is solitary, furtive, and I know all about those things" (Eugenides 319). Smart protagonist, that Cal(lie). And I'd say that she, as a fictional person, makes a more successful—not to mention more hilarious and entertaining—argument for understanding than having OBC members read an intersexual memoir, or having an in-studio panel of hermaphrodites onstage to attempt the same.

The Oprah Book Club web pages devoted to discussion of Eugenides's novel also do their part to encourage people to understand that good writers use their imaginations, and that good readers should feel free to do the same. "What are the most unusual questions you've been asked about *Middlesex?*" asks one of the Q's in the extensive *Middlesex* Q and A section. "They usually involve my pants," replies Eugenides. "People want me to remove them. It's difficult to convince some people that I make things up for a living. They think all this really happened to me, which it didn't." (Oprah.com)

Beyond fiction's obvious ability to fight the good fight in favor of imagination and creativity, nonfiction doesn't currently need Winfrey's help to find a readership, whereas fiction stands to benefit more from her Midas touch. Winfrey struck a blow against "truthiness" with her selection of McCarthy's novel, and seems—for now—to have wisely returned to the honest lie of fiction, turning her back on the actual lies and sensationalism of so much memoir being promoted today.

I'll have more on Eugenides soon, but for now, I want to touch on the last, but not the least of my reactions to Laura's blog post. Part of the function of the *Ploughshares* blog is to get people talking. Our tag line, after all, promises "ramblings, gossip, and disinformation about the literary world from the staff readers and editors of *Ploughshares*." One surefire way to provoke people to post comments is to get them riled up. So I understand where Laura was coming from in terms of being a solid blog editor, but her final sentence, "The real question is if Oprah's readers will know what the fish mean at the end" struck me as a cheap shot. To my delight, the very first comment, by a blogger named "hermit greg," retorted, "I wouldn't limit the question of the fish to Oprah's readers alone."

I am pleased to report that now, after over a dozen years of recommending estimable books, and just as many years of runaway popular acclaim, it seems as though Winfrey's club is at last beginning to enjoy the critical respect it has deserved all along. Finally, the self-appointed literary elite have allowed themselves to take an honest look at the history and influence of OBC and admit that Winfrey's literary project is intelligent and worthwhile, and even that OBC readers can be as smart as they consider themselves to be.

Sure, there are those such as the members of the Williamsburg Book Club who still feel the need to tell the world that they are hipper than Oprah. These people do not spend all that money on their apartments in one of Brooklyn's most self-consciously artistic neighborhoods to be mistaken for the hoi polloi. "We've chosen *Middlesex* by Jeffrey Eugenides, winner of the Pulitzer Prize. (Okay, and maybe an Oprah book selection, too . . . peel the sticker off and get on with it.)" says the online posting advertising its August 13, 2007, meeting.

But for the most part, even hipsters feel secure acknowledging, as a blogger named Scotter does on the *Detroit Metro* blog, that "Oprah doesn't pick crappy books for her book club." Scotter also remarks that "As for Oprah, yeah, I know. I too was a hater. And although I'm no longer a hater, I'm still not much of a liker." In fairness, there remains plenty to criticize about *The Oprah Winfrey Show* itself. But by now, OBC should no longer fall victim to prejudices or assumptions that have more to do with the talk show than with

Winfrey's literary project. For the most part, it no longer does; more and more non-OBC members are beginning to acknowledge the beneficial influence of OBC. Except, that is, for a few stragglers and high-brow holdouts—some of whom, to my chagrin, happen to be among my close friends.

Here I need to flash back to yet another discovery of an OBC selection via the blogosphere. On June 5, 2007, the same day as her landmark interview with McCarthy, Winfrey announced her summer selection, declaring, "I promise it will grab you from the first sentence." Once again, I didn't learn this via the show itself, since I was driving cross-country from Tacoma to Chicago at the time, and planned to watch the interview—multiple times—through the Oprah.com website later. No, it was once again the trusty *Ploughshares* blog that alerted me to Winfrey's latest pick.

This time, I was surprised less by the choice of author and book—*Middlesex,* a Pulitzer prize-winning epic, tragicomic family saga of self-discovery, is logical fit with Winfrey's list—and more by the way the news was delivered to me. In a post entitled "Cannon ball!" my coeditor Elisa Gabbert concluded, "And can I just say that I hate when books I like get made into movies or land on Oprah's bedside table" (Gabbert, screen 1). She was of course referring to *Middlesex.* I sat in front of my laptop, trying to convince myself she was just being provocative, and that I didn't have to rise to the bait. My self-restraint lasted for about thirty seconds before I jumped in and added the first comment: "You know where I stand on the whole Oprah thing, but I still have to ask: *why* do you hate it when good books get picked for OBC (which, I might add, happens quite frequently, and has been happening for over 10 years now)?"

This kicked off a lively twenty-three-comment debate, which evoked a range of responses. The poet Chris Tonelli, another coeditor, replied, "It's because they get lumped in with crap. She equates GAP CREEK by Robert Morgan with Morrison's BELOVED. This confuses the America that watches TV at 4pm." I resisted the urge to point out that he was actually among the confused, since *Beloved* was never an OBC selection. But I couldn't resist coming back with the question, "How do you know they're confused? How can you lump millions of people together and say they're all the same, which is to say dumb and undiscriminating? That's inaccurate and unfair."

Several comments later, Elisa returned with "Chris's answer is pretty good, about lumping crap and non-crap together in a false category. It just seems like a meaningless stamp of approval. I don't get why Oprah is qualified to tell people what to read," prompting me to say, "I don't see how anybody is qualified or disqualified to tell someone else what to read. Your cabdriver might tell you what to read, and you can take his recommendation or leave it. Who do you think *is* qualified, and what exactly are the qualifications?" Even the managing editor of the journal, Rob Arnold, weighed in, deciding, "Oprah's an avid reader who uses some portion of her vast wealth to promote reading mainly-good fiction to the general public. That sticker means sales, not prestige, in the publishing industry. If Oprah were choosing the National Book Award, I'd worry maybe. But shouldn't we be encouraging other media moguls to follow suit? Shouldn't we, as writers, welcome the Keilors [sic] and Winfreys of the world who push their favorite books/poems (some of which are our own favorite books/poems too) to their sizable audiences? Oprah has a pretty good track record for mixing interesting fiction into her book lists. That fact alone gives me faith in her qualification (or her staff's qualifications) for telling people what to read."

And so on, back and forth, until we exhausted ourselves on the subject and agreed to disagree. I've said it for many pages and many years now, but I'll say again it one more time: Oprah Winfrey is a smart reader who picks smart books for a smart audience. I realize that it is neither possible, nor even necessary, to convince every person in the world of this fact, but I do wish that those individuals—including my blogging friends—who still hold a hostile opinion of OBC could be more open to and less insecure about Winfrey's literary project.

And speaking yet again of blogs, you've probably noticed by now that I've been leaning rather heavily on them for supporting material in this chapter. I have been. This is not because I'm a lazy researcher, but rather because these are the sources where the material can be found, and where debate on these topics is taking place.

When Winfrey chose Gabriel García Márquez's 1988 novel *Love in the Time of Cholera*—her second Marquez pick, after her selection of *100 Years of Solitude* back in 2004—in October 2007, searching for information on the subject proved, as usual of late, to be a study in media consolidation. I found the same AP wire story all over the web, popping up on links in every major American newspaper from the *Chicago Tribune* to the *Washington Post*. "If you love love, this book is the best love story ever," they all quoted Winfrey as saying. "Vintage Books, a paperback imprint of Random House Inc., announced a new printing of 750,000 copies for the novel, and an additional 30,000 for the original Spanish-language text," some of them—the ones that didn't get truncated by space-saving editors—added (AP News). The only individual viewpoints providing opinions or analyses of the latest OBC pick came from the blogosphere.

"Gabriel García Márquez? Oprah picked Gabriel García Márquez? An author who's won the Nobel Prize? Who's got a movie coming out next month? Who's already been an Oprah pick? Good God," ranted novelist Jennifer Weiner, on her aptly named blog SnarkSpot. "Could Oprah have tapped a book, or an author, who's got more going for it, and for him?" she wondered. "Is there anyone left in America who hasn't heard of García Márquez, or who wouldn't have heard of him once the movie promotion swung into gear? Seriously, what's the Girlfriend Of Us All going to choose next? The Bible? " (Weiner).

Meanwhile, over on Vivir Latino, whose motto is "US Latino Life in Blog Form," it was more sour grapes, delivered with less wit and more anger. The post was headlined "Oprah 'discovers' García Márquez" and was dated, fittingly, Monday, October 8, the federal holiday in honor of Columbus's having "discovered" America. "It is so beautifully written that it really takes you to another place in time and will make you ask yourself—how long could you, or would you, wait for love?" the post author quoted Winfrey as saying during Friday's announcement of the novel. "I can almost hear Oprah saying that last line, her hypnotic voice leading the Anglo women of America to their local Barnes and Noble for a copy," Jennifer Woodard Maderazo seethed before dismissing the *Cholera* selection as "pure PR and marketing, as the movie version of the book is set to premiere next month" (Maderazo). And that was about it, in terms of lively, provocative, opinionated coverage of Winfrey's most recent selection.

Mainstream print coverage of both Oprah's Book Club and—even more dishearteningly—books in general has been on a dramatic decline in America of late.

Observing this phenomenon in *Blog Critics* magazine, Ted Gioia writes of Winfrey's selection of Eugenides's novel, "Now Oprah's club will have its chance at this rich work. The attention has already pushed *Middlesex* up to the sixth position on Amazon's best seller list. God bless Oprah for continuing to promote quality fiction at a time when newspapers are slashing their book review pages and publishers are retrenching. The smart money says that, after a taste of Eugenides' great writing, more than a few readers will turn off the television and start checking out the action on the library shelves."

The National Book Critics Circle is among many organizations concerned about the threat this decline poses to the health of American culture. "We're getting tired of it," writes NBCC president John Freeman on the group's website:

> We're tired of watching individual voices from local communities passed over for wire copy. We're tired of book editors with decades of experience shown the exit. We're tired of shrinking reviews. We're tired of hearing newspapers fret and worry over the future of print while they dismantle the section of the paper which deals most closely with the two things which have kept them alive since the dawn of printing presses: the public's hunger for knowledge and the written word. (Freeman, screen 1).

As an individual voice in a local community myself, I sympathize with their worry and their weariness. And I commend their efforts in launching a "Campaign to Save Book Reviews" in response to, for example, the *Atlanta Journal-Constitution*'s firing of their books editor and the *Los Angeles Times*'s folding its stand-alone book review into another section of the paper. But to date it does not appear as though they have been able to save much of anything, and individual voices find themselves speaking more and more on the virtual pages of the Internet as opposed to the inky printed ones of the newspaper.

Yet even as literary criticism and discussion moves to the blogosphere, many bloggers themselves acknowledge that this is an unfortunate development, highlighting a further decline in the relevance of literature to American culture. Critic Adam Kirsch, a sometime contributor to the online journal *Contemporary Poetry Review,* writes that "the future of literary culture does not lie with blogs—or at least, it shouldn't. The blog form, that miscellany of observations, opinions, and links, is not well-suited to writing about literature, and it is no coincidence that there is no literary blogger with the audience and influence of the top political bloggers" (Kirsch, screen 1). He continues, "Literary criticism is only worth having if it at least strives to be literary in its own right, with a scope, complexity, and authority that no blogger I know even wants to achieve. The only useful part of most book blogs, in fact, are the links to long-form essays and articles by professional writers, usually from print journals" (screen 1).

I do not share his entirely dim view of blogs, but I do wish that blogs could be more of a supplement to—and not a substitute for—other sources of news and dialogue about literature in America. And I want to point out that even as book sections get cut or folded into entertainment sections, one mainstream source of literary discussion and promotion remains powerfully independent and influential, and that, of course, is Oprah's Book Club. Obviously, OBC is not a reviewing outlet, but it is a source of news and insight for millions of Americans on books and authors. Winfrey herself knows that she is not serving the function of a writer, or a book reviewer, and she is fine with that.

Early in her vaunted televised interview with Cormac McCarthy, she illustrates her comfort with her role. In response to a question from Winfrey about his reclusive behavior—"It's nothing against the press or the media?" she asks—he replies, "You work your side of the street and I'll work mine."

This comment may look harsh in writing, but McCarthy delivered it with a smile, and Winfrey replied in kind. She knows, she seemed to be saying, exactly how to work her side of the street, and she works it in a way that no one else possibly could. She must know, too, that she is serving a much-needed function, not just with these televised segments, but also with the online written components of OBC, which began to flower with her turn to the classics, and have continued to bloom now with her return to contemporary fiction.

The complementary materials—the discussion boards, the summaries, the reading schedules, the synopses, the interview, the Q and A's, and the special topics—that abound on the book club section of her Oprah.com website are thorough, thought-provoking, and comprehensive in a way that few blogs, and few newspaper book reviews for that matter, bother to be. A curious reader of *Middlesex,* for example, can get happily lost amid information on genetics and gender as they relate to the experiences of the novel's intersexual protagonist. So too can that reader learn what Eugenides has to say about his experience winning the Pulitzer Prize and grappling with the ethereal notions of fame and success. Readers can write in with their own responses and questions, and many of them do, crafting complex queries such as the following from a Jessica F. who is struggling with the best way to describe the novel to other inquisitive readers. "I have been an absolute fanatic about this book for about five years now," she begins:

> As a part-time library clerk, full-time second-hand bookstore owner and overtime avid reader, I am constantly recommending *Middlesex* to other readers—but I can't ever say what it is about because it is so epic in scope. I usually end up saying something like, "Well, the flap copy says it is about a hermaphrodite—but it's really not . . ." Not the best description to get others to read it! I am curious how you explained this book (prior to its current status) to those who asked what it was about? (Oprah.com)

And Jessica's discerning question is just one of many on the site.

All this is not to say that Oprah's Book Club is perfect, nor that it is the sole solution to the problem of what to do to promote active readership in an America whose newspapers at least seem to have little time to spend on literature. There are still questions to be asked of the club and criticisms to be raised, and the fact that individuals

---

continue to raise them speaks to the lively position OBC currently occupies on the public stage. With Winfrey's return to fiction, for instance, there has been speculation as to whether perhaps her latest shift is a bid to recover from the James Frey fiasco. So too has there been some grumbling about the fact that her two most recent picks have been by white men—established, Pulitzer Prize-winning white men, at that.

OBC is such a rich phenomenon that I could go on and on in this chapter, in this book, examining more of its many aspects. But I'll stop here and leave that for my fellow readers to continue.

For now, I'll close with one of my favorite exchanges from Winfrey's interview with Cormac McCarthy, an interview in which both of them strike me as totally charming. Neither of them is posing or posturing, neither he as the Great Writer, nor she as the Great Reader. They are each doing their best to behave authentically as two people committed to having a decent televised discussion of literature.

In response to Winfrey's question about his passion for his vocation, McCarthy laughs shyly, seems to sink even lower in his chair, and replies:

> I don't know. Passion . . . it sounds like a pretty fancy word. I like what I do, and I suppose I . . . some writers have said in print that they hated writing, it was a chore and a burden, and I certainly don't feel that way about it. Sometimes it's difficult. You always have this image of the perfect thing, which you can never achieve, but which you never stop trying to achieve. But I think at the core of it there's this image you have, this interior image, of something that is absolutely perfect, and that's your signpost, your guide. You'll never get there, but without it, you won't get anywhere.

Winfrey has helped us as readers get somewhere. For over a dozen years now, she has done her best to accomplish what perhaps in her mind was this perfect thing, this way to help serious literary works reach a serious audience, and to help awaken hundreds of thousands of people to the pleasures of reading. Neither the journey nor the destination has ever been perfect, but the somewhere she's been trying to take us has always been worth attempting to reach.

APPENDIX A

The Oprah Books In Order of Selection for the Club

Mitchard, Jacquelyn. *The Deep End of the Ocean.* New York: Penguin Group, 1996. Selected September 1996.

Morrison, Toni. *Song of Solomon.* 1977. London: Vintage / Random House, 1998. Selected October 1996.

Hamilton, Jane. *The Book of Ruth.* 1988. London: Black Swan, 1997. Selected November 1996.

Lamb, Wally. *She's Come Undone.* New York: Washington Square Press Pocket Books, Simon and Schuster, 1992. Selected January 1997.

Hegi, Ursula. *Stones From the River.* New York: Scribner Paperback Fiction, Simon and Schuster, 1994. Selected February 1997.

Reynolds, Sheri. *The Rapture of Canaan.* New York: Berkeley Books, 1995. Selected April 1997.

Angelou, Maya. *The Heart of a Woman.* 1981. London: Virago Press, Little, Brown and Company, 1998. Selected May 1997.

Morris, Mary McGarry. *Songs in Ordinary Time.* New York: Penguin Books, 1996. Selected June 1997.

Gaines, Ernest. *A Lesson Before Dying.* New York: Random House Vintage Contemporaries, 1993. Selected September 1997.

Gibbons, Kaye. *A Virtuous Woman.* 1989. New York: Random House Vintage Books, 1990. Selected October 1997.

———. *Ellen Foster.* 1987. London: Virago of Little, Brown and Company, 1998. Selected October 1997.

Cosby, Bill. *The Best Way to Play.* New York: Cartwheel Books, 1997. Selected December 1997.

———. *The Treasure Hunt.* New York: Cartwheel Books, 1997. Selected December 1997.

———. *The Meanest Thing to Say.* New York: Cartwheel Books, 1997. Selected December 1997.

Morrison, Toni. *Paradise.* New York: Alfred A. Knopf, 1998. Selected January, 1998.

Hoffman, Alice. *Here On Earth.* 1997. London: Random House Vintage, 1998. Selected March 1998.

Quindlen, Anna. *Black and Blue.* New York: Random House, 1998. Selected April 1998.

Danticat, Edwidge. *Breath, Eyes, Memory*. 1994. New York: Random House Vintage, 1998. Selected May 1998.

Lamb, Wally. *I Know This Much Is True*. New York: HarperCollins, 1998. Selected June 1998.

Cleage, Pearl. *What Looks Like Crazy On an Ordinary Day*. New York: Avon Books, Inc., 1997. Selected September 1998.

Bohjalian, Chris. *Midwives*. 1997. New York: Random House Vintage, 1998. Selected October 1998.

Letts, Billie. *Where the Heart Is*. 1995. New York: Warner Books, 1996. Selected December 1998.

Lott, Bret. *Jewel*. 1991. New York: Washington Square Press, Simon and Schuster, 2000. Selected January 1999.

Schlink, Bernard. *The Reader*. London: Phoenix House, 1997. Selected February 1999.

Shreve, Anita. *The Pilot's Wife*. 1998. New York: Little, Brown and Company, 1999. Selected March 1999.

Fitch, Janet. *White Oleander*. London: Virago, Little, Brown and Company, 1999. Selected May 1999.

Haynes, Melinda. *Mother of Pearl*. 1999. New York: Washington Square Press Pocket Books, Simon and Schuster, 2000. Selected June 1999.

Binchy, Maeve. *Tara Road*. 1998. New York: Random House, 1999. Selected September 1999.

Clarke, Breena. *River, Cross My Heart*. New York: Little, Brown and Company, 1999. Selected October 1999.

Ansay, A. Manette. *Vinegar Hill*. 1994. New York: Harper Collins Avon Books, 1998. Selected November 1999.

Hamilton, Jane. *A Map of the World*. New York: Anchor Doubleday, 1994. Selected December 1999.

Morgan, Robert. *Gap Creek*. New York: Algonquin Books of Chapel Hill/ Workman Publishing, 1999. Selected January 2000.

Allende, Isabelle. *Daughter of Fortune*. New York: Harper Collins, 1999. Selected February 2000.

O'Dell, Tawni. *Back Roads*. New York: Viking Penguin, 2000. Selected March 2000.

Morrison, Toni. *The Bluest Eye*. 1970. New York: Penguin Books, 2000. Selected April 2000.

Miller, Sue. *While I Was Gone*. London: Bloomsbury, 2000. Selected May 2000.

Kingsolver, Barbara. *The Poisonwood Bible*. New York: Harper Collins, 1999. Selected June 2000.

Berg, Elizabeth. *Open House*. New York: Random House, 2000. Selected August 2000.

Schwarz, Christina. *Drowning Ruth*. New York: Doubleday Random House, 2000. Selected September 2000.

Dubus III, Andre. *House of Sand and Fog*. 1999. New York: Vintage, Random House, 2000. Selected November 2000.

Oates, Joyce Carol. *We Were the Mulvaneys*. New York: Plume / Penguin Group, 1997. Selected January 2001.

Rubio, Gwyn Hyman. *Icy Sparks*. 1998. New York: Penguin Books, 1999. Selected March 2001.

Oufkir, Malika. *Stolen Lives*. New York: Miramax, 2002 (paperback ed.) Selected May 2001.

Tademy, Lalita. *Cane River*. New York: Warner Books, Inc., 2001. Selected June 2001.

Franzen, Jonathan. *The Corrections*. New York: Farrar, Strauss, and Giroux, 2001. Selected October 2001.

Mistry, Rohinton. *A Fine Balance*. New York: Vintage International, Random House, 1995. Selected November 2001.

McDonald, Ann-Marie. *Fall on Your Knees*. New York: Simon and Schuster, 1996. Selected January 2002.

Morrison, Toni. *Sula*. 1973. New York: Alfred A. Knopf, 2001. Selected April 2002.

Steinbeck, John. *East of Eden*. 1952. New York: Penguin USA, 2003. Selected June 2003.

Paton, Alan. *Cry the Beloved Country*. 1948. New York: Simon and Schuster, 2003. Selected September 2003.

Márquez, Gabriel García. *One Hundred Years of Solitude*. 1970. New York: Harper Perennial, 2004. Selected February 2004.

McCullers, Carson. *The Heart is a Lonely Hunter*. 1940. New York: Houghton Mifflin, 2004. Selected April 2004.

Tolstoy, Leo. Trans. Pevear, Richard and Volokhonsky, Larissa. *Anna Karenina: A Novel in Eight Parts*. Penguin Books: New York, 2002. Selected May 2004.

Buck, Pearl S. *The Good Earth*. 1931. New York: Washington Square Press, 2004. Selected September 2004.

Faulkner, William. *As I Lay Dying*. 1930. New York: Vintage Books Box Set, 2005. Selected Summer 2005.

———. *The Sound and the Fury*. 1929.

———. *A Light in August*. 1932.

Frey, James. *A Million Little Pieces*. 2003. New York: Anchor, 2005. Selected September 2005.

Wiesel, Elie. *Night*. 1958. New York: Hill and Wang; Revised Edition, 2006. Selected January 2006.

Poitier, Sidney. *The Measure of a Man: a Spiritual Autobiography*. 2000. San Francisco: HarperSanFrancisco, 2006. Selected January 2007.

McCarthy, Cormac. *The Road*. 2006. New York: Vintage Books, 2007. Selected March 2007.

Eugenides, Jeffrey. *Middlesex*. 2002. New York: Picador, 2007. Selected June 2007.

Márquez, Gabriel García. *Love in the Time of Cholera*. 1985. New York: Vintage Reprint Edition, 2007. Selected October 2007.

Follet, Ken. *The Pillars of the Earth*. 1989. New York: NAL Trade, 2007. Selected November 2007.

BIBLIOGRAPHY

Abbott, Charlotte. "Oprah taps Faulkner." *Publishers Weekly* 6 June 2006 http://www.publishersweekly.com/article/CA606196.html?pub-date=6%2F6%2F2005&display=archive

Abramson, Marla et. al. "Ten People Who Decide What America Reads." *Book* magazine July-August 2001: 37–41.

Allen, Brooke. "The Promised Land." Rev. of *Paradise,* by Toni Morrison. *New York Times Book Review.* 11 Jan. 1998: 6.

Angel, Karen. "Starbucks Has Strong Showing With Oprah Books." *Publishers Weekly* 10 Nov. 1997: 21.

AP News. "Marquez's 'Cholera' is Oprah's latest book pick: Winfrey says Nobel winner's tome is one of greatest love stories she's read." 5 Oct. 2007. http://www.msnbc.msn.com/id/21150387/

Arnold, Martin. "For Readers, Online Clubs." *New York Times* 28 June 2001: E3.

Baker, Jeff. "Oprah's Stamp of Approval Rubs Writer in Conflicted Ways." 12 Oct. 2001. http://www.oregonian.com.

Barrientos, Tanya. "Unconventional Wisdom: Reading Drives Need Oprah's Fire." *The Philadelphia Inquirer* 27 Apr. 2002. 20 July 2002 http://www.philly.com/mld/inquirer/news/columnists/3149970.html.

Barton, Laura. "The Man Who Rewrote His Life" the *Guardian* 15 Sept. 2006 http://books.guardian.co.uk/news/articles/0,,1873009,00.html

Bauer, Susan Wise. "Oprah's Misery Index." *Christianity Today* 7 Dec. 1998: 70–74.

Bayard, Louis. "The Soundbite and the Fury." Salon.com 23 Apr. 2003 http://dir.salon.com/story/mwt/feature/2003/04/19/frey/index.html

Bayles, Martha. "Imus, Oprah, and the Literary Elite." *New York Times Book Review* 29 Aug. 1999: 35.

BBC News. "Harper Lee makes print appearance." 28 June 2006 http://news.bbc.co.uk/2/hi/entertainment/5122376.stm

Beha, Chris. "Oprah and the dregs." Huffington Post 19 June 2007 http://www.huffingtonpost.com/chris-beha/oprah-and-the-dregs_b_52911.html

Berg, Elizabeth. Letter to the author. 29 June 2001.

Blais, Jacqueline. "Oprah's the Toast of Book Publishers." *USA Today* 11 Feb. 1999: 4D.

———. "Oprah Tackles Hefty 'Anna Karenina'. *USA Today.* http://www.usatoday.com/life/books/news/2004-06-09-oprah-anna_x.htm. screen 1. 9 June 2004. 11 June 2004.

Bloom, Harold. "Dumbing Down American Readers." http://www.boston.com/news/globe/editorial_opinion/oped/-articles/2003/09/24/dumbing_down_american_readers?mode=PF. 24 Sept. 2003. 2 June 2004

Bohjalian, Chris. Postcard to Author. 6 Nov. 2001.

"The Bookseller: Conflicted About the Hype Machine." *Bookseller* 9 Nov. 2001: 22.

Bordieu, Pierre. *The Field of Cultural Production: Essays on Art and Literature (European Perspectives)*. New York: Columbia University Press, 1993.

———. *Distinction: a Social Critique of the Judgement of Taste*. Cambridge: Harvard University Press, 2002.

Canellos, Peter S. "Popular Winfrey Looks Beyond TV." *Boston Globe* 29 May 1997: 1A.

Carey, John. "Enquiry." E-mail to the author. 5 Nov. 2001.

———.*The Intellectuals and the Masses: Pride and Prejudice among the Literary Intelligentsia, 1880–1939*. London: Faber and Faber, Ltd., 1992.

———. *Pure Pleasure: A Guide to the 20th Century's Most Enjoyable Books*. London: Faber and Faber, 2000.

Carr, David "Oprahness trumps truthiness." *New York Times* 30 Jan. 2006 http://select.nytimes.com/search/restricted/article?res=F50A14FD355B0C738FDDA80894DE404482

Chevannes, Ingrid, McEvoy, Dermot, and Simson, Maria. "Oprah's Tender Takeover of Paperbacks." *Publishers Weekly* 23 Mar. 1998: 56.

Chin, Paula. "Touched by an Oprah." *People Weekly* 20 Dec. 1999: 112–122.

Cleage, Pearl. "Pearl Cleage Responses to Oprah Book Club Questions." E-mail to the author. 24 Aug. 2001.

Clementson, Lynette. "Oprah on Oprah." *Newsweek* 8 Jan. 2001: 38–48.

Cloud, Dana L. "Hegemony or Concordance? The Rhetoric of Tokenism in 'Oprah' Winfrey's Rags-to-Riches Biography." *Critical Studies in Mass Communication* 14 (June 1996): 115-137.

CNN.com "Winfrey stands behind 'Pieces author: writer has been accused of exaggerating memoir." 12 Jan. 2006 http://www.cnn.com/2006/SHOW-BIZ/books/01/11/frey.lkl/

———. "Oprah to author: 'You conned us all.'" 27 Jan. 2006. http://www.cnn.com/2006/SHOWBIZ/books/01/27/oprah.frey/index.html

———. "James Frey, publisher settle lawsuit." 7 Sept. 2006. http://www.cnn.com/2006/SHOWBIZ/books/09/07/authorlies.settlement.ap/index.html

Colford, Paul. "Tolstoy top seller, thanks to Oprah." http://www.nydailynews.com/business/story/201661p-174030c.html. 11 June 2004. 11 June 2004.

Conklin, Mike, and Mills, Marja. "Winfrey Turns Page in Cutting Book Picks." *Chicago Tribune*. 6 Apr. 2002: 1, 14.

Coomes, Mark. "Literary Eyes Focus on Oprah's Version of 'Classics.'" *Olympian* 24 Aug. 2003. 26 Oct. 2003 http://www.theolympian.com/home/news/20030824/living/83303.shtml.

Crossen, Cynthia. "Read Them and Weep: Misery, Pain, Catastrophe, Despair . . . and That's Just the First Chapter." *Wall Street Journal* 13 July 2001: W15.

Daspin, Eileen. "The Tyranny of the Book Group: Scores of Once-Genteel Groups Have Degenerated into Infighting, One-Upmanship and Shear Social Terror." *Wall Street Journal* 15 Jan. 1999: W1.

Davidson, Cathy, ed. *Reading in America: Literature and Social History*. Baltimore: Johns Hopkins University Press, 1989.

"Deconstruct This: Jonathan Franzen and Oprah, a Novelist, a Talk-Show Host, and Literature High and Low." *Chronicle of Higher Education* 30 Nov. 2001: B4.

Dedman, Bill. "Amazon.com's Oprah-Opera Oops." *Chicago Sun Times* 26 Feb. 2001: 5.

DeMoraes, Lisa. "Same Plot, Different Setting: 'Today' adopts Oprah's Book Club idea." *Washington Post* 9 Apr. 2002. 16 Apr. 2002 http://www.washingtonpost.com.

DiCarlo, Lisa. "Ye Oprah Book Club Returneth." Forbes.com 27 Feb. 2003. 26 Oct. 2003 http://www.forbes.com/2003/02/27/cx_ld_0227 bookclub.html.

Donahue, Deirdre. "Steinbeck on Oprah? He Would be 'Tickled.'" *USA Today* 26 June 2003. 26 June 2003 http://www.usatoday.com.

"Dumbing Up (How Oprah Winfrey Has Influenced People to Read More Through Her Television Show)." *The Economist* 17 Oct. 1998: 76.

Egan, Jennifer. "Why Oprah Picked The Road: Why here new book club selection isn't as surprising as you think." Slate.com 29 Mar. 2007 http://www.slate.com/id/2162975/

Eugenides, Jeffrey. "Eugenides Q and A." Oprah.com http://www.oprah.com/obc_classic/featbook/middlesex/qa/middlesex_qa_01.jhtml

Farley, Christopher John. "Queen of All Media." *Time* 5 Oct. 1998: 82–84.

Fitzgerald, Kate. "Inside Oprah's Book Club." *Writer's Digest* Oct. 2000: 24–27.

"Forbes 400." Forbes.com 18 Sep. 2003. http://www.forbes.com/richlist2003/rich400land.html

Forster, E.M. *Aspects of the Novel*. 1927. New York: Harcourt Inc, 1985.

Fowler, Geoffrey. "For This Summer's Hottest Books, Readers Head for Nonfiction Section." *Wall Street Journal* 18 Jul. 2001: B1.

Frankfurt, Harry G. *On Bullshit*. Princeton: Princeton University Press, 2005.

Franzen, Jonathan. "Perchance to Dream: In the Age of Images, a Reason to Write Novels." *Harper's Magazine* Apr. 1996: 35-54.

———. "Meet Me in St. Louis: A Writer's Televised Homecoming." *New Yorker* 24 & 31 Dec. 2000: 70–75.

———. Letter to the author. 6 December 2001.

"Franzen's Dilemma." *Flak* magazine 26 Oct. 2001. 20 Dec. 2001 http://www.flakmag.com/opinion/franzen.html.

Freeman, John. "The National Book Critics Circle's Campaign to Save Book Reviews." http://www.bookcritics.org/?go=saveBookReviews

Freeman, Judith. "Blessed Are the Ordinary." Rev. of *Jewel,* by Bret Lott. *New York Times Book Review.* 1 Mar. 2001: 21.

Frey, Hillary. "Oprah's book flub" Salon.com 11 Oct. 2005 http://dir.salon.com/story/books/feature/2005/10/11/frey/index.html

Gabbert, Elisa. "Cannon ball!" *Ploughshares* blog 8 June 2007 http://pshares.blogspot.com/2007_06_01_archive.html

Gamerman, Amy. "Behind the Scenes at Oprah's Book Club." *Wall Street Journal* 8 Apr. 1997: A20–21.

Garner, Dwight. "Inside the List." *New York Times* 5 Oct 2005 http://www.nytimes.com/2005/10/09/books/review/09tbr.html?ex=11 56737600&en=f9f129633e8803df&ei=5070

———. "This Old House." *New York Times Book Review.* 10 Oct. 1999: 10.

Gates, David. "She Speaks Volumes." *Newsweek Special Edition.* 1996: 76–77.

Gerzina, Gretchen Holbrook. "White Oleander." Rev. of *White Oleander,* by Janet Fitch. *New York Times Book Review.* 2 May 1999: 21.

Giles, Jeff. "Errors and Corrections: Brash Best Seller Stumbles into Dustup With Oprah." *Newsweek* 5 Nov. 2001: 68–69.

Gillin, Beth. "The Incredible Bulk: This Summer's Books Have Heft. And Reading Lists Abound with Oprah Hooked on Classics This Time Around." *Philadelphia Inquirer* 7 July 2003. 15 July 2003 http://www.philly.com/mld/inquirer.

Gioia, Ted. "Oprah's Book Club Picks Middlesex for its Summer Selection." *Blog Critics* 9 June 2007 http://blogcritics.org/archives/2007/06/09/173152.php

Gray, Paul. "Winfrey's Winners." *Time* 2 Dec. 1996: 84.

Grogan, David. "The Future of Book Clubs is Today." *ABA Bookselling this Week* 11 Apr. 2002. 28 July 2003 http://www.news.bookweb.org/news/415.html.

———."*Good Morning America* Asks Book Clubs to "Read This!" *ABA Bookselling this Week* 13 June 2002. 28 July 2002 http://www.news.bookweb.org/news/567.html

Gross, Terry. "Transcript from *Fresh Air* Interview with Jonathan Franzen on 15 Oct. 2001." 15 Oct. 2001: 1-10.

Grossberg, Josh. "Oprah Hits the Books!" *e!* online 19 June 2003. 26 June 2003 http://www.eonline.com.

Grosso, Joseph. "A Match Made in Neutrality: Oprah & Elie Wiesel." *Counterpunch* 1 Feb 2006 http://www.counterpunch.org/grosso02012006.html

Hamilton, Jane. Letter to the author. 23 Aug. 2001.

Heffernan, Virginia. "Critic's Notebook; Ms. Winfrey Takes a Guest To the Televised Woodshed." *New York Times* 27 Jan. 2006 http://select.nytimes.com/search/restricted/article?res=F60911FD3A5B 0C748EDDA80894DE404482

Hume, David. "Of the Standard of Taste." *Essays: Moral, Political, and Literary.* Indianapolis: Liberty Classics, 1889. 226-49.

Jamison, Laura. "Carry-On Baggage." Rev. of *The Pilot's Wife,* by Anita Shreve. *New York Times Book Review.* 7 June 1998: 37.

Jefferson, Margo. "Oprah Goes to Press With Ideas on Living Well." *New York Times* 7 Aug. 2000: E2.

Johnson, Marilyn. "Oprah Winfrey: A Life in Books."*LIFE magazine* Sept. 1997: 44–60.

Karbo, Karen. "Heathcliff Redux." Rev. of *Here on Earth,* by Alice Hoffman. *New York Times Book Review.* 14 Sept. 1997: 25.

"Keepers of the Word" Rev. of *The Business of Books,* by A. Schiffrin. *The Nation* 25 Dec. 2000: 25.

Keller, Julia. "Author's Rejection of Winfrey Book Logo Stirs Literary Tempest." *Chicago Tribune* 25 Oct. 2001 sec. one: 20.

———. "Franzen vs. the Oprah Factor: The 'Dissing' of Winfrey Hovers Over Author's Talk." *Chicago Tribune* 12 Nov. 2001: 3.

———. "Dear Oprah: A Few Humble Recommendations." *Chicago Tribune* 10 Apr. 2002: 1+.

Keller, Julia and Mills, Marja. "Where Have All the Good Books Gone? Good Question." *Chicago Tribune* 10 Apr. 2002: 1+.

Kennedy, Randy. "IDEAS & TRENDS; My True Story, More or Less, And Maybe Not at All." *New York Times* 15 Jan. 2006. http://www.nytimes.com/2006/01/15/weekinreview/15kenn.html?_ r=1&oref=slogin

Kingsolver, Barbara. Letter to the author. 29 Aug. 2001.

Kinsella, Bridget. "Is Oprah Bringing in New Readers?" *Publishers Weekly* 20 Jan. 1997: 276.

———. "The Oprah Effect." *Publishers Weekly* 20 Jan. 1997: 276–278.

Kirsch, Adam. "The Scorn of the Literary Blog." *New York Sun* 12 June 2007 http://www.nysun.com/article/56368

Kirkpatrick, David D. "Winfrey Rescinds Offer to Author for Guest Appearance." *New York Times* 24 Oct. 2001. http://www.nytimes.com.

———. "'Oprah' Gaffe by Jonathan Franzen Draws Ire and Sales." *New York Times* 24 Oct. 2001. 29 Oct. 2001 http://www.nytimes.com.

Kleiner, Carolyn. "In the Book World, it's Raining Women." *U.S. News and World Report* 28 June 2001: 46.

Lacayo, Richard. "Oprah Turns the Page." *Time* 15 Apr. 2002: 63.

Lamb, Wally. "Oprah Book Club Experience Questionnaire." E-mail to the author. 24 July 2001.

Lauerman, Connie. "The Story Behind What We Read: Are Women's and Men's Tastes in Books Really That Different?" *Chicago Tribune* WomaNews 21 Nov. 2001: A1+.

Lazere, Donald. "Literacy and Mass Media: The Political Implications." *Reading in America: Literature and Social History.* Baltimore: Johns Hopkins University Press, 1989: 259-284.

Lehman, Chris. "The Oprah Wars (the Critics Literati)." *American Prospect* 3 Dec. 2001: 40.

———. "Oprah's Book Fatigue: How Fiction's Best Friend Ran Out of Stuff to Read." *Slate* magazine 10 Apr. 2002. http://www.slate.com.

Levine, Lawrence W. *Highbrow/Lowbrow: The Emergence of Cultural Hierarchy in America.* Cambridge: Harvard University Press, 1988.

Lippman, Laura. "Melodramatic Mistake: Second Effort from Mitchard Disappointing." *Chicago Sun-Times* 28 June 1998: 19.

"Little O's Book Club." *Reading Today* 16.12 (October 1998): 1+.

Lyall, Sarah. "The British Version of Oprah's Book Club." *New York Times* 27 July 2006. http://select.nytimes.com/search/restricted/article?res=F30F12F6395B0C7A8EDDAE0894DE404482

Maderazo, Jennifer Woodard. Vivir Latino blog. "Oprah 'discovers'" Garcia Marquez." 8 Oct. 2007. http://vivirlatino.com/2007/10/08/oprah-discovers-garcia-marquez.php

Margolis, Rick. "Oprah's Book Club, Jr." *School Library Journal* 46.9 (Sept. 2000): 18.

Maryles, Daisy. "Oprah's Echo Effect." *Publishers Weekly* 15 June 1998: 17.

———. "Full Circle for Viking Penguin." *Publishers Weekly* 23 June 1997: 20.

———. "Oprah Raises Cane." *Publishers Weekly* 25 June 2001: 17.

———. "More Oprah Clout." *Publishers Weekly* 12 Mar. 2001: 20.

———. "New Year, New Oprah Pick." *Publishers Weekly* 29 Jan. 2001: 22.

———. "Mass Movements." *Publishers Weekly* 15 Jan. 2001: 18.

———. "New 'House' for Oprah." *Publishers Weekly* 20 Nov. 2001: 19.

———. "Oprah, Meet Ruth." *Publishers Weekly* 2 Oct. 2000: 24.

———. "Oprah's 'Open'-ing." *Publishers Weekly* 28 Aug. 2000: 21.

————. "It's Miller Time at Oprah." *Publishers Weekly* 29 May 2000: 30.

————. "Starbucks to Stock Oprah Book Club Picks." *Publishers Weekly* 2 June 1997: 19.

————. "Oprah's For Barbara." *Publishers Weekly* 26 June 2000: 20.

————. "Toppling Grisham." *Publishers Weekly* 10 Apr. 2000: 20.

————. "Irish Eyes Are Smiling." *Publishers Weekly* 13 Sept. 1999: 20.

————. "The Creek is Rising." *Publishers Weekly* 24 Jan. 2000: 178.

————. "Pietsch's in Cream." *Publishers Weekly* 10 May 1999: 30.

————. "LB's Triple Play." *Publishers Weekly* 18 Oct. 1999: 22.

————. "Two Authors Owe Oprah." *Publishers Weekly* 3 May 1999: 18.

Max, D. T. "The Oprah Effect." *New York Times Magazine* 26 Dec. 1999: 36-41.

McCormick, Patrick. "Oprah Throws the Book at Us." *US Catholic* Feb. 1997: 38–40.

Meadows, Susannah. "The Producer." *Newsweek* 17 Nov. 2001: 64–65.

Melnyczyuk, Askold. "*Shadowboxing:* An Open Letter to My Students About Captain Violin, Saul Bellow, the War, and the Art of Fiction." *AGNI* 62.

Miller, Sue. "Letter to the author." 15 Aug. 2001.

Miller, Laura. "Book lovers' quarrel." *Salon* 26 Oct. 2001. 29 Oct. 2001 http://dir.salon.com/books/feature/2001/10/26/franzen_winfrey/index.html.

————. "After Oprah: Her Imitators and Her Critics Misunderstand How She Sold Books." *Salon* 18 Apr. 2002. 1 Aug. 2002 http://www.salon.com/books/feature/2002/04/18/oprah/index.html.

Mills, C. Wright. "The Cultural Apparatus." *The Collected Essays.* New York: Oxford University Press, 1963: 405-21.

Mills, Marja. "Oprah's Book Club to Take Classic Spin: Selections Could Mean Millions for Publishers, Lead to Rediscovery of High School, College Reading." *Akron Beacon Journal* 17 Mar. 2003. 26 June 2003 http://www.ohio.com/mld/ohio/entertainment/5411049.htm.

Miner, Lisa Friedman. "Getting a Read on *Book*: New Magazine Targets Lovers of Good Writing." *Chicago Daily Herald* 4 May 1999: 1.

Mitchard, Jacquelyn. Interview with the author. 28 June 2001.

Mojtabai, A. G. An Accidental Family. Rev. of *A Fine Balance,* by Rohinton Mistry. *New York Times Book Review.* 23 June 1996: 29.

Morgan, Robert. "Oprah Book Club." E-mail to the author. 15 July 2001.

New York Times. Editorial. "On Oprah's Couch." 27 Jan. 2006 http://select.nytimes.com/search/restricted/article?res=F30F11FC3A5B0C748EDDA80894DE404482

Noah, Timothy. "Defining Bullshit: a philosophy professor says it's a process, not a product." Salon.com 2 Mar. 2005. http://slate.com/id/2114268/

"Not a Member of the Club: Jonathan Franzen." *People* 31 Dec. 2001: 86.

Nguyen, Lan N. "Touched by an Oprah." *People Weekly* 2 Dec. 1996: 36.

O'Dell, Tawni. "A Writer's Dream, a Mother's Nightmare." *Ladies Home Journal* February 2001: 44–48.

O'Hara, Delia. "Overnight Success Author Tawni O'Dell Learns the Power of Oprah's Monthly Book Club." *Chicago Sun-Times* 14 May 2000: 5.

"O No." ABC News 8 Apr. 2002. 8 Apr. 2002 http://www.ABCNEWS.com.

Oprah.com. "Oprah's Questions for James Frey and His Publisher." http://www2.oprah.com/tows/slide/200601/20060126/slide_20060126_350_115.jhtml

Oprah Web site. http://www.oprah.com.

"Oprah Demurs." *New York Times* 10 Apr. 2002. 10 Apr. 2002 http://www.nytimes.com.

"Oprah's Book Club Gets the Country Reading." *American Libraries.* 28.3 (Mar. 1997): 6.

"Oprah Heads 'East of Eden.'" AP online 18 June 2003. 18 June 2003 http://www.ap.org.

"Oprah Relaunches Book Club With East of Eden." Write News 20 June 2003. 26 June 2003 http://www.writenews.com.

"Oprah Revives Book Club With Steinbeck." *Associated Press* 17 June 2003. 17 June 2003 http://www.ap.org.

"Oprah Reviving Her Book Club: New Discussion to Focus on Classics." CNN.com 27 Feb. 2003. 28 Feb. 2003 http://www.cnn.com.

Oprah Winfrey Show. 5 Apr. 2002. (Author attended 4 Apr. 2002 taping of this episode.)

Ott, Bill. "Oprah Cure: Bill's Book Club." *American Libraries* 32.4 (April 2001): 102.

Peck, Janice. "The Oprah Effect: Texts, Readers, and the Dialectic of Signification." *Communications Review* 5.2 (2002): 143-78.

Pesci, David. "Poor Little Johnny." *Chicago Tribune* 28 Oct. 2001 sec. one: 21.

Peyser, Marc. "The Ugly Truth. *Newsweek* 23 Jan. 2006 http://www.msnbc.msn.com/id/10854740/site/newsweek/

Poulet, Georges. "Criticism and the Experience of Interiority." Trans. Catherine and Richard Macksey. *Reader–Response Criticism: From Formalism to Post-Structuralism.* Ed. Jane P. Thomas. Baltimore: The Johns Hopkins University Press, 1994. 41–49.

Putnam, Robert. "Bowling Alone: America's Declining Social Capital." *Journal of Democracy* 6.1 (January 1995): 65–78.

Quindlen, Anna. "oprah." E-mail to the author. 23 July 2001.

Quinn, Judy. "Georgetown's New Twist on the Oprah Effect." *Publisher's Weekly* 8 Nov. 1999: 20.

"TV's Oprah to Scale Back Club." Reuters 7 Apr. 2002. 15 Apr. 2002
http://www.washingtonpost.com.

Rabin, Nathan. "Interview With Stephen Colbert." The Onion A.V. Club 25
January 2006 http://www.avclub.com/content/node/44705

Radway, Janice. "The Book-of-the-Month-Club and the General Reader: The
Uses of Serious Fiction." *Reading in America: Literature and Social History.*
Baltimore: Johns Hopkins University Press, 1989: 259-284.

Reichgott, Megan. "Oprah Picks Cormac McCarthy's 'The Road.'" Associated
Press 28 Mar. 2007 http://www.sfgate.com/cgi-
bin/article.cgi?f=/n/a/2007/03/28/entertainment/e080836D25.DTL

———. "Oprah Book Club's Latest Pick." Chicago Sun-Times 29 Mar. 2007
http://www.suntimes.com/entertainment/books/318261,CST-NWS-
oprah29.article

Rilke, Rainier Maria. "On an Archaic Torso of Apollo." *Poems to Read: A New
Favorite Poem Project Anthology.* Eds. Robert Pinsky, Maggie Dietz. New
York: W. Norton and Company, 2002: 238.

"The Ripa Effect." ETOnline. 15 May 2002. 20 July 2002
http://www.etonline.com.

Roeper, Richard. "Oprah's Sheep Ready to Follow Every Whim." *Chicago Sun-
Times* 22 Jan. 1998: 11.

Rotenberk, Lori. "Winfrey Windfalls." *Chicago Sun-Times* 23 June 1998: 29.

Rubin, Joan Shelley. *The Making of Middlebrow Culture.* Chapel Hill: University of
North Carolina Press, 1992.

Runyon, Keith. "Oprah selects Jeffrey Eugenides' 'Middlesex.'" *Louisville Courier-
Journal* blog 5 June 2007 http://www.courier-
journal.com/blogs/books/2007/06/oprah-selects-jeffrey-eugenides.html

Ruta, Suzanne. "The Secrets of a Small German Town." *New York Times Book
Review* 20 Mar. 1994: 2.

Santich, Kate. "Book Clubs Fill Oprah's Absence." *The Orlando Sentinel* 26 June
2002. 20 July 2002
http://www.azcentral.com/ent/arts/articles/0627oprah.html.

Schindehette, Susan. "Novel Approach: Author Jonathan Franzen Insults
Oprah—and Gets Dumped from Her Show." *People* 12 Nov. 2001: 83-4.

Schlink, Bernhard. "Letter to the author." 31 Jul. 2001.

Schmich, Mary. "Oprah Should Book Writer, Not Turn Page." *Chicago Tribune* 26
Oct. 2001 sec 2: 1.

Scotter. *Detroit Metro* blog
http://detroit.metblogs.com/archives/2007/06/join_oprahs_boo.phtml

Schultz, Susy. "Oprah Renews Our Love of Reading: Book Club Show Sets New
Trend." *Chicago Sun-Times* 24 Feb. 1997: 6.

Schwarz, Christina. Phone interview with the author. 18 Nov. 2001.

Schwarzbaum, Lisa. "The Crusader." *Entertainment Weekly* 21 Mar. 1997: 65–66.

———. "Join the Club." *Entertainment Weekly* 31 July 1998: 65–66.

Sellers, Patricia. "The Business of Being Oprah: She's Talked Her Way to the Top of Her Own Media Empire and Amassed a $1 Billion Fortune. Now She's Asking, 'What's Next?'" *Fortune* magazine 1 Apr. 2002. 31 July 2002 http://www.fortune.com.

Senna, Carl. "Dying Like a Man." Rev. of *A Lesson Before Dying,* by Ernest Gaines. *New York Times Book Review.* 8 Aug. 1993: 21.

Sharma-Jensen, Geeta. "Publishers Find New Money in Old Classics." *Milwaukee Journal Sentinel* 31 Aug. 2003 http://www.jsonline.com.

Shone, Tom. "The Last Time They Met." Rev. of *The Last Time They Met,* by Anita Shreve. *New York Times Book Review* 22 Apr. 2001: 34.

Siklos, Richard. "MEDIA FRENZY; I Cannot Tell a Lie (From an Amplification)." *New York Times* 5 Feb. 2006. http://www.nytimes.com/2006/02/05/business/yourmoney/05frenzy.html

Simon, Daniel. "Keeper of the Word." the *Nation.* 7 Dec. 2000: 25.

Smith, Russel Scott. "Oprah's Beloved Author on Top." *Us Weekly* 19 June 2000: 36.

Sontag, Kate and David Graham, editors. *After Confession: poetry as autobiography.* Saint Paul: Graywolf Press, 2001.

Spivak, Gayatri Chakravorty. *The Post-Colonial Critic: Interviews, Strategies, Dialogues.* Ed. Sarah Harasym. London: Routledge, 1990.

Stamaty, Mark Alan. "Boox." *New York Times Book Review* 9 Dec. 2001: 35.

Stevens, Heidi. "When Oprah Talks, People Listen." *Chicago Tribune* 23 June 2003. 23 June 2003 http://www.chicagotribune.com.

Stone, Tanya Lee. *Oprah Winfrey: Success With an Open Heart.* Brookfield, Conn.: The Millbrook Press, 2001.

Streitfield, David. "Queen of all Media." *Mirabella.* 1997: 48–50.

Striphas, Ted. "A Dialectic With the Everyday: Communication and Cultural Politics on Oprah Winfrey's Book Club." *Critical Studies in Media Communication.* 20.3 (September 2003): 295–316.

Suellentrop, Christopher. "John Steinbeck: Should He Be Afraid of Oprah?" *Slate* magazine 26 June 2003. 26 Oct. 2003 http://www.slate.com.

Sullivan, Andrew. "Book Club Update." *The Daily Dish.* 5 Mar. 2002.

Suskind, Ron. "Without a doubt." *New York Times* 17 Oct. 2004 http://select.nytimes.com/search/restricted/article?res=F30F1EF93A5F0C748DDDA90994DC404482

Tannen, Deborah. "The TV Host: Oprah Winfrey." *Time* 8 June 1998: 196–198.

Tauber, Michelle. "Catching Up With . . . Icy Sparks." *People Weekly.* 23 Apr. 2001: 48.

Thomas, Mike. "Oprah means business for authors." *Chicago Sun Times* 8 Aug. 2006.

Tipper, Bill. "What America's Reading: Book Talk." Barnes and Noble 20 July 2002. 20 July 2002 http://www.barnesandnoble.com.

Trachtenberg, Jeffrey. "Author James Frey publishes letter apologizing to readers" *The Wall Street Journal*. 2 Feb. 2006.http://online.wsj.com/public/article/SB113881165041262277-LInyKMox4VIkRbqh8MNsqJawKM8_20070202.html

Trachtenberg, Jeffrey A. and Lawton, Christopher. "Would You Be a Member of These Book Clubs?" *The Wall Street Journal* 26 June 2002. 1 Aug. 2002 http://www.onlinewsj.com/public/us.

Tressider, Jody. "The Adventures of James Frey." *Ploughshares* Blog. http://pshares.blogspot.com/2006_09_01_pshares_archive.html

van den Berg, Laura. "Oprah Strikes Again." *Ploughshares* blog 29 Mar. 2007 http://pshares.blogspot.com/2007_03_01_archive.html

Vincent, Norah. "Good Riddance to Oprah's Book Club, and Her Literary Amateurism." *Los Angeles Times* 11 Apr. 2002. 15 Apr. 2002 http://www.latimes.com.

Wallace, David Foster. "E Unibus Pluram: Television and Fiction." *A Supposedly Fun Thing I'll Never Do Again*. New York: Little, Brown and Company, 1997: 21-82.

Wapshott, Nicholas. "Oprah Winfrey Goes Literary: Oprah Embraces Classics in New Club." *The Halifax Herald Limited* 16 Mar. 2003. 26 June 2003 http://www.hearld.ns.ca.

Weeks, Linton. "Oprah-Pick Franzen Wins National Book Award." *The Washington Post*. 15 November 2001: C1+.

Weich, Dave. "Jonathan Franzen Uncorrected." Powells 4 Oct. 2001. 29 Oct. 2001 http://www.powells.com/authors/franzen.html.

Weiner, Jennifer. SnarkSpot blog. 5 Oct. 2007. http://jenniferweiner.blogspot.com/2007/10/gabriel-garcia-marquez-oprah-picked.html

Weiss, Michahel J. "Oprah and the Book Club Boom." *U.S. News and World Report* 17 Feb. 1997: 18.

Whitcomb, Robert. "Clear it With the Queen." *Providence Journal*. 13 Nov. 2001: 5.

White, Kate. *If Looks Could Kill*. New York: Warner Books, 2002.

Williamsburg Book Club. 22 July 2007 http://bookclub.meetup.com/839/

Wikipedia.org. "Truthiness." http://en.wikipedia.org/wiki/Truthiness

"Winfrey Cancels Dinner With Author." *New York Times* 23 Oct. 2001. 24 Oct. 2001 http://www.nytimes.com.

Wood, James. "Abhorring a Vacuum: The Corrections and Jonathan Franzen." *The New Republic* 15 Oct. 2001: 32–40.

Woodward, Richard. "Cormac McCarthy's Venomous Fiction." *New York Times.* 19 Apr. 1992 http://www.nytimes.com/1992/04/19/books/mccarthy-venomous.html?ex=1185249600&en=3f50419ebfb6f685&ei=5070

Woolf, Virginia. *A Room of One's Own.* 1928. ed. Mary Gordon. New York: Harcourt Brace Jovanovich, 1981.

Word of Mouth: an Association of Women Authors, http://www.wordof-mouthwriters.org/

Wyatt, Ed. "For Oprah's Book Choice, Lots of Sound, a Little Fury." *New York Times* 6 Jun. 2006 http://select.nytimes.com/search/restricted/article?res=F50A15FB3E5C0C758CDDAF0894DD404482

———. "Oprah's Book Club to Add Contemporary Writers." *New York Times* 23 Sept. 2005. http://www.nytimes.com/2005/09/23/books/23oprah.html

———. "Best-selling memoir draws scrutiny." *New York Times* 10 Jan. 2006 http://select.nytimes.com/search/restricted/article?res=F20B10F934540C738DDDA80894DE404482

———."Writer says he made up some details." *New York Times* 12 Jan. 2006 http://select.nytimes.com/search/restricted/article?res=F70C11F63D5B0C718DDDA80894DE404482

———. "Next book for Oprah is 'Night' by Elie Wiesel." *New York Times* 17 Jan. 2006   http://select.nytimes.com/search/restricted/article?res=F60E16F83F5B0C748DDDA80894DE404482

———."Treatment Description in Memoir Disputed." *New York Times* 24 January 2006   http://www.nytimes.com/2006/01/24/books/24frey.html?ex=1156737600&en=754dea3079259f57&ei=5070

———."Live on 'Oprah,' a Memoirist gets kicked out of the book club." *New York Times* 27 Jan. 2006 http://select.nytimes.com/search/restricted/article?res=F00811FD3A5B0C748EDDA80894DE404482

———. "Frey says falsehood improved his tale." New York Times 2 Feb. 2006 http://select.nytimes.com/search/restricted/article?res=F30C17FB345B0C718CDDAB0894DE404482

Wyatt, Edward. "Tolstoy's Translators Experience Oprah's Effect." *New York Times.* 7 June 2004: E1.

Yardley, Jonathan. "The Story of O, Cont'd." *The Washington Post* 5 Nov. 2001: C2.

———. "Oprah's Bookend." *The Washington Post* 15 Apr. 2002: C2.

Zeitchick, Steven. "J-Franz Oprah Show Nixed: Host Doesn't Want to Make Him Uncomfortable." *PWNewsline.* October 2001.

INDEX

Grammer, Kelsey, 204

Grapes of Wrath, The (J. Steinbeck), 155, 191

Grass, Günter, *The Tin Drum,* 81

Gray, John, 141

great books, 12, 16, 32, 165, 173, 183, 185, 187, 190, 194–97, 199, 201, 202; online reading lists, 190. *See also* classics

Great Expectations (Dickens), 209

Great Gatsby, The (Fitzgerald), xii, xiii, 210

Grisham, John, 7, 177

Gross, Terry, 42, 43, 44, 155

Grove, Robert, 169

Gutenberg, Johann, 51

Halifax Herald Limited, 193

Hamilton, Jane, 11, 138; *The Book of Ruth,* 10–11; *A Map of the World,* 78, 138

Hammett, Dashiel, 19

Handler, Daniel, *The Basic Eight,* 18

Hardy, Thomas, 70

HarperCollins, 175

Harper's, 36, 42, 48, 56, 75

Harpo Productions, xi, 77, 104, 114, 120, 129, 135–36, 149, 160, 164, 170, 219

Harrison, Kathryn, 222

Harry Potter and the Order of the Phoenix (Rowling), 187

Harry Potter and the Half-Blood Prince (Rowling), 216

Hawthorne, Nathaniel, 188

Haynes, Melinda, 123

Hazelden, 227

Heaney, Seamus, *Beowulf,* 127

Heartbreaking Work of Staggering Genius, A (Eggers), 214

Heart is a Lonely Hunter, The (McCullers), 194, 199, 202, 221

Heart of a Woman (Angelou), 77, 225

Heath, Shirley Brice, 75

Heffernan, Virginia, 214

Hegi, Ursula, *Stones from the River,* 80, 81

Heller, Joseph, *Catch-22,* 80–81

Hemans, Felicia, 200

Hemingway, Ernest, 155, 191, 193

Here on Earth (Hoffman), 78, 85, 86–87

Herron, Jerry S., 60, 77

Highbrow/Lowbrow (Levine), 5–6, 194–95

highbrow vs. lowbrow. *See* cultural hierarchies

Hillenbrand, Laura, 222; *Seabiscuit,* 178

Hirsch, E. D., Jr., *Cultural Literacy,* 15

Hoffman, Alice, *Here on Earth,* 78, 85, 86–87

Homes, A. M., 222

Horace, 195

Hours, The (Cunningham), 187

House of Sand and Fog, The (Dubus), 96

Howarth, Richard, 221

Hudgins, Andrew, 229

Hume, David, "Of the Standard of Taste," 58

Huntington, Samuel, 133

Hussein, Saddam, 233

Huxley, Aldous, 25

I Know This Much is True (Lamb), 80, 83–84

I Know Why the Caged Bird Sings (Angelou), 29

If Looks Could Kill (White), 180

Imus, Don, 132

Inside the Mouse, 182

Instant Intellectual, The (Vincent), 173

Intellectuals and the Masses, The (Carey), 29

Iraq, American-led invasion of, 220, 233, 234

Jackass, 215

Jacobsohn, Rachel, 14–15

Jamison, Laura, 88

Jay, Debra, 227

Jefferson, Margo, 202

Jewel (Lott), 75, 93, 94, 167

Jiles, Paulette, 181; *Enemy Women,* 178

Johnson, Kristen, 179

Johnson, Marilyn, 109, 122, 157

Johnson, Samuel, 106

Jones, Quincy, 160
Joyce, James, 25, 37; *Finnegans Wake,* 7;
    Ulysses, 82
Julie, ou la nouvelle Heloise (Rousseau), 212

Kafka, Franz, 98
Kakutani, Michiko, 20, 238
Kamp, David, 215
Karbo, Karen, 86–87
Katsoulis, Carol, 186
Keats, John, 200
Keillor, Garrison, 250
Keller, Helen, 158
Keller, Julia, 49–50
Kennedy, Randy, 228–29
Kennedy, Susan Petersen, 187
Kerouac, Jack, 189
King, Gayle, 82, 168
King, Larry, 228, 238
King, Martin Luther, Jr., 238
King, Stephen, 37, 211
Kingsolver, Barbara, 69; *The Poisonwood*
    Bible, 17, 95–96, 97
King World Productions, 170
Kinsley, Michael, 236
Kirkpatrick, David, 54
Kirsch, Adam, 253
Knopf, 67, 178, 209, 242
Kramerbooks, 34

Lacayo, Richard, 172–73
Lachey, Nick, 220
Lamb, Wally, 52, 112–13, 138; *I Know*
    This Much Is True, 80, 83–84; *She's*
    Come Undone, 75, 92, 94
Landon, Laetitia, 200
Lang, Adele, *Confessions of a Sociopathic*
    Social Climber, 180
Lapham, Lewis, 56
Larry King Live, 227–28
Last Time They Met, The (Shreve), 68
Late Show with David Letterman, The, 134
Latimer, Nicholas, 209
Lazere, Donald, 115–16, 133, "Literacy
    and Mass Media," 115

Lazy B (O'Connor and Day), 179
Lee, Harper, 245
LeGuin, Ursula, 19
Lehane, Dennis, 19
Lehmann, Chris, 47–48, 55–56, 61
Lesson Before Dying, A (Gaines), 92–93
Lester, Irving, 159
Letts, Billie, *Where the Heart Is,* 78
Levine, Lawrence, 14, 31, 79–80, 85, 172,
    197–98, 212; *Highbrow/Lowbrow,* 5–6,
    194–95
Life magazine, 109, 111, 157
Lifetime network, 87
Light in August (Faulkner), 221
"Literacy and Mass Media" (Lazere), 115
Little, Brown and Company, 176
Live with Regis and Kelly, 163, 179
Lolita (Nabokov), 18
London Times, 13
Los Angeles Times, 252
Lott, Bret, 167–68; *Jewel,* 75, 93, 94
Love in the Time of Cholera (García
    Márquez), 251–52

MacDonald, Ann–Marie, 130, 140,
    146–47, 152–53; *Fall on Your Knees,*
    104, 105, 130, 140, 151, 152, 154, 164
Maderazo, Jennifer Woodard, 251
Mander, Jerry, *Four Arguments for the*
    Elimination of Television, 115
Mann, Thomas, 98
Map of the World, A (Hamilton), 78, 138
Mapplethorpe, Robert, 55
Maryles, Daisy, 74, 124
Massachusetts Bay Company, 15
Matthews, Carole, 189
Max, D. T., 118, 120, 122, 125, 143,
    146, 155
McCarthy, Cormac, ix, 239, 241–46, 253,
    255; *All the Pretty Horses,* 243; reputa-
    tion for reclusiveness, 245–46, 253;
    The Road, 241–46
McCullers, Carson, 196; *The Heart is a*
    Lonely Hunter, 194, 199, 202
McGee, Alice, 14
McGraw, Phil, 48, 51

McLuhan, Marshall, 132

McNett, Gavin, 71

The Measure of a Man (Poitier), 239, 242

"Meet Me in St. Louis" (Franzen), 64–66

Mekons, 39

Melnyczyuk, Askold, *"Shadowboxing:* An Open Letter to My Students About Captain Violin, Saul Bellow, the War, and the Art of Fiction," 239

Melville, Herman, 209, 213

Memmott, Carol, 177

memoir, 216–18, 223–27, 228–32, 235, 238–40, 246–47

Messitte, Anne, 168

Middlesex (Eugenides), 241, 247–49, 252, 254

Midwestern United States, 64–65, 101–3, 145

Midwives (Bohjalian), 55, 85, 87–88, 104, 123

Miers, Harriet, 233

Miller, Laura, 35, 58–59, 166, 167, 182

Miller, Sue, 69, 74, 155–56, 222; *While I Was Gone,* 74, 155

Million Little Pieces, A (Frey), 214, 215–19, 224–28, 230–32, 237–38; note to the reader, 237; refund offer, 237–38

Milliot, Jim, 174

Millman, Michael, 195

Mills, C. Wright, "The Cultural Apparatus," 127, 128

Minow, Newton, 113

Mirabella, 30

Mistry, Rohinton, *A Fine Balance,* 97, 130, 164

Mitchard, Jacquelyn, 3, 14, 15, 20, 89, 117, 125; *The Deep End of the Ocean,* 3, 15, 121; *A Theory of Relativity,* 3

Mitchell, Joni, 14

Modern Fiction Studies, 194

Mojtabai, A. G., 97

Monteith, Joanna, 186

Moody, Rick, 56, 61

Moraes, Lisa de, 180Morgan, Robert, 4, 9, 69, 142, 249; *Gap Creek,* 4, 75, 94–95, 249

Morgan, Susan, 166–67

Morris, Mary McGarry, *Songs in Ordinary Time,* 78, 125

Morrison, Toni, xii, 19, 51, 68, 74, 120, 122–23, 172, 173, 174, 198, 249; *Beloved,* 60, 81, 161, 249; *The Bluest Eye,* 82, 95; *Paradise,* 80, 81–82; *Song of Solomon,* 11, 75, 77, 81–82, 123, 147; *Sula,* x, 154, 165, 172

Moseley, Walter, *Bad Boy Brawly Brown,* 178

Mostly We Eat (book club), 178

Mount Vernon Love Story (Clark), 189

Mrs. Dalloway (Woolf), 18, 187

Murakami, Haruki, *The Wind-Up Bird Chronicle,* 18

Murphy, William, 189

Murray, Gloria, 192–93

My Friend Leonard (Frey), 216

Nabokov, Vladimir, *Lolita,* 18

Name of the Rose, The (Eco), 19

Nasshan, Bill, 188

Nation, 139

National Book Awards, 50–51, 122, 129, 250

National Book Critics Circle, 252

National Book Critics Circle Award, 244

National Book Foundation, 120, 211

National Public Radio, 41, 155, 183

National Security Book List, 190

Nausea (Jean–Paul Sartre), 106

New Criticism, 25, 79

New Republic, 106

Newsweek, 30, 50, 53

New York Observer, 214, 219

New York Times, 33, 35, 41, 46, 47, 49, 54, 115, 126, 173, 174, 175, 177, 187, 191, 207, 213, 216, 219, 223, 225, 226, 229, 236, 238, 245; book reviews, 2, 10, 78, 81, 86, 88, 93, 94, 95, 97, 129, 160, 215; magazine, 118, 228, 234

New Yorker, 48, 64, 67

Nielsen Book Scan, 189, 243

Nietzsche, Wilhelm Friedrich, 29

Night (Wiesel), 238, 239

Nin, Anaís, *Delta of Venus,* 19

Williams, Raymond, ix
Wilska, Erik, 166
Wind-up Bird Chronicle, The
    (Murakami), 18
Winfrey, Oprah, ix–xiii, 2–3, 5, 8–16,
    20–31, 33–55, 57–62, 65–66, 67–69,
    71–72, 74–79, 82, 85, 104–8, 109–11,
    114–15, 117–35, 137, 139–51, 153–61,
    163–77, 179–83, 185–212, 214–20,
    224, 226–27, 238–39, 245–46, 253–55;
    childhood, 29, 30, 75, 120, 156–59;
    criticism of James Frey, 214–20,
    232–33, 236, 238; defense of James
    Frey, 227–28, 231; disinvitation of
    Franzen, xiii, 26, 33, 34, 46, 48, 51–52,
    60–62, 63, 164, 170–72, 220; as an
    intellectual, xii, 13, 21–23, 174; as a
    reader, x, xi, 28–29, 30, 75–76, 77,
    111, 120, 145, 155, 157–61, 163,
    166–67, 168–69, 205, 250; respect for
    writers, 62, 118, 156, 172; selection of
    OBC titles, ix–x, 36, 37, 68, 77, 82,
    107, 119, 125, 163, 165–68, 205; as a

teacher, 13, 107, 119, 186–87, 197,
    200–203, 205–7; television viewing
    habits, 30, 109, 134, 168–69; wealth,
    3, 10, 124–25, 169, 170, 188, 193, 250
Wittgenstein, Ludwig, 245
Wolff, Virginia Euwer, *True Believer,* 50
Women and Children First, 119
Wood, James, 106, 107
Woolf, Virginia, "A Room of One's
    Own," 10; *Mrs. Dalloway,* 18, 187
Word of Mouth, 222–23, 239
Wordsworth, William, 200
Writer's Digest, 109
Wuthering Heights (E. Brontë), 86–87

Yankee Bookshop, The, 167
Yanni, 148
Yardley, Jonathan, 53, 67–68, 115, 173
Yates, Richard, *Revolutionary Road,* 73

Zeitchik, Steven, 45

KATHLEEN ROONEY is a founding editor of Rose Metal Press and the author of the upcoming University of Arkansas Press title *Live Nude Girl*. She has cowritten the collaborative poetry collections *Something Really Wonderful* and *That Tiny Insane Voluptuousness* with Elisa Gabbert. Her poems and essays have appeared in many publications, including the *Nation, Gettysburg Review, Harvard Review, Another Chicago Magazine*, and *Contemporary Poetry Review.* She lives in Chicago.